Everybody's Autonomy

MODERN AND CONTEMPORARY POETICS

Everybody's Autonomy

CONNECTIVE READING and COLLECTIVE IDENTITY

JULIANA SPAHR

The University of Alabama Press

Tuscaloosa and London

Copyright © 2001
The University of Alabama Press
Tuscaloosa, Alabama 35487-0380
All rights reserved
Manufactured in the United States of America

2 4 6 8 9 7 5 3 1
02 04 06 08 07 05 03 01

Designer: Michele Myatt Quinn
Typeface: Galliard and Syntax
Typesetter: J. Jarrett Engineering, Inc.
Printer and Binder: Thomson-Shore, Inc.

∞

The paper on which this book is printed meets the minimum
requirements of American National Standard for Information
Science–Permanence of Paper for Printed Library Materials,
ANSI Z39.48-1984.

Library of Congress Cataloging-in-Publication Data

Spahr, Juliana.
   Everybody's autonomy : connective reading and collective identity /
Juliana Spahr.
      p.   cm.
Includes bibliographical references (p. 195) and index.
   ISBN 0-8173-1053-3 (alk. paper)—ISBN 0-8173-1054-1 (pbk. : alk.
paper)
   1. American poetry—20th century—History and criticism. 2. Language
and culture—United States—History—20th century. 3. Authors and
readers—United States—History—20th century. 4. Stein, Gertrude,
1874–1946—Criticism and interpretation. 5. Andrews, Bruce, 1948—
Criticism and interpretation. 6. Mullen, Harryette Romell—Criticism
and interpretation. 7. Identity (Psychology) in literature. 8. Cha, Theresa
Hak Kyung. Dictâee. 9. Group identity in literature. 10. Hejinian, Lyn.
My life. 11. Reader-response criticism. I. Title.
   PS310.L33 S63 2001
   811'.509—dc21

                                                            00-009859

British Library Cataloguing-in-Publication Data available

Contents

Acknowledgments   ix

Introduction   1

1 "There Is No Way of Speaking English"
    The Polylingual Grammars of Gertrude Stein   17

2 "Make It Go with a Single Word. We."
    Bruce Andrews's "Confidence Trick"
    and Lyn Hejinian's *My Life*   51

3 "What Stray Companion"
    Harryette Mullen's Communities of Reading   89

4 "Tertium Quid Neither One Thing Nor the Other"
    Theresa Hak Kyung Cha's *DICTEE* and the
    Decolonization of Reading   119

Conclusion
An Unquiet House, An Uncalm World   153

Notes   161

Works Cited   195

Index   215

Acknowledgments

I believe I should have been almost stupefied but for one circumstance.

It was this. My father had left a small collection of books in a little room upstairs, to which I had access (for it adjoined my own) and which nobody else in our house ever troubled. From that blessed little room, Roderick Random, Peregrine Pickle, Humphrey Clinker, Tom Jones, the Vicar of Wakefield, Don Quixote, Gil Blas, and Robinson Crusoe, came out, a glorious host, to keep me company. They kept alive my fancy, and my hope of something beyond that place and time,—they, and the Arabian Nights, and the Tales of the Genii,—and did me no harm; for whatever harm was in some of them was not there for me; I knew nothing of it. It is astonishing to me now, how I found time, in the midst of my porings and blunderings over heavier themes, to read those books as I did. . . . This was my only and my constant comfort. When I think of it, the picture always rises in my mind, of a summer evening, the boys at play in the churchyard, and I sitting on my bed, reading as if for life.

—Charles Dickens, *David Copperfield*

I owe a huge debt to various readers of this manuscript over many years. Charles Bernstein, Susan Howe, Stacy Hubbard, Joan Retallack, and Neil Schmitz all read and reread earlier drafts with patience. A loosely formed writing group of Michelle Burnham, Gail Brisson, Eric Daffron, Anna Geronimo, and Julia Miller provided friendship, read earlier drafts of these chapters, and generously discussed ideas with me while we were at Buffalo. Later versions of these chapters were read by Hawai'i colleagues Cynthia

Franklin, Susan Schultz, and Rob Wilson. Sections of this manuscript were also thoughtfully commented on by Hawai'i graduate students—Carlo Arreglo, Jacinta Galeai, Alonso Garcia, Miriam Gianni, Kathleen McColley, Jill Sprott—in a fall 1999 Critical Writing Workshop. Earlier versions of these chapters appeared in *American Literature, College Literature, Second Thoughts: A Focus on Rereading,* and *Pro Femina* (translated by Dubravka Djuric). The anonymous readers' reports I received from these publications were of great help. Hank Lazer and Joan Retallack caught numerous errors and provided insightful comments on final drafts. I am lucky enough to be writing on works whose authors are readily available, and I benefited greatly from conversations with Bruce Andrews, Lyn Hejinian, and Harryette Mullen about their work. Other friends, outside readers, and e-mail acquaintances sent me articles or citations, discussed ideas with me, pointed me to things to read, read chapters and responded, or gave me a forum to discuss these ideas at conferences. Among them are Sherry Brennan, Steve Carll, Maria Damon, Michael Davidson, Ulla Dydo, Steve Evans, Renee Gladman, Yung-Hee Kim, Walter Lew, Suzanne MacElfresh, Jonathan Monroe, Mark Nowak, A. L. Nielsen, Jeffrey Nealon, Jena Osman, Marjorie Perloff, Doris Sommer, Ron Silliman, Brian Kim Stefans, and John Zuern. Bill Luoma and Charles Weigl both gave this work their argumentative attention and also made coming home and working on it a good thing.

I'm immensely grateful to these various and personal attentions. All errors are, of course, my own.

I was talking to Lee Ann Brown the other day and she was saying how Paul Connolly took her seriously as a teacher and that was a great thing for her. I owe a similar debt to Paul, who died last year. During the years I was associated with the Institute for Writing and Thinking at Bard College, he included many of the works I discuss here among the teaching materials for the institute and thus provided a space for extended discussion of the pedagogical possibilities of these works with colleagues and students. Similarly, I feel lucky to have had students at various institutions over the years—not only at Bard College but also at Siena College, State University of New York at Buffalo, and University of Hawai'i at Manoa—who have responded to these works with generosity and productive interest. Although I have avoided quoting directly from student writing (mainly because I did not get adequate permission before I lost track of them), student input and discussions have informed much of this work. Much of my conviction that these works are productive of reading rather than the reverse comes from classroom experience.

I also owe a debt to family. My parents have always been unusually supportive of my obsessions. And have also been readers of example. My father, who also died while this book was in production, grew up in an orphanage. Each year he was allowed to ask for a Christmas gift which was then provided by a patron. My father tells of asking, much to the nun's puzzlement, for a set of Dickens's novels as his Christmas gift one year. In some ways, my father's attraction to Dickens's work is obvious. His novels must have meant both literature and representation. When my father got old and quit working, he volunteered to teach adults to read. Most of these adults were men who had been promoted at the paper mill and needed a basic literacy so they could read a machine's instructions. David Copperfield calls reading his "only and constant comfort"; he claims he read "for life." I have thought often about what reading can mean for life, about my father's unschooled obsession with reading, in writing this.

Finally, a note on form. As this book is about reading, I've tried to leave the reading in: in endnotes, in marginal quotations, in the text itself. That part has been fun. The harder part has been the more personal one of who I am when writing this. I have often felt caught between an academic scene and a poetry scene that are often antithetical in desires and intents. I remain committed to both, and appreciate the pressures of both, but I often felt that I could please neither master. When I looked one way, the other way went out of focus. And then when I looked the other way, the one way went out of focus. Please forgive, then, the awkward, bifocal moments that are this work. At the same time, while this book is clearly academic criticism, it draws heavily from ideas that are under discussion in the various poetry communities with which I have loosely and luckily been a part of (especially as manifested in e-mail lists such as subpoetics-l, where poetry's relation to larger questions of how we live has been discussed daily).

Permissions

Grateful acknowledgment is made for permission to reprint material from the following sources:

From Bruce Andrews's *Give Em Enough Rope* (Los Angeles: Sun & Moon Press, 1987). Reprinted by permission of Sun & Moon Press.

From Theresa Hak Kyung Cha's *DICTEE,* copyright © 1982, by Third Woman Press.

From the Clovers's "Lovey Dovey," copyright © 1956 by Unichappell Music.

From T. S. Eliot's "The Waste Land" by the Eliot Estate and Faber & Faber.

From Cynthia Franklin's "Recollecting *This Bridge* in an Anti-Affirmative Action Era: Literary Anthologies, Academic Memoir, and Institutional Auto-biography." Unpublished manuscript.

From Cynthia Franklin's "Turning Japanese/Returning to America: Race and Nation in Memoirs by Cathy Davidson and David Mura." Unpublished manuscript.

Excerpt, as submitted, from "Wichita Vortex Sutra" from *Collected Poems, 1947–1980* by Allen Ginsberg, copyright © 1966 by Allen Ginsberg. Re-printed by permission of HarperCollins Publishers, Inc.

From personal e-mail by Renee Gladman.

From Lyn Hejinian's *My Life* (Los Angeles: Sun & Moon Press, 1987) by Lyn Hejinian. Reprinted by permission of Sun & Moon P.

From Myung Mi Kim's *The Bounty,* copyright © 1996 by Chax Press.

From Bill Luoma's e-mail to the subpoetics list, "Scanner Dan."

From Edouard Manet's *Olympia,* Paris, Musée d'Orsay.

From The Steve Miller Band's "Gangster of Love," copyright © 1990 by Warner Brothers Publications.

From *Muse & Drudge* by Harryette Mullen, copyright © 1995 by Singing Horse Press.

From *S*PeR M**K*T* by Harryette Mullen, copyright © 1992 by Singing Horse Press.

From Harryette Mullen's *Tree Tall Woman,* copyright © 1981 by Harryette Mullen.

From *Trimmings* by Harryette Mullen, copyright © 1995 by Tender Buttons Press.

From Aldon Lynn Nielsen's "Black Margins: African-American Prose Poems," in *Reading Race in American Poetry: "An Area of Act,"* ed. Aldon Lynn Nielsen, copyright © 2000, U of Illinois P, Champaign.

From Carl Perkins, "Matchbox," copyright © 1957, Warner Chappell Music.

From "Fragment #34; First Voice" from *Sappho: A New Translation*, translated by Mary Barnard, copyright © 1958 by The Regents of the University of California; copyright renewed 1986 Mary Barnard.

From personal e-mail by Ron Silliman.

From the work of Gertrude Stein, various copyrights, by the Estate of Gertrude Stein, care of Calman A. Levin.

From Wallace Stevens's "The House Was Quiet and the World Was Calm," in *Collected Poems* by Wallace Stevens. Reprinted by Permission of Alfred A. Knopf, a Division of Random House, Inc.

Photograph of students gathered around Gertrude Stein by Carl Van Vechten from the Carl Van Vechten Trust.

From Cecilia Vicuña's Quipoem: *The Precarious: The Art and Poetry of Cecilia Vicuña,* copyright © 1997 by Wesleyan University Press.

Photograph of Gertrude Stein, seated below portrait, from UPI/Corbis-Bettmann.

Photograph of Stein and Basket II with Marie Laurencin's portrait of Basket, ca. 1940–46, from The Yale Collection of American Literature, Beinecke Rare Book and Manuscript Library.

Introduction

As I read, however, I applied much personally, to my own feelings and condition. I found myself similar yet at the same time
strangely unlike to the beings concerning whom I read and to
whose conversation I was a listener. I sympathized with and partly
understood them, but I was unformed in mind; I was dependent
on none and related to none. "The path of my departure was
free," and there was none to lament my annihilation. My person was hideous and my stature gigantic. What did this mean?
Who was I? What was I? Whence did I come? What was my
destination?

—the creature in Mary Shelley's *Frankenstein*

Very soon after I went to live with Mr. and Mrs. Auld, she very
kindly commenced to teach me the A, B, C. After I had learned
this, she assisted me in learning to spell words of three or four
letters. Just at this point of my progress, Mr. Auld found out what
was going on, and at once forbade Mrs. Auld to instruct me further, telling her, among other things, that it was unlawful, as well
as unsafe, to teach a slave to read. To use his own words, further,
he said, "If you give a nigger an inch, he will take an ell. A nigger
should know nothing but to obey his master—to do as he is told
to do. Learning would spoil the best nigger in the world. Now,"
said he, "if you teach that nigger (speaking of myself) how to
read, there would be no keeping him. It would forever unfit him
to be a slave. He would at once become unmanageable, and of
no value to his master. As to himself, it could do him no good,
but a great deal of harm. It would make him discontented and
unhappy." These words sank deep into my heart, stirred up sen-

timents within that lay slumbering, and called into existence an entirely new train of thought. It was a new and special revelation, explaining dark and mysterious things, with which my youthful understanding had struggled, but struggled in vain. I now understood what had been to me a most perplexing difficulty—to wit, the white man's power to enslave the black man. It was a grand achievement, and I prized it highly. From that moment, I understood the pathway from slavery to freedom.

—Frederick Douglass, *Narrative of the Life of Frederick Douglass, an American Slave, Written by Himself*

"What Was My Destination?"

In *Frankenstein*, the creature learns to read by trickery. He looks through a peephole onto a family who is teaching Safie, who has come from afar, to read and speak in English, and learns her lessons. When he learns to read, he has a series of questions: "What did this mean? Who was I? What was I? Whence did I come? What was my destination?" He is, after all, a creature. So his learning to read is not expected or necessary. Rather, his reading allows him to ask those all-important questions about identity, allows him an identity, and allows readers to identify with him.

Less than fifteen years later but in the United States, Frederick Douglass asserts that reading is "the pathway from slavery to freedom" (49). Similar to the creature, Douglass in his narrative ponders the relationship between literacy and subjectivity and the political rights that accompany these. His narrative points out that to gain literacy is not only to master a cultural symbolic system but also to participate in a culture. He makes this relationship literal in his narrative: literacy is a pathway to freedom. As is often noted, Douglass reads himself to emancipation, writes himself to subjectivity. In his narrative, reading is figured as productive and active, bound with agency: "The reading of these documents enabled me to utter my thoughts, and to meet the arguments brought forward to sustain slavery" (55). Douglass does not learn that slavery is an evil through reading. This is readily evident to him. But he does learn how white culture talks about slavery; he learns the vocabulary of abolitionism; and he learns how one talks with others immersed in this culture. But at the same time, Douglass's narrative is not completely naive about reading. While recognizing reading as an agent of socialization that allows entry into the freedoms controlled by white culture, he also figures it as a potential predatory learning process that perpetuates assimilation. Douglass has moments when he is ambiguous about reading and notes that reading brought on the "very discontentment which Master Hugh had predicted would follow my learning to read." He continues, "I would at times feel that learning to read had been a curse rather than a blessing. . . . It opened my eyes to the horrible pit, but to no ladder which to get out" (55).

One way Douglass counters this discontentment is through realizing reading as a communal, not individual, act. There are several examples of this. Douglass's life as a reader begins with Mrs. Auld's teaching him, but soon she is told to abandon this project by her husband, and Douglass, who realizes he still needs others to learn to read, turns to his own wits and masters the system through communal trickery. He learns to read by trading bread for words with poor white children he meets on the street: "This bread I used to bestow upon the hungry little urchins, who, in return, would give me that more valuable bread of knowledge" (53–54). And he finishes the unfinished lessons in Thomas Auld's *Webster's Spelling Book*. But neither of these is the ladder that leads out of the pit in which Douglass finds himself. This ladder is the word "abolition," which Douglass hears people using but does not understand. His response is to do the individualistic act and look it up in the dictionary, but this leads to little success because the dictionary just defines it by tautology as "the act of abolishing." It is only when he encounters the word used in the discussion of slavery in the newspapers that, as he notes, "the light broke in upon me by degrees" (56). Or one moves from reading as a curse to reading as bread, as a liberatory ladder, as one learns through and with others, as one exchanges and as one converses with a culture. Once reading is recognized as dependent on community, and on the relationship between readers and works as a form of community itself, reading turns into a force that can be manipulated and used as a tool of resistance to respond to the inhumanity of slavery.[1]

I have put two unrelated stories—one fictional, one not—beside each other here as a beginning because both point to a link between reading and identity that emerges in the nineteenth century. It is emblematic, for instance, that the creature learns to read. Modern Western consciousness, these examples illustrate, is tied up with reading. This relation between consciousness and reading has a complex history, riddled with related stories of class, educational access, missionaries, and alternate cultural literacies. This book does not tell these stories, for they are huge stories, demanding historical, sociological, and legal knowledges beyond my scope. However, the general outlines of these stories point to something crucial and wonderful and also something dangerous in the intersection between reading and identity. The works I examine in this book tell similar stories: stories that acknowledge the dangers and stories that suggest possibilities for escaping the dangers through collective and connective models of reading, through collective identities.

"Getting Out of the Way"

1. Do you love the audience?
Certainly we do. We show it by getting out of the way.

—Bruce Andrews (quoting John Cage), "Index"

What sort of selves literary works influence, encourage, or create is what this study is about.

The creature reads Milton's *Paradise Lost* and learns to act as if he were in a grand drama between good and evil. He did not learn the in-between. Thus his failure.

Douglass reads and as he reads he learns to ask others about the word "abolition." Thus his success.

I argue in *Everybody's Autonomy* that what we read and how we read it matters. That a heavily plotted and symbolic novel, for example, encourages a different sort of reading practice than mixed-genre writing. While either work might affect readers in many different ways, the formal aspect of each must play a role in any consideration of reading.

I argue here that when we tackle literary criticism's central question of what sort of selves literary works create, we should value works that encourage connection. By "connection" here I mean works that present and engage with large, public worlds that are in turn shared with readers.[2] I mean forms of writing that well represent and expand changing notions of the public, of everybody. And I mean forms of writing that take advantage of reading's dynamic and reciprocal nature. "You read," Theresa Hak Kyung Cha writes, "you mouth the transformed object across from you in its new state, other than what it had been" (*DICTEE* 131). In this context, it is crucial that the creature and Douglass both learn to read only with others. This most necessary of acts in modern society is also one we must learn with others, arduously. It has nothing natural about it. It is bound with exchange (the first things written supposedly are records of sale). It is a difficult translation— this move from symbol to letter to sound. And yet it is, as these stories suggest, a defining one for how we think of ourselves.

My emphasis in this book is less on deciphering works, and more on what sorts of communities works encourage. It has not been unusual to argue that reading leads to transcendence in forms like the novel because it allows identification with others.[3] Similarly, I am interested in works that encourage communal readings. I would include identificatory moments in this, but I would also want to include moments that are non-identificatory: moments when one realizes the limits of one's knowledge; moments of partial or qualified identification; moments when one realizes and respects unlikeness; moments when one connects with other readers (instead of characters). I am interested in works that look at the relation between reading and identity in order to comment on the nature of collectivity. Works that recognize reading's dangers, its potential exclusions, and work to make this relationship more productive. I am interested in works that use reading to contribute to, contest, and expand how we think of public (and thus cultural) spheres. I am interested in works that pursue cosmologies diverse enough for individual contestation and evaluation, yet still have as their ultimate goal considerations of what sorts of humans the experience of reading encourages us to be.

I am not arguing here for a model reader or for a recognizable community, like my mother's reading group that meets every other Sunday. I have avoided writers whose work tends to be seen as representative of certain well-defined group concerns (the way, say, Adrienne Rich's work represents a feminist community or Gloria Anzaldúa's a Chicana). My argument is more formal than sociological, and many of the works I examine here have been critiqued as apolitical formalism and for not adequately taking up representational concerns. Yet my turn to a different canon of works to address representational concerns is not because I feel that well-defined collective gestures are unimportant, but rather because I feel that expanding the range of works under consideration would also expand and add much to current discussions of identity, especially how individual identities negotiate within collectivities.

The main story of this book is told through the work of Gertrude Stein, Lyn Hejinian, Bruce Andrews, Harryette Mullen, and Theresa Hak Kyung Cha. By concentrating on works that use nonstandard English, multilingualism, puns, disconnected syntaxes, and repetition, *Everybody's Autonomy* argues for anarchic—in the sense of self-governing—approaches to reading. The works of these writers, rather than guiding readers through developmental structures to a neat box of a conclusion, encourage dynamic participation. Rather than rewarding readers for well-deciphered meaning and allusion, they reward readers for responsive involvement and for awareness of their limitations. Andrews, to choose just one example here, argues that reading at its best is a form of co-production. His writing, instead of having a clear poetic voice, has voices in the plural. And it is often composed of phrases and sentences that are multiply connected within the work (they tend to be joined by dashes, and it is hard to tell where one ends or begins). This work only makes sense if one sees reading as dramatically reciprocal, as shareable, as connective.

While this attention to reading's connective moments is a value in its own right, I argue that this attention to readers has much to add to discussions of subjectivity. It is no coincidence, I argue, that the emphasis on reading as connective and communal in these works parallels the rise of a literature that addresses gender, ethnicity, and race. I also argue that there is a close relationship between this literature and consciousness-raising. While it is often said that these works are inaccessible because they are too experimental or too avant-garde and thus dissolve subjectivity, I maintain that these writers instead directly engage the complicated claims around identity that come to the forefront of large social concerns in the late 1960s.[4] But rather than the clear, singular voice and narrative of much of the literature that gets categorized as consciousness-raising, these works propose group identities with room for individualistic response. Thus, my concentration in this study has been on the tension in these works between collectivity and individualism. For, in a crucial move, these works repeatedly relate reader autonomy to social, political, and cultural autonomy. Mullen's work, for example, concentrates not on an essential African-American culture, but rather locates the distinctiveness of African-American culture in its gathering and use of various cultures and in its respect for various sorts of autonomy. Her work avoids placing essentialist identities against performative identities and avoids juxtaposing orality against textuality by concentrating instead on cultural flows and exchanges without abandoning a racial consciousness.

A few of the questions I asked as I began writing were: Is reading (and forms of writing other than prose) still relevant in the age of cultural studies? What sort of cultural information does the formal construction of a work carry? That an attention to reading went more or less out of style after the 1980s and did not play much of a role in the turn to studies of literature's cultural roles concerned me. And so this book is an attempt to propose a theory of reading that is in dialogue with the concerns of race and ethnic studies. I argue that these works of autonomy are a rich yet often overlooked tradition in the literature of minority, immigrant, exile, and/or postcolonial experience. Thus, one other goal of this book is to place what are often considered marginal forms of American literature in a larger, cross-cultural context.

It is worth noting in this context that the works on which I have concentrated in this study defy genre conventions. Most often these works are considered poetry, but in some ways that seems less representative of the actual forms of these works and more indicative of how bookstores shelve anything that is not conventional prose in the poetry section. Still, I have been torn over whether or not to make this book an argument for poetry.

On the one hand, calling works poetry throws them off the radar of much academic discourse. As Carrie Noland notes, "As attention shifts from canonical texts and formalist methodologies to the contextualized study of more popular forms, poetry appears to be the genre whose traditional status within the humanities curriculum is most seriously threatened" (40).[5] Anecdotally, I see this trend reflected in the courses taught in my university. There are few poetry courses, and when poetry does appear it does so as a part of historically based survey classes. Courses that examine concepts of race, ethnicity, nation, and culture in literature, if they teach any poetry at all, tend to say something after a long list of novels like "the reading for this course will be supplemented by some poems."

On the other hand, the works I examine in this study are often written by writers who identify themselves as poets, and that is probably telling. These works—the ones that come after Stein—all have roots in the huge growth of various grassroots, non-university-affiliated poetry scenes that developed in the United States after the 1950s. While some of these writers teach in the university (Andrews in political science at Fordham University; Mullen in English at UCLA), their work is not rooted in the M.F.A./creative writing scene but rather in communities gathering outside traditional institutions. My response in this study has been to more or less leave these issues of genre behind, as these writers have done in their own work. Yet I bring issues of genre up here because they do have some larger resonance. I realized this the other day when listening to a colleague talking about the death of poetry (she was referencing books like Dana Gioia's *Can Poetry Matter?*) and student disinterest. Her conviction—even while it was said in lament—that poetry was irrelevant to the time pointed out to me how dramatically different poetry's role in the university is from its role outside academia. One of the more interesting sociological moments genre studies has yet to examine is how the decline of poetry in the academy has been accompanied by a growth in the attention, publication, and programming of poetry by non-university venues.[6] Poetry in these venues has become an unusually politicized genre. And as Maria Damon notes, "[t]hese forms, consciousnesses, and communities are not, however, mere acultural novelties but carry with them the traces and influences of many dissident or socially subordinated traditions as well as evolving new ones" ("Avant-Garde or Borderguard" 479). The issues and concerns of collectivity and critique that are dominant discussions in these various grassroots poetry scenes have greatly defined and influenced the writers of this study.

A recent talk by Grace Molisa at the University of Hawai'i at Manoa made me think more about what is to be gained from poetry. Molisa, a writer from Vanuatu, spoke movingly on the role of poetry in a country of eighty islands with over one hundred languages (three national languages) and a population of 170,000. Her poetry, a poetry of memo, made me think a lot about poetry's role as information. One of Molisa's poems, for instance, is called "Democracy" and explains very clearly that democracy is using a stanzaic form. Molisa talked of how she began writing poetry in order to be able to get information out to isolated villages. Her work interests me because it is so divorced from the conventions of postcolonial poetry even while it is directly rooted in a postcolonial state. While I want to avoid genre essentialism, her attention to the sorts of work poetry can do in various contexts was one that I saw as useful for thinking about works of autonomy and poetry's unique role outside the academy.

Finally, this book also is a defense of literature, of poetry, in an age of critique. When I sat down to write this study, I wanted to point to works that I found important pedagogically and personally, works that shifted conventions of thinking for the students I encountered and for myself. While literary criticism has done valuable work of critique, successfully investigating how literature can reify racism and sexism, it has less often explored the ways literature might avoid such damages. This book looks at works that concentrate on possibilities of response to various forms of oppression. These are works that are emblematic of the world's growing connectiveness, yet ones that do not see these connections as unifying or homogeneous. They are works that negotiate between the dire worries of homogeneity and loss and the utopian hopes of diversity and invention.

I develop these arguments through a series of chronologically ordered close readings, beginning with Stein's claim to write for everybody, with her use of fragmentation to encourage reader autonomy. Stein's work is an ideal place for any consideration of reading's politics and possibilities because it is so extreme, so extremely repetitive, so extremely fractured, and so extremely lengthy. In this chapter I begin by placing this much-noted extremity and multivalence of Stein's experimental works in an urban, polyglot context. And I conclude by looking at Stein's claims that she wrote for everybody.

In the second chapter I look at language writing in general and the work of Andrews and Hejinian in particular. In this chapter I examine not only the already-mentioned connective possibilities of Andrews's work, but also the investigation of privilege that is often overlooked in discussions of experimental works. For instance, I examine how Hejinian uses identification in *My Life* to move her readers in, through, and out of her autobiographical "I." Hejinian's switch of autobiography from narcissistic and individualistic to the constructed nature of collective memory is a deliberate reinterpretation of the bourgeois history of the autobiography. The twist of *My Life* is how it points out that even the most narcissistic and self-privileging of genres has possibilities for outward connection. Andrews's "Confidence Trick" extends the work of *My Life* into racial critique. The "I" in this work is not allowed to be generic. And whiteness is never allowed to be neutral in this poem. It is mocked and always exposed as connected to larger systems of power. The moments of reader connection in Andrews's work are, thus, also moments where readers are required to question their own affiliations.

In the third chapter I turn to the work of Harryette Mullen. Mullen's later works—and these are the ones I concentrate on—turn to puns, samplings, and other sorts of wordplay to examine and challenge overly limiting constructions of race, ethnicity, class, and gender. As her work illustrates, the difficult and necessary work of challenging limiting subjectivities requires also that one challenge the strictures of grammar and rigorous narrative.

In the final chapter I look at Cha's *DICTEE*. Cha talks about reading frequently in *DICTEE*. In her preferred model, reading involves not simply identifying and assigning meaning to certain works, but also entering into a creative and self-reflexive relation with them. Both readers and works matter. *DICTEE* is a complicated work. It is multilingual (it is mainly written in a nonstandard English and French); it is more collage than narrative; it is highly allusive; it often tricks and lies to its readers. My argument in this chapter is that Cha pursues and presents not simply a critique of colonization on the level of content (much of the book is about the colonization of Korea by Japan), but that she also writes her work so as to decolonize reading. Her work challenges the forms of reading that subtly remove literature from cultural concerns, from the world that produces and surrounds it. As political decolonization's intent is to dislodge dominant and externally imposed ideas and ideologies, so Cha wants to dislodge dominant and externally imposed methods of reading. I conclude by arguing for alliances, by suggesting that the concerns of reading and identity that I locate in this book can be found in a number of twentieth-century works.

"Clear as Mud, But Mud Settles"

My writing is clear as mud, but mud settles and clear streams run on and disappear, perhaps that is the reason but really there is no reason except that the earth is round and that no one knows

the limits of the universe that is the whole thing about men and
women that is interesting.

—Stein, *Everybody's Autobiography*

The creativity of the reader grows as the institution that controlled it declines.

—Michel de Certeau, *The Practice of Everyday Life*

It has been a good, heady century for readers. In fact, one of the sad ironies
of contemporary life is that while a new world order constantly asserts its
might (the writing of this book was sandwiched between the Gulf War and
the bombing of Serbia), there has been at the same time a vigilant, if often
overlooked, tendency of art and culture that continually reacts against au-
thoritarianism in the name of autonomy. I am not sure what to make of this.
Some might argue that culture has become so irrelevant under global capitalism that its resistances are ignored, but I think one could just as easily
argue that things could be much worse without cultural resistance and reclamation, without literature that presents a way out of the abyss.

In this context, some well schooled in reader response and deconstruction
might reply to my arguments that reading is always free, always impossible
to pin down.[7] Even literary criticism, one of the genres more slow to change,
reflects this move to autonomy that defines twentieth-century culture. After
New Criticism's intense respect for the work, literary theory celebrates reading in a series of quick changes that begin in the 1970s with deconstruction
and continue to this day. Readers gain so much power that, by 1980, Stanley
Fish asks *Is There a Text in This Class?* and answers no.

But it is worth noticing, as the language acquisition sections of Cha's
DICTEE so poignantly suggest, that reading is also a learned and regulated
act. Reading is usually taught in school so as to walk hand in hand with
assimilation. And it is at its most oppressive when taught through principles
of absolute meaning. Beginning reading exercises tend to emphasize meaning
as unambiguous and singular; the word "duck" in the primer means the bird,
not the verb.[8] Further, as a learned and regulated act, reading socializes readers not only into the process of translating symbol into word with a one-to-

one directness, but also into specific social relationships. Dick and Jane, to use the most clichéd example of a primer, teach how to live the normalized lives of the nuclear family as much as they teach how to read. Further, much of what is read does not fully engage the resistant possibilities within reading, and as a result it tends to perpetuate reading's conventions.

So while one of the major lessons of poststructuralism has been that readers construct meanings and texts, these works that pursue reader autonomy point to how this construction does not take place on an entirely blank slate. Too many arguments about reading end with the mere observation that reading is variable and sidestep the responsibility for assessing the politics and dynamics of reading itself. Readers can, after all, read variably only to find themselves choosing between two forms of containment. To ignore the formal characteristics of the work is to ignore one of the crucial ways works carry meaning. Further, such an approach reads all works as bland and apolitical.

Undeniably, my attention to reading here draws heavily from deconstructive and reading response theory that developed in the 1980s. I have learned a lot from the attention in these discussions to the more practical moments of reading, and from the attention to how reading is a variable act. But while reader-orientated theory has been of undeniable influence to both my work and my teaching, I have found its distrust of readers' potential for anarchic rebellion of limited applicability to the works I examine here. The fear of anarchy has led a number of critics—the very critics most concerned with resisting readerly restrictions—to conceive of readers as one of them, as literary critics who categorize and follow reading's conventions. Umberto Eco's "model reader," Wolfgang Iser's "implied reader," Michael Riffaterre's "super reader," Jonathan Culler's "ideal reader," and Stanley Fish's "community of readers" are all examples of this sort of model reader.[9]

While the character of the model readers that these critics present often varies, and requires more attention than I dedicate here, Fish's turn to a community-oriented model of reading that limits individual response provides a succinct example of the potentially repressive possibilities of such models. When he asks "Is there a text in this class?" and answers no, there are only readers; but since he also fears the anarchy that could happen when there are only readers, he proposes readers who will not misbehave. Fish's introduction to *Is There a Text in This Class?* presents him wrestling constantly with the question of a reader's potential anarchy (which he calls "subjectivity") and continually sidestepping the issue until he reconceives "the reader in such a way as to eliminate the category of 'the subjective' altogether" (10). Instead of seeing reading's difficult relation to subjectivity as a crucial part of reading's power, he establishes the kinder, gentler authority of a dominant community. Readers may create the work, but not individually, only through their input into this larger interpretive community. His model also assumes the members of this community to be critics. This community, as Elizabeth Meese notes, establishes "a strong insider-outsider dynamic, a gender-based literary tribalism, that comes into play as a means of control" (7). In contrast, the works of reader autonomy that I concentrate on here invert literary tribalism and insist on crossed interpretative moves and communities.

For the works I discuss here, I have found it useful to think of reading as anarchic. There is in these works a collective attention to the multiple, an attention to the diversity of response in the name of individual rights. David Weir points out in *Anarchy and Culture* that "anarchism succeeded culturally where it failed politically" (5), and the works that I discuss in this book are best explained with an anarchic frame. I am thinking here of reading as a form of self-governing that resembles Peter Kropotkin's territorial and functional decentralization. Stein, for instance, writes for anarchic individualism when she writes the word "one" one hundred times—like this: "one and one and one . . . "—so as to emphasize individuals within communities (*Useful Knowledge* 150–151). And Andrews riffs off of Stein to connect reading and this multiplicity of position: "We can take our well-developed attention to signs & our desire for their dishevelment & expose it to a social dialogue, to networks of meaning understood as thoroughly socialized, to questions about the making of the subject (Reading as Writing & Writing as Reading): the making of Americans—the making of me, myself, & I—of you, yourself, & *us*" (*Paradise & Method* 52). And Cha urges simply, "More. Others." (*DICTEE* 65). These one-word sentences of Cha's, with their content of pluralism yet a rejection of collective inclusion into the sentence's hierarchies, well exemplify much of what interests me about these works.

Often the criticism of these works of reader autonomy misreads them as individualistic. Again and again, for instance, Stein's work has been called nonsense, or private, or encoded, or presymbolic. Instead, I like to think of her work as using reading to encourage a sort of anarchy, not the sort the Sex Pistols called for where all the rules are abandoned in the name of chaos, but rather one where the work allows readers self-governance and autonomy, where the reading act is given as much authority as the authoring act. As Emma Goldman writes, "Individuality is not to be confused with the various ideas and concepts of Individualism; much less with that 'rugged individualism' which is only a masked attempt to repress and defeat the individual and his individuality" (112). These works value the individual meanings readers bring to works and abandon much of the authority of the author. They, like anarchism, work to have both individuality and community. And from them a new discursive economy emerges, one that does not subordinate readers to explicative functions.

For similar reasons, I have also found useful theories of reading that come out of anthropology's concern with cultural negotiations and which figure it as cooperative storytelling. This would include Paulo Friere's various pedagogies. And Michael Taussig's emphasis on reading as "excesses of interpretation" (x). And Smadar Lavie's attention to how the Mzeina are "able to transcend world politics by means of local poetics" (39). And Greg Sarris's attention to reading's relation to dialogues or conversations "that can open the intermingling of the multiple voices within and between people and the texts they encounter, enabling people to see and hear the ways various voices intersect and overlap, the ways they have been repressed or held down because of certain social and political circumstances, and the ways they can be talked about and explored" (*Keeping Slug Woman Alive* 5). And outside anthropology, certainly Roland Barthes's *The Pleasure of the Text,* required undergraduate reading for any English major of my age, resonates here.

I should stress here, however, that I turn to these theories for their attention to reading, for their attention to how poetry and other forms of writing matter. Clearly, the role of language writing in the United States is not in any way the same sort of role that Mzeina tribal poetry or Pomo baskets or stories have to those cultures.[10] But still, I have found these critics' turn away from a work's "literariness" and toward its collective resonances and uses more useful for thinking about reading's connective moments. These theories have also helped me to understand the importance (pedagogically; personally) of a series of often overlooked works in the United States.

Mainly, this book is an attempt to figure out my own story, to understand what happened when I was in high school and found Stein's work in an anthology of twentieth-century writing and everything that I thought I knew about reading changed. While one reading of this moment would be assimilationist (Stein's work representing everything that the rural Midwestern town I was growing up in was against), I have not been willing to dismiss this early moment that easily. So this book is, fourteen years later, a continuation of the paper I wrote my senior year in high school in which I attempted to figure out what it was that *Tender Buttons* meant.

"There Is No Way of Speaking English"

The Polylingual Grammars of Gertrude Stein

The United States is invaded by aliens, thousands of whom constitute so many acute perils to the health of the body politic. Modernism is of precisely the same heterogeneous alien origin and is imperiling the republic of art in the same way. It began, as our excessive immigration began, in an insidiously plausible manner. . . . Such movements!—crude, crotchety, tasteless, abounding in arrogant assertion, making a fetich of ugliness and, above all else, rife in ignorance of the technical amenities. These movements have been promoted by types not yet fitted for their first papers in aesthetic naturalization—the makers of true Ellis Island art.

—Royal Cortissoz, *American Artists*

We have the illusion of a stronger vitality and of a greater intellectual freedom, but we are polyglot, parvenu, hysterical and often only semi-literate. When time shall have weeded out our less important writers, it is probable that those who remain will give the impression of a literary vaudeville.

—Edmund Wilson, *The Shores of Light*

There is something precisely *ominous* about Miss Stein. Her books of "about one thousand pages" may, and will, remain unread; but Miss Stein is going to make trouble for us just the same. In this Hogarth Essay of fifty-nine pages [*Composition as Explanation*] the atom is dissociated. . . . Moreover, her work is not improving, it is not amusing, it is not interesting, it is not good for one's mind. But its rhythms have a peculiar hypnotic power not met with before. It has a kinship with the saxophone. If this is of the future, then the future is, as it very likely is, of the barbarians. But this is the future in which we ought not to be interested.

—T. S. Eliot, "Charleston, Hey! Hey!"

[Stein] became the people she wrote about, adopting their illiteracies and colloquialisms. . . . [She] gives proof of all the false "revolutionary," propagandist *plainmanism* of her time. The monstrous, desperate, soggy *lengths* of primitive mass-life, chopped off and presented to us as a never-ending prose-song, are undoubtedly intended as an epic contribution to the present mass-democracy.

—Wyndham Lewis, *Time and Western Man*

Gertrude Stein, living in France, has apparently forgotten English—at least the kind of English this reviewer speaks.

—*Detroit News,* qtd. in an advertisement for *Transition*

There is no way of speaking english. I say there is no way of speaking English. What do you mean. I mean that anybody can begin and go on. And finish. It's easy enough and especially hard when there is a use. Why do you say exchange. I do not know what they say exchange. They say they believe in exchange. I often talk about nothing.

What have I to say.

—Stein, "He Said It," *Geography and Plays*

"There Is No Way of Speaking English"

The years of Gertrude Stein's childhood were a time of unprecedented immigration. Five and a half million people immigrated to the United States in the 1880s; four million in the 1890s.[1] These immigrants moved to cities. Farmers joined them. As Howard Zinn notes, "[b]etween 1860 and 1914, New York grew from 850,000 to 4 million, Chicago from 110,000 to 2 million, Philadelphia from 650,000 to 1½ million" (248). In 1910 it is estimated that German was the native tongue for about nine million people living in the United States.[2] Those who moved from the country to the city and who spoke English did so in different, regionally specific dialects. It was thus a time of unprecedented language contact in the United States. People with different language skills, different accents, and different dialects gathered together in closely packed cities. They gathered with their localisms intact, yet they immediately entered into dialogue with speakers of other Englishes and other languages. Some were hopeful about this contact. As Marc Shell notes, "Many German-American writers and visual artists of the 1920s and 1930s were interested in developing a tradition at once multilingual and cosmopolitan" ("Hyphens" 259).

But language politics were also intense and, at times, ugly. English was changing as a result of disparate language knowledges and practices, and this caused various sorts of linguistic anxieties. Michael North charts the other side of Shell's story in *The Dialect of Modernism: Race, Language, and Twentieth-Century Literature*. He recounts the reactive founding of organizations such as the English Society for Pure English and the American Academy of Arts and Letters, both of which mandated the preservation of the English language from the foreign influence perpetuated by immigration. The publications of these groups present inflammatory rhetoric against foreign influences. As North notes, "The boom in linguistic criticism in the United States coincided with the increased immigration of the 1880s and was one manifestation of the reaction against it" (17). The established figures of literary criticism reacted similarly. As North also notes, Royal Cortissoz complained about "Ellis Island art" and Edmund Wilson, in a mixture of complaint and observation, pointed to an American literature that is "polyglot" and a form of "literary vaudeville" (18, 246, 246).

Stein's parents were part of this mass immigration, and like many other immigrants, they spoke English as their second language. In 1875, when Stein was eight months old, her family moved to Vienna for four years. Then they briefly moved to Paris before returning to the United States when she was five. So Stein's prime language learning years would have immersed her in languages other than English. Once an adult, Stein reimmersed herself in the polyglot with her move to Paris in 1904. At the salon she held at 27, rue de Fleurus, many different languages were spoken, and the Anglo-modernist literary culture that she had constant contact with was one of linguistic cosmopolitanism. Raymond Williams notes that one cannot make sense of modernism without seeing it as the literature of the émigré, that "a very striking feature of many Modernist and avant-garde movements [was] that they were not only located in the great metropolitan centres but that so many of their members were immigrants into these centres, where in some new ways all were strangers" (78). As North and others point out, this literature of the émigré is now often indicted as guilty of elitism and racism. T. S. Eliot and Ezra Pound, two of modernism's most indicted, often use languages other than English in their work to shore up their sense of hierarchies of knowledge. Eliot ends "The Waste Land" with a series of polyglot and worldly references.[3] Pound's *Cantos* move among Chinese, English, Greek, Latin, Italian, and other languages. But there is another side to this story, much of it collected in Eugene Jolas's journal *Transition*. Published from 1927 to 1938, *Transition* has a uniquely utopian, if at times almost quaint, take on the political possibilities of nonstandard language practices. While showcasing Stein and James Joyce (with long excerpts from *Finnegans Wake*) in its early issues, it places beside these more established figures work by emerging international avant-gardists such as Gustavo Barroso, Hart Crane, A. Lincoln Gillespie, Jr., Sidney Hunt, St.-John Perse, Laura Riding, Kurt Schwitters, and William Carlos Williams. Editorial statements, almost always concerned with what Jolas would later call "the revolution of the word,"[4] propose nonstandard grammars as challenges to the troubled racial and class politics of standard English and high modernism. (Eliot and Pound are interestingly missing from *Transition*.) In issue number 2, Victor Llona predicts that those in the future will say that the "most striking characteristic [of post–World War I writing] was a determined straining towards an interpenetration of languages and other racial elements such as had never before been attempted or even dreamed of" (169). In issue number 24, Jolas introduces a section called "Inter-Racial Documents" that begins to appear regularly in the journal. He notes: "[The poet] builds the creative language of the future by consciously welding together the elements of all the languages in flux due to the interracial synthesis now going on. He seeks a new syntax and vocabulary in order to give voice to the enormously complicated world of psychic changes that are the result of the biological and politico-economic metamorphoses today" (112). This same issue includes an essay by Luis E. Valcarel which claims that "there are several Americas" (131).

Although North does not directly address *Transition*, he does argue that this modernist rhetoric of liberation was just rhetoric, and he argues that the war between liberation and anxiety over other languages in the 1880s and beyond "was fought over the body of a third figure, a black one" (27). He points to how much modernism aligned the deviance of the nonstandard language of the artist with the dialect of African America. But despite this rhetorical alignment, he notes that its possibilities were "never fulfilled" (129). He writes, "the Americanist avant-garde demonstrated instead a persistent inability to understand how race fit into its conception of modern America, or how the language of African America fit into its conception of 'plain American'" (129). He is right. Anglo-modernism failed on resolving race issues, on actually building a linguistic coalition of attack on dominant culture's exclusivity. Even *Transition* does not live up to its rhetoric, and at times work there seems to foster rather than avoid stereotype.[5] Stein is part of this failure.

Yet while Stein personally failed, her work is more complicated on these issues than North and many other writers assume. North limits his examination of Stein to the undeniably racially troubling "Melanctha."[6] But, her later work (which is a huge amount of work) abandons her appropriation of black culture and all that North notes that it represents at the time. In 1914 she begins, with *Tender Buttons*, to write a series of works that have more complicated takes on issues of language and liberation.[7] And while her work from 1914 to 1933 may not be the "epic contribution to the present mass-democracy" that Wyndham Lewis notes with disdain, the endless (and still strong) anxiety around language issues that it provokes deserves more careful and wide-ranging attention (62). Further, while her work reads to many as divorced from immigrant concerns, I think it could not help but be concerned with the cultural situation where the growth of German-speaking peoples and their productivity result in an anti-German hysteria that begins with World War I and culminates in the United States with Theodore Roosevelt's banning of German-language schools in 1917.[8] Her work is an ideal place for any consideration of reading's politics and possibilities because it is so extreme, so extremely repetitive ("Business in Baltimore"), so extremely fractured (*Tender Buttons*), and so extremely lengthy (*The Making of Americans*). In this chapter I place this much-noted extremity and multivalence of Stein's experimental works in a polyglot historical context, support her claims that she wrote for everybody, and conclude by arguing that what is most resonant about Stein's work is not its radical experimentalism but rather how she, with her attention to reading's autonomy, aligns her work with immigrant and other nonstandard Englishes.

"Fuss Is Spell with s
So Is Business"

Fuss is spell with s
So is business.

—Stein, *A Primer for the Gradual Understanding
of Gertrude Stein*

A grammar is a cause of poplars wire. By this I mean an island
of whether green with attached whether finally knotted carried
all reachable by after at a distance. Now let us know distance is
grammar by after at a plain is description. Dealing is description
detained is grammar. Appointed is grammar at and when is description.

—Stein, "Arthur A Grammar," *How to Write*

It has been a commonplace of Stein criticism to note its multivalence,[9] what Marjorie Perloff first calls the "poetics of indeterminacy" in her book of the same name. And coming at Stein's work from an entirely different direction, Catharine Stimpson calls this multivalence "the lesbian lie." Multivalence, according to Stimpson, is what fools "a public that is both vigilant and unwary as it patrols the borders of permissible speech and behavior" (163). Multivalence is also what Maria Damon, respectful of Stein's ethnicity, notes when she argues in *Dark End of the Street* that Stein's work is like Yiddish.[10] But Stein's multivalence is merely artistic excess (even Stimpson concludes that the lesbian lie is theatrical) unless one sees it as fully engaged with the polylingual politics of immigrant experience. Often the criticism of Stein seems caught between readings of her work as "sui generis"[11] and readings of it as cultural. Yet what I find most useful about Stein's work is how she refuses to see art and culture as separate. Stein's experimental works turn the language patterns of immigrants into art. And, as I will argue in more detail in later sections, she uses this nonstandard English as a reply to grammar's authorities. Stein's works are connective ones. Their content often explores how people with different levels of fluency speak to each other, but they also encourage readers to bring to them different levels of connection, of meaning, of resonance. My argument here draws from Peter Quartermain's observation in the introduction to *Disjunctive Poetics: From Gertrude Stein and Louis Zukofsky to Susan Howe* that Stein, William Carlos Williams, and Louis Zukofsky all either "learned English as their second (or third) language or grew up bilingual" (10).[12]

This reading of Stein's work might seem funny in the context of her professed patriotism about American English,[13] but this patriotism is a good place to begin because it is, like much of Stein's writing, playfully complicated. In *The Autobiography of Alice B. Toklas*, Stein claims that "english was her only language" (91). However, this claim, written in the voice of Toklas, comes at the end of a passage that situates Stein's English in a polyglot context: "Her father having taken his children to Europe so that they might have the benefit of a european education now insisted that they should forget their french and german so that their american english would be pure. Gertrude Stein had prattled in german and then in french but she never read until she read english. As she says eyes to her were more important than ears and it happened then as always that english was her only language" (91).

Similarly, in a much-quoted statement, Stein writes of her self-imposed exile in France as allowing her to be all alone with "english" and herself. But the passage as a whole reads (again in Toklas's voice):

When I first knew Gertrude Stein in Paris I was surprised never to see a french book on her table, although there were always plenty of english ones, there were even no french newspapers. But do you never read french, I as well as many other people asked her. No, she replied, you see I feel with my eyes and it does not make any difference to me what language I hear, I don't hear a language, I hear tones of voice and rhythms, but with my eyes I see words and sentences and there is for me only one language and that is english. One of these things I have liked all these years is to be surrounded by people who know no english. It has left me more intensely alone with my eyes and my english. I do not know if it would have been possible to have english be so all in all to me otherwise. And they none of them could read a word that I wrote, most of them did not even know that I did write. No, I like being with so very many people and being all alone with english and myself. (*Autobiography of Alice B. Toklas* 85–86)

Thus Stein's English is, from the onset, impure, and her ability to be "alone" with it is predicated on the other languages that surround her.

The impurity of American English is, for Stein, related to the unique conditions of its "national" formation:

Always before the language of each nation who had a narrative to make a story to tell a life to express a thing to say did it with a language that had gradually become a language that was made gradually by them to say what they had to say. But here in America because the language was made so late in the day that is at a time when everybody began to read and to write all the time and to read what was written all the time it was impossible that the language would be made as languages used to be made to say what the nation which was coming to be was going to say. (*Narration* 7)

Or, Stein's American English is a language that is not made by "them" but by "everybody." And, perhaps a bit optimistically, she claims it as a language that is not complicit with national government.

This concern with other languages—the languages of nations other than the United States—and the fluency they require is evident throughout Stein's more experimental works. It is so prevalent as to be almost relentless. For instance, what is most striking about *Geography and Plays*, a collection of pieces written between 1908 and 1920 and the first collection that Stein selected for publication, is its constant attention to the specificities of knowledge that fluency in other languages requires. While it has not been unusual for critics to note Stein's concerns with languages in general,[14] her examination of specific languages is often overlooked. And it is important to note here that Stein does not assume fluency. Rather, in her work, fluency in these other languages is presented as unreachable. While communication is continually attempted in these works, there is also lots of anxiety and confusion. "In Marseilles," she writes, "I cannot understand words. Cannot you" (255). "Can you pronounce it," she asks in "The King or Something (The Public Is Invited to Dance)" (131). This piece begins:

Letting me see.
Come together when you can.
Have it higher. You mean that lake.
What was that funny thing you said.
I am learning to say a break.
I am learning to say a clutch.
I am learning to say it in french. (122)

And "Turkey and Bones and Eating" presents this dialogue:

The french language.
Who is it.
What was I saying.
You were saying that you were able to be at home.
Yes I am able to be at home.
Then this is what troubles you.
No it does not trouble me. It makes me realize that I do not wish to leave.
Of course you do not wish to leave.
Yes that was understood.
Did you say that you listened.
Were you speaking what did you wish.
I wish not to be disturbed.
Oh yes we will leave in the spring.
I am not satisfied with what is right. (250–251)

These dialogues are fraught with confusions. They represent, to a certain extent, an anxiety about specific language fluency that might be a result of Stein's self-imposed exile in France and the linguistic cosmopolitanism she would have found there. But it would be a mistake to read these works as merely anxious. What is crucial about them is not that they endlessly register their author's anxiety, but rather that they turn the language tendencies of second-language speakers into a respectful art. Stein approaches the anxiety that accompanies any venture into different language systems from a different angle than do many other writers of ethnically marked literature. The literature of immigrant experience has tended to either smooth over this anxiety and deny the signs of its existence (much immigrant literature is published in grammatically standard English) or, in more populist forms, to lampoon it with exaggeration.[15] Instead of exaggerating the "mistakes" of second-language speakers, Stein composes her works around such nonstandard grammatical variations. "I am a grammarian," she says in *How to Write,* "I do not hesitate but I rearrange prepositions" (109).

Rather than using segregated and ethnically representational models, Stein's experimental works refuse to mark their linguistic engagements as the property of a specific ethnicity. While specific languages are marked as puzzles or tainted by misunderstandings, Stein engages an English that is largely, and widely, immigrant-based. So, while "Melanctha" is undeniably a representation of Black English, the "The Good Anna" of lower-class English, and "The Gentle Lena" of German-immigrant English, the works that come after *Three Lives* entangle the language tendencies of various ethnicities and cultures. Stein's work turns away from specificity and its relation to ethnic parody and burlesque. And she turns to creating works that enact linguistic interaction, polylingualism, and bastardization. In this context, it makes sense to read Stein's work as documenting the decline of English as a language that represents the nation of England. Her work is one among many that begin to take advantage of the rise of many different Englishes as economic imperialism and mass immigration play havoc with any idea of a linguistic standard.

One could use this mixing of different languages as an argument for a new national standard. Walt Whitman, for instance, argues that what makes American English and its literature unique is how it is "enriched with contributions from all languages, old and new" (*American Primer* 2). But Stein avoids such nationalism in her experimental works by turning the ephemeral usages of second-language speakers into the terrain of art.[16] Her works catalog the semantic and syntactic tendencies of a range of second-language speakers. And while one could trace only Germanic and Romantic sentence structures in her works (or privilege Yiddish as Damon does), to do so would be finally misleading. Stein's interest is in the inauthentic and the transitional. She does not reinscribe authentic and national narratives onto her nonstandard English. And thus her work does not exclude the large amount of non-European influences on American English. The ephemeral tendencies of second-language speakers—which include unusually inclusive and complex sentences, phrases or incomplete sentences, nonstandard qualifier and verb usage, duplicate words and/or a restricted vocabulary, and word confusion (such as spelling inconsistencies and homonym confusion)—show up in various forms throughout Stein's work. I want to briefly catalog Stein's use of these techniques to demonstrate how what in many readings appears as mere linguistic polysemy can resonate differently in the context of tendencies of second-language speech patterns.

1. Unusually Inclusive and Complex Sentences

Stein composes most of *The Making of Americans,* her novel of immigrant experience, in complex sentences that violate the grammatical decency and segregation of the English language:

> These certain men and women, our grandfathers and grandmothers, with their children born and unborn with them, some whose children were gone ahead to prepare a home to give them; all countries were full of women who brought with them many children; but only certain men and women and the children they had in them, to make many generations for them, will fill up this history for us of a family and its progress. (3–4)

2. Phrasal or Incomplete Sentences

Stein often fills her work with nonstandard punctuation that mimics the stuttering of someone speaking in an alien or foreign language. In "We Came. A History," one of several works by Stein that skeptically investigate historical reportage, she uses the equal sign as a disrupter:

> How do you like what you have heard.=History must be distinguished=From mistakes.=History must not be what is=Happening.=History must not be about=Dogs and ball in all=The meaning of those=Words history must be=

Something unusual and=Nevertheless famous and=Successful. History must=Be the occasion of having=In every way established a=Precedent history must=Be all there is of importance=In their way successively=History must be an open= Reason for needing them= (*Reflections on the Atomic Bomb* 148–149)

And in "No" she uses periods and line breaks:

Left.
Left.
Pretty.
I
had
pretty
a
good
pretty
like if
room
pretty
all
and
I fire
chairs
pretty
silver
good
left. (*As Fine as Melanctha* 35)

The disruptive nature of the passage is further perpetuated by the context of the piece, in which a military marching song ("I had a good wife and she left, right, left," which itself uses a disruptive technique by doubling the meaning of "left"), is very literally torn apart. These unconventional line or phrasal breaks insert a pause or a silence after each word to draw attention to reading's disruptions. Here Stein draws her reader into reading like someone who lacks a conventionally fluent flow of reading.

3. *Nonstandard Qualifiers and/or Verb Use*

In an attention to the sentence's more minor words, Stein turns qualifiers (relative pronouns, adverbs, future passive verbs: all words that provide grammatical agency and the words that are most difficult to master when learning another language) into the excess of "Patriarchal Poetry":

> Never which when where to be sent to be sent to be sent to be never which when where never to be sent to be sent to be sent never which when where to be sent never to be sent never to be sent never which when where to be sent never to be sent never to be sent which when where never to be sent which when where never which when where never which to be sent never which when where to be sent never which when where to be sent which when where to be sent never to be sent never which when where to be sent never which when which when where to be sent never which when where never which when where which when where never to be sent which when where. (122)

4. *Duplicate Words and/or a Restricted Vocabulary*

At times Stein multiplies helping verbs, as in "Business in Baltimore":

> If he had had and had had given and had had given to him what he had had how many more are there to have held it in this way away. (*Useful Knowledge* 70)

At other times she challenges the boundaries of correctness through deliberate alternate usage:

> What is the difference between a verb and their altering it. If there is a difference between their verb and their altering a verb is not a word. A verb is not a word. Having been what they need their verb is not a word. A word with it. What is a verb. A verb is right away. Therefor there is no need of it. This is why they may upon it. This is a verb. Do be used this is a verb. They will see that they do not defer to not to need. This is a verb in disappearing. This is still a verb and an allowance. Always when there is a verb they do not need a noun. They do not need a verb. With a verb. They have led a life. They have led the life. They have led their life. (*How to Write* 153)

Or she duplicates words as if representing a limited vocabulary:

> Interlude of a dictionary. Spell bells spell best. Spell and spell wishes. Spell sets
> spell such as at once. Spell final and spell felt. Spell rice and spell reality. Spell
> prepare and spell prepared. Spell sale and spell station, spell height and spell
> her spell anticipate and spell shall, spell slate and spell cardinal and spell tell and
> spell well. Spell well as well. Spell what there is to tell. ("Natural Phenomena,"
> *Painted Lace* 176)

5. *Word Confusion*

Stein deliberately plays with code confusion by puzzling over linguistic inconsistencies confusing to second-language speakers:

> Eyes are a surprise
> Printzess a dream
> Buzz is spelled with z
> Fuss is spell with s
> So is business. (*A Primer* 69)

Similarly, even while she claims that "grammar makes no mistakes," Stein
pursues the "mistake" (*How to Write* 81). In this passage, from one of Stein's
books for children, a first reader, the puns are numerous:

> So, now sew and so, so is so and sew is not so, you see to know whether sew
> is so or so is sew how necessary it is so that is to read is so necessary so it is.
> And read just think of read if red is read, and read is read, you see when all is
> said, just now read just then read, do you see even if a little boy or a little girl
> is very well fed if they do not read how can they know whether red is read and
> read is red. How can they know, oh no how can they know. (*First Reader and
> Three Plays* 11)

Here the sight-centered pun registers irregularities that trouble those new to
a language: "read" (present tense), "read" (the past tense), and "red"; "sew"
and "so"; "no," "know," and "now." It has always delighted me that Stein,
who was a champion of child rights, called this a first reader. But the term

also resonates as a primer for those just learning a language, no matter what age.

Stein's insistence that her work is rooted in an immigrant U.S. tradition, and not in the cosmopolitan or worldly or international European-centered one that so enamored T. S. Eliot, Henry James, and Ezra Pound, is telling.[17] Her tendency to align with and kindly mimic the language patterns of second-language speakers is in itself a revision of what it means to be writing an American literature. While it has not been unusual to note the conjunctions between nonstandard English, language politics, and art in writers writing out of colonial experiences,[18] it has been less common to see the same poly-lingual tendencies as a vibrant part of white immigrant American literature. The national narratives told make white immigrant writers look as if they arrived with a standard English fully intact. Immigrant literature tends to mean a tale of assimilation, a transitional story of an ethnically defined iden-tity moving into a larger whole: a United States and white identity, an Ameri-can English that is static. But this identity, this English, was something in the midst of creation. If we are willing to locate something "new" in Stein's writing, and I am willing to do this with the usual qualified reservations, then this new thing is her exploration of what it means to get off a boat and enter into a completely different language system that is most likely learned through a terrifying immersion, not through orderly classrooms. Stein's work points to a polylingual American literature rooted in the localities of dialect and idiolect. It suggests that English (and languages in general) is always fluctuating, always defined by users and the contested field of daily conver-sation, not by grammar handbooks or literatures of standardization. Diaspora as it is figured in these works is not in any way associated with an essential or traditional ethnic identity. Instead, it is something transnational that com-municates across boundaries. Further, Stein's works redefine white immi-grants' relation with American English so as to point to how this relationship has been at times difficult and appropriative. And her work's insistence that "there is no way of speaking english" requires a rethinking of the aesthetics of cultural critique, especially as it relates to immigrant experience. Stein's experimental works present a story of American immigrant literature that is anti-assimilation, that celebrates mistake and insists that there is no hope for a monolingual United States or literature.

"By Any One I Mean Every One"

By any one I mean every one.

—Stein, *Lectures in America*

You see I tried to convey the idea of each part of a composition being as important as the whole. It was the first time in any language that anyone had used that idea of composition in literature. Henry James had a slight inkling of it and was in some senses a forerunner, while in my case I made it stay on the page quite composed. You see he made it sort of like an atmosphere, and it was not solely the realism of the characters but the realism of the composition which was the important thing, the realism of the composition of my thoughts.

After all, to me one human being is as important as another human being, and you might say that the landscape has the same values, a blade of grass has the same value as a tree.

—Stein, *A Primer for the Gradual Understanding of Gertrude Stein*

One could argue that even though Stein's work is rooted in a polylingualism, it is still exclusionary of basic readers because of its very strangeness. Stein, however, denies such accusations when she claims a relation between her "composition" and the fact that "one human being is as important as another human being" (*A Primer* 16). In this section I examine Stein's claims that her writing is for everybody. Or as Stein phrases it, "I am writing for myself and strangers" (*The Making of Americans* 289).

It seems that in the reception of Stein's work a great deal depends on whether one accepts these claims or not. If one does not, Stein is the elitist artist building a career by confounding the masses and propping up the tenure bids of academics. If one does, then Stein is still an ambiguously complicated figure, but one that has something to say about, something to add to, modernism. Bob Perelman has not accepted these claims. He argues against Stein's claim of writing for everybody in *The Trouble with Genius: Reading Pound, Joyce, Stein, and Zukofsky*. Perelman offers a new twist on the

Photograph by Carl Van Vechten in Stein's *Everybody's Autobiography* shows Gertrude Stein surrounded by students at the College of William and Mary in Williamsburg, Virginia, February 8, 1935. (The Yale Collection of American Literature, Beinecke Rare Book and Manuscript Library, from the Carl Van Vechten Trust)[19]

endlessly recurring argument that Stein is all nonsense by arguing that Stein's work is elitist (Leo Stein's and B. L. Reid's arguments of unreadability accuse Stein's writing of being infantile).[20] Perelman writes: "Rather than explicating, evaluating, selecting out thematic coherence, or using the works of these four writers [Pound, Joyce, Stein, and Zukofsky] to articulate an argument as to the nature of language, I want to keep strange the strangeness of their verbal surfaces and extreme rhetorical strategies, and at the same time see how this intensely specialized language is continually at the service of the most ambitious attempts at totalization and social authority" (10). While one could argue that Perelman's position here is evidence of how academic criticism, like fashion, recirculates variations on the argument of unreadability year after year, that is finally too easily dismissive. Perelman's study is careful in its concern for and attention to the cultural meanings of forms in the academy. But despite his critique of the industry of literary criticism, he tends to give most of his attention to what Stein said about her writing and her self rather than to her actual writing or those academics who write about her writing.[21] He sees Stein as lacking any strategy, any irony. In Perelman's reading, there is no possibility of parodic revisionary feminism in a statement of Stein's like "In the month of February were born Washington Lincoln and I" (*Geographical History of America* 45).[22] But one could also argue that Stein's comparisons in this quote suggest an I that flexibly invokes and aligns itself with others. In essence, Stein's comparisons echo Walt Whitman's claim in "Song of Myself" that he contains multitudes: "With the twirl of my tongue I encompass words and volumes of worlds" (*Complete Poems* 89). One could just as easily see Stein's statements as complicitous with the fundamental irony of her work. For instance, she tends to bury her grandiose comparisons in the works that most strongly deny the authority of her self, and even goes so far as to question its existence. A more gracious reading might look at these statements as incantations to banish the insecurity that dominant culture instills in those doing something different, similar to Muhammad Ali's pre-fight boasts. And, as Barrett Watten points out, "Stein can claim to be a genius for the manner in which her *oeuvre* was built, one innovation at a time, so that she could claim, in the displacements of the *Autobiography* to be one: 'What a genius!' in an everyday, open-ended, democratic sense" (19). I do not want to overemphasize Perelman's reading. Rather, I want to point out that Stein's work is to this day, despite numerous successful critical readings, still haunted by claims of unreadability. If Stein's writing remains "obviously unusual and obscure" (150) to someone so steeped in the avant-garde as Perelman, a pioneering language writer, his study seems eerily indicative of a crisis in contemporary visions of reading. And while some might say that linguistic polysemy and dissonance have won the day, reading works like Stein's remains counter-intuitive and unsettling to many.

Stein, however, was very much aware of the accusations of the unreadability of her work (how could she not be, since her brother was making them?), and she provides a series of interesting and often overlooked responses to them throughout her autobiographies, especially *Everybody's Autobiography*. Basically, Stein uses the genre of autobiography to discuss how she wants to be read. She denies her self (which can be read also as a denial of the bourgeois authorial self of autobiography) and compares her self with overlooked and unincluded immigrant or foreign selves, selves that are not where they belong. And it is perhaps exemplary of the wonderful perversity of her work that she presents her theories of reader autonomy in autobiography, the genre that is the most individualistic.

The story I am telling about these autobiographies is one that develops in the history of their reception and the dissonance between the two works. Stein's first autobiography, *The Autobiography of Alice B. Toklas*, made her a celebrity. As many critics have noticed, while this work appears to be yet another traditional autobiography, it is one of trickery, of substitution. Stein writes her own life story under the guise of Toklas's autobiography. Neil Schmitz notes this when he argues that the photograph by Man Ray that opens the book, in which Stein is shown, in shadow, at her desk writing and Toklas, in the light, coming through the door, "returns us to the beginning of Alice's tale, to reread, to review" (204). To follow Schmitz and reread is to realize that *The Autobiography of Alice. B. Toklas* is not only a work written to expose the difficulties—the lies—in the form of autobiography, but that the end result of this deceit reformulates readerly agency in the autobiographical work. Evidence of this is in those very first photographic pages where Stein begins not by taking advantage of readers' trust, but by challenging readers' preconceptions. She communicates the autobiographical joke to readers, not through the authority of her voice, but through sight, the action that mediates reading. She exposes the "I" in autobiography through the reader's eye that looks at the photograph as deceit.[23]

The public liked the book. Some of Stein's friends did not.[24] But both the public and her friends more or less ignored or overlooked Stein's pointed mocking of the cult of personality in this book. So in 1937 Stein published *Everybody's Autobiography*. She wrote it partly in exchange. Alfred Harcourt, the publisher of *The Autobiography of Alice B. Toklas*, wanted another autobiography to publish, but she wanted him to publish her other—to her, more important—works. She offered him another autobiography in the hopes that it would pave the way to publication of these other works.[25] As *The Autobiography of Alice B. Toklas* made Stein and Toklas celebrities, *Everybody's Autobiography* pointedly avoids telling the story of Stein's life and instead tells the story of her work's reception. The first chapter begins with Stein's life after the publication of *The Autobiography of Alice B. Toklas*, and the last ends with her return to France—a period of about a year. Instead of telling about her life, Stein uses the forum of autobiography and its popularity to defend her more experimental work from accusations of unreadability. Her argument is simple: her writing (her self) is not unreadable but rather hyper-readable; it is not elitist but rather written for everybody.

In *Everybody's Autobiography,* Stein's rhetoric is one of inclusion: "Anyway autobiography is easy like it or not autobiography is easy for any one and so this is to be everybody's autobiography" (6). "Everybody" speaks of a collectivity and of an autobiography that denies the exclusivity of the self. The specific "yourself," as she writes, is suspect, "funny":

> And identity is funny being yourself is funny as you are never yourself to yourself except as you remember yourself and then of course you do not believe yourself. That is really the trouble with an autobiography you do not of course you do not really believe yourself why should you, you know so well so very well that it is not yourself, it could not be yourself because you cannot remember right and if you do remember right it does not sound right and of course it does not sound right because it is not right. You are of course never yourself. (68)

The self—or at least the possessed self of "yourself"—dissolves throughout this work. She constructs herself as a negative ("you are never yourself"). In the course of discussing how peau de chagrin (the skin of a calf, a horse, or a mule) came to be called by that name, she gets asked, "how did you happen to be called Gertrude Stein?" (115). Stein's answer: "Identity always worries me and memory and eternity" (115). Stein is similarly worried by people who recognize her on the street and by a film made of her reading "Pigeons on the Grass." At another moment she encounters her name directly:

> we saw an electric sign moving around a building and it said Gertrude Stein has come and that was upsetting. Anybody saying how do you do to you and knowing your name may be upsetting but on the whole it is natural enough but to suddenly see your name is always upsetting. Of course it has happened to me pretty often and I like it to happen just as often but always it does give me a little shock of recognition and non-recognition. It is one of the things most worrying in the subject of identity. (175)

Just as seeing your name is suddenly upsetting and brings on a "funny feeling," Stein presents herself as composed of signs that create a puzzle, a complexity, of identity. *Everybody's Autobiography,* instead of having the conventional photographs of the author at various ages within its pages, has a photograph of Stein that shows her as a crowd, or surrounded by a crowd, by everybody. And she sees naming, the thing that she once thought defined a person, as flexible and variable. "I used to think the name of anybody was very important," Stein writes, "and the name made you and I have often said so. Perhaps I still think so but still there are so many names and anybody nowadays can call anybody any name they like" (10).

Rather than focusing on the singular name, this work is centered on the multiple, the mobile, the names of "everybody." When Stein writes of Picasso's many names, they multiply. Or as Stein phrases it, "finally the names pile up and you take your choice" (10). And the Chinese servants that Stein describes in *Everybody's Autobiography,* for whom "the name they say they are has nothing to do with what they are they may have borrowed or gambled away their reference," are multiply named (10). (I should note here that race in Stein's work is never an easy issue. Stein's stereotyping of the Chinese immigrants as gambling servants is undeniably troubling even if her interest in them is identificatory and she celebrates how they fool the Europeans by duplicating or switching names.)

So Stein switches from the singular duplicity of *The Autobiography of Alice B. Toklas* (Toklas = Stein) to the encompassing yet standoffish duplicities of *Everybody's Autobiography* (Stein = everybody). Both Stein's autobiographies and her experimental works make no sense unless they are read almost as the opposite of autobiography, as tales of the inability to write a narrative of individualism. These works are written to deny the name of the author and her identity as singular. In *Everybody's Autobiography,* Stein literally walks, or drives, away from mimetic representation to pursue the question mark of identity. She has the voice of Toklas explain the relationship between motion and autobiography in *The Autobiography of Alice B. Toklas:* "Wrong or right, said Gertrude Stein, we are going on. She could not back the car very successfully and indeed I may say even to this day when she can drive any kind of a car anywhere she still does not back a car very well. She goes forward admirably, she does not go backwards successfully" (214). Stein's attention to motion speaks to the mutable in a static genre, to an avoidance of identity's usually carefully constructed histories. Stein's travels are a guiding trope for the change of scenes in *Everybody's Autobiography:* she literally walks, drives, and flies readers across the Atlantic to the United States and then across the continent. Yet, while her work may be geographically grounded, her rendering of landscape is absent of any detail. The path Stein takes as she tells the story of her travels is difficult, at times impossible, to map. The introduction, for instance, starts in Los Angeles, at the end of the American tour, returns to New York, at the beginning of the American tour, and then moves back, before the tour, to France. Stories appear in the autobiography at times without chronology or context. Often stories begin with "I was out walking . . . " or "When I was walking the other day . . . " At times Stein uses walks as transitions. In the first chapter, for instance, she concludes one paragraph with "Now I am still out walking. I like walking" and then begins the next with "Yesterday when I went out walking" (12). All this has left critics who attempt to match an anecdote in the autobiography with Stein's travel itinerary in the not uncommon position of Borges's mapmaker, who cannot make a map except to reproduce it on a scale of one to one.

By wandering instead of mapping, the questions this autobiography asks are not "Who is Stein?" but "Who is anybody?" and "Who is everybody?" These are difficult, challenging questions that interrogate pluralism as merely a form of homogeneous inclusion. With them Stein rejects the sort of pluralism that accepts others only under the condition that they adopt the dominant culture's concerns. What interests her about "everybody" is its lack of fixity. In "Poetry and Grammar" she writes that she likes pronouns because they are not fixed: they "represent some one but they are not its or his name. In not being his or its or her name they already have a greater possibility of being something" (*Lectures in America* 213–214). As pronouns let someone be something by not representing someone, so Stein attempts to write an autobiography that invokes this flexibility by emptying out the self of autobiography to acknowledge and encourage instead the everybody of autobiography. Stein presents a pluralism of exclusion rather than one of inclusion. She suggests a pluralism of specificity in "An Instant Answer or a Hundred Prominent Men" when she writes,

> I tell their names because in this way I know that one and one and one and
> one and one and one and one and one and one and one and one and one and
> one and one and one and one and one and one and one and one and one and

one and one and one and one and one and one and one and one and one and
one and one and one and one and one and one and one and one and one and
one and one and one and one and one and one and one and one and one and
one and one and one and one and one and one and one and one and one and
one and one and one and one and one and one and one and one and one and
one and one and one and one and one and one and one and one and one and
one and one and one and one and one and one and one and one and one and
one and one and one and one and one and one and one and one and one and
one and one and one and one and one and one and one and one and one and
one and one and one and one and one and one and one make a hundred. (*Useful Knowledge* 150–151)

Here the names are emptied of prominence, gathered as "ones" to add up to one hundred. Similarly, Jennifer Ashton notes how "*Everybody's Autobiography* is simply a 'history of every one,' but unlike *The Making of Americans,* whose account (in precisely the numerical sense of the term) of everyone derives from additive experience, the autobiography of 'everybody' isn't based on experience at all, but rather on a logical principle of substitutability" (325). Using substitutability rather than individuation, Stein avoids turning the pronoun into a sort of repressive and homogenous über-body by continually filling it with multiple possibilities, multiple images. Similarly, she fills the introduction of *Everybody's Autobiography* with lists of potential anybodies and everybodies. Alice B. Toklas begins one list that continues with Dashiell Hammett, Miss Hennessy, David Edstrom, Mrs. Ehrman, Carl Van Vechten, Charlie Chaplin, the Emersons, Knopf, Charlotte Brontë, George Eliot, Jenny Lind, Grace Darling, Florence Nightingale, Helen, Max White, Lindley Hubbell, Mary Pickford, Belle Greene, Nathalie Barney, Whistler, and Mr. Mathews. Some might call this name-dropping, but this list interests me because of how it crosses gender, race, class, sexuality, and levels of fame. Here Stein has chosen to treat the noun—in this case the proper noun—as she does all nouns, to "refuse them by using them" (*Lectures in America* 228). For in the midst of all these names, it is impossible to equate the representation of everybody with anybody in particular, with any particular identity category. Everybody is rather an embracing of subjectivities.

Everybody is Stein's way of seeing self, friends, acquaintances, and strangers as funny, as foreign. And *Everybody's Autobiography* is one of irony, of anti-ego. In a sense, Stein turns the tables on pluralism. Instead of embracing everyone, she distances the specific from everyone in an attempt to create an egalitarian inclusion that does not smother. Her faith is in the community of the alien or foreign self. It is a conception of community that is not bound with samenesses of nation, race, sexuality, or gender, but rather with the moments that everybody has when they feel they do not fit.[26] Multiplication of the self means there is no true connection with the self. So Picasso and the Chinese servants know with all their names. So Stein realizes as she herself becomes a "name" in the sense of product with the publication of *The Autobiography of Alice B. Toklas.* And this pluralism of exclusion, the escape from specificity that Stein espouses, has at its heart an abandonment of the authority that pluralisms of inclusion tend to leave in place or even at times prop up.

"Grammar Is in Our Power"

As I say commas are servile and they have no life of their own, and their use is not a use, it is a way of replacing one's own interest and I do decidedly like to like my own interest my own interest in what I am doing. A comma by helping you along holding your coat for you and putting on your shoes keeps you from living your life as actively as you should lead it and to me for many years and I still do feel that way about it only now I do not pay as much attention to them, the use of them was positively degrading.

—Stein, "Poetry and Grammar," *Lectures in America*

Authority is afternoon and after grammar. Grammar is in our power.

—Stein, "Arthur A Grammar," *How to Write*

In the last section, I looked at Stein's autobiographies because she presents her philosophy of writing for everybody in these works both by example and by fairly direct statement. But the ramifications of what it means to write for everybody are more dramatically enacted in her experimental, less traditionally narrative works. My argument here is that Stein's works are not subversive, as is often assumed, but are rather connective. They connect with readers. They deny authorial authority and instead encourage readers to be their own authors.

While the disjunction and fragmentation of Stein's work are common to modernism, she uses these techniques in very different ways than do her modernist peers. She exhibits, for instance, an undeniable willful simplicity. This simplicity is crucial to her work. The words she uses tend to be resolutely common, never obscure or archaic. While this does not necessarily make her completely clear to all readers, it does suggest an intent different from much of high modernism. A useful comparison, for example, is how Stein uses the word "rose" to demonstrate her linguistic pyrotechnics in her "rose is a rose is a rose is a rose" phrase, while James Joyce uses the word "bababadalgharaghtakamminarronnkonnbronntonnerronntuonnthunntrovarhounawnskawntoohoohoordenenthurnuk" to demonstrate his in *Finnegans Wake*. I am deliberately choosing an extreme example, but as I point out to students when teaching Stein's work, it is always useful to remember that what makes Stein's work sound strange is not a vocabulary so rich that one must be well schooled in English's half million lexemes to understand it. Her words are intentionally common, simple, and never esoteric. They do not make Joyce's claims for a learned internationalism, but rather privilege what can be done with a limited vocabulary.

Further, and one reason why it is crucial to consider Stein's work in the context of the immigrant language tendencies of the time, in order to understand Stein's work as something other than dadaist, one needs to look at what it builds, at its alliances, and not merely at its resistance or subversion. The tendency has been to read disjunctive or avant-garde works as shattering, not building. These works are associated with resistance or subversion of established norms. They resist the Queen's English, or resist patriarchal language practices, or resist the symbolic. The word "subversive," for example, has often been used to describe Stein's work. Marianne DeKoven describes "the intentional subversiveness of Stein's experimental writing" in her reading of Stein's language as a "'militantly unintelligible' surface" (xxiv). Lisa Ruddick, who decodes *Tender Buttons* with a gnostic frame, writes of how "Stein's gnosticism . . . recreates from the Bible a subversive message about and for women" (10). Even Sandra M. Gilbert and Susan Gubar, who are more than skeptical of Stein's work, write (in a sketchy hypothetical argument) that *The Autobiography of Alice B. Toklas* is "a subversive gift from Alice B. Toklas" (254). While I do not want to hold literary criticism to too high a standard, the endless assertion of resistance or subversion that is attached to Stein's nonstandard language seems indicative of what Meaghan Morris has called the "banality" of cultural studies which reduces all action to resistance (3). No wonder there are constant questions about the value of such a practice.

But I want to insist that Stein's work is as much one of building as of subverting. In this passage from *Tender Buttons,* for example, Stein mocks the act of creation in a series of puns that the reader creates:

> Pain soup, suppose it is question, suppose it is butter, real is, real is only, only excreate, only excreate a no since.
>
> A no, a no since, a no since when, a no since when since, a no since when since a no since when since, a no since, a no since when since, a no since, a no, a no since a no since, a no since, a no since. (58)

Here a word like "excreate" appears to be only bordering on sense, but zooms into sense upon reading the obvious puns of "excretion," "creation," and a possible negative of something like x-creation. "A no since" similarly makes little sense unless read for the nuances of "nonsense" and "innocence"; "when sense" for "winces."

At other moments she splits words in half or adds onto them. This is from a piece called "In":

(I)   Was. Cream
               Pear——ery.
               Cut——ery
               Slice ear——ie
               A creamerie. (*Bee Time Vine* 44)

In this passage, the reader is left with the question of how to read. There is no indication of what, if anything, should be created out of the words. One can, for instance, add an "l" to "Cut——ery" to make "cutlery," but the reference the fractured word makes is multiple, for one could as easily create "cutchery."

On an anecdotal level, I have had amazing experiences teaching Stein to students in introductory-level composition courses. While the students' first response is often laughter, I have also found that, when encouraged and after the laughter dies down, they can produce fascinating readings of the work that are grounded in their own experience. Many are, like Stein, immigrants. Many of them hear or speak another language at home. And they can easily take advantage of Stein's mandate in *Tender Buttons* to "re letter and read her" and bring their own concerns to the work (59). In a recent class, for instance, one student argued that "GLAZED GLITTER" (a section of *Tender Buttons*) was about counterfeiting and the falseness of money (centered around the phase "Nickel, what is nickel" that begins the passage [9]); another argued that it was about racial categories in twentieth-century America (this one concentrating on "There can be breakages in Japanese. That is no programme. That is no color chosen. It was chosen yesterday . . . " [9]); another that it was a critique of cleanliness (this one quoting " . . . very charming is that clean and cleansing. Certainly glittering is handsome and convincing" as speaking to the superficial values of cleanliness [9]). This is an exceptional range of readings for an introductory writing class, and it illustrates what readers can do once they are encouraged to push past their initial resistance.

Similarly, I have found that this work encourages students of English as a second language to overcome their fear that poetry is too allusive, too dense with doubled meaning for their level of language and cultural knowledge. Stein's work serves as an empathic relation for second-language speakers. They see a reflection and validation of their sense that English is unusually structured, almost as if her works had been written for the cross-lingual skills of second-language speakers. While student evidence is necessarily anecdotal and tainted by classroom politics, I include it here as a counter to arguments made by literary critics who often assume that because Stein's work does not fully utilize their well-developed close reading skills, it must also be too difficult for students to read. Or worse, irrelevant to student experience.

Stein's work suggests that questions of authorial intent are not a priority. It is not that the author is dead, just never really in control. Throughout her work she challenges the definitional closeness between the words "author" and "authority." For instance, she places the author behind the door in *Tender Buttons*: "The author of all that is in there behind the door and that is entering in the morning" (64). This same work urges the translation of authority so as to show a choice: "Dance a clean dream and an extravagant turn up, secure the steady rights and translate more than translate the authority, show the choice and make no more mistakes than yesterday" (76). At other moments, she self-reflexively explains how to escape this authority: "Largely additional and then completely exploding is one way to deny authorisation" (*GMP* 98). In this play with the word "authority" Stein abandons her own authorship and turns it over to readers, who, when reading the work actively, participate by constructing their own readings. Her work does not deny authority but instead advocates its dispersal (decentralization), a dispersal that relies on the multiple possibilities and interpretations distributed among different readers, and one that has, literally, to do with not knowing the language. "Any and every one is an authority," she writes in "A Little Novel" (*A Novel of Thank You* 262). She writes also of how "Nouns are the name of anything and anything is named, that is what Adam and Eve did and if you like it is what anybody does" (*Lectures in America* 229). Here it is not merely, as it is in Genesis, that Adam names, but Eve joins him, and even she is not alone as they are both pointedly joined by the nongendered "anybody," a common person, the reader. For Stein, the author is an agent or facilitator. While the author cannot help but be a creator, he or she is just one of many and also the one who remains behind the door when the work leaves and becomes read by others.

In this context, the often-noted disjunctions of Stein's work are not yet another example of a dadaist destruction. Instead, they show multivalence as they jolt readers out of the conventional patterns of reading in order to show other possibilities. As Priscilla Wald points out, it is interesting to consider Stein's early experiments with "normal motor automatism" in this context. In the 1890s when Stein was still in medical school, she did several experiments with Leon M. Solomons. The object of these experiments, Solomons and Stein note in their write-up of the study, "was primarily to determine the limits of normal automatism, and, if possible, show them to be really equal to the explanation of the second personality; and incidentally to study as carefully as possible the process by which a reaction becomes automatic" (9–10). Solomons and Stein had their subjects hold a pen and rest their hand on a planchette covered with paper. As a result, the subjects could easily move their arm without much will. Then Solomons and Stein read out loud to put their subjects in a state that would allow them to access the automatism. As they write, "[t]he words read must be familiar for the automatism to work well. Dialect stories do not go well at all" (19). It is probably not without coincidence that Stein, ever interested in disrupting the hypnotism of reading's conventions, begins her publishing life with *Three Lives*'s dialect stories and then later turns this work into the more extremely disjunctive experimental works.

But such literal examples are minor. The real importance of Stein's works is in the alternate grammars they build. Correct grammar is most obviously one of society's more dramatic class markers. Proper usage is required for entry into even menial jobs and social situations. Yet proper usage is often obtained by those new to learning English only after years of immersion. But Stein's work embraces grammatical deviance, opposes standards. She, for instance, rejects certain grammatical conventions because they restrict agency. She denounces commas because they keep "you from living your life as actively as you should lead it" and are thus "positively degrading" (*Lectures in America* 220). Her statements about grammar in the punningly titled "Arthur A Grammar" in *How to Write* are expansive. They veer in and out of conventional sense yet are also at moments wonderfully sloganistic and reformatory. "Attack attach grammar," the work proclaims at one point (75). The point of many of these statements is that when one authors a grammar—one's own grammar, not *the* grammar of the standard—grammar turns into a way of joining and a metaphor for community. So Stein writes, "Grammar is the art of reckoning that it is by themselves that they are one and two" (48). Or "Grammar unites parts and praises. In just this way" (63). Such utopian hopes in grammar are built out of a reckoning that "Grammar is a conditional expanse" (55). Similarly, in works like *Lifting Belly* it is often a small step between respect for grammatical deviance and respect for what is considered by some to be sexual deviance. And while I do not want to make too much of Stein's complicated marginality, there is a probable connection between her lack of respect for social and grammatical convention and her own status as an outsider: a woman, a Jew, and a lesbian.

I have been arguing that such grammatical deviance is related to the speech patterns of those new to English or those who have learned the Englishes created by economic imperialism and migration. And that Stein's twist is to make her own immigrant experiences into art. In this context, Stein's statement of writing for herself and strangers is not, as it is often read, one of hubris, but rather one of empathy with those new to English's grammatical geographies. But for those of us schooled in Dick and Jane, Stein's writing also provides an unsettling challenge to our reliance on our mastery of English conventions when reading. Her works turn our reading into the stumbles and turns of second-language speakers. We are encouraged to abandon our fluency, the very thing we have worked so hard to hone. We are allowed to acknowledge language's disruptions and the art they make. We are challenged to reformulate the connection between aesthetic beauty and conventions of correctness.

For those reluctant to give up the mastery of fluency, Stein provides two wonderful examples of how to read. In *The Geographical History of America,* she tells of getting her hair cut one afternoon and having to take her glasses off. In this passage, Stein writes that reading becomes pleasurable when one has one's glasses off and uses them as a magnifying glass to enlarge and distort each individual word:

> reading word by word makes the writing that is not anything be something.
>> Very regrettable but very true.
>> So that shows to you that a whole thing is not interesting because as a whole well as a whole there has to be remembering and forgetting, but one at a time, oh one at a time is something oh yes definitely something. (143)

The second anecdote occurs in *The Autobiography of Alice B. Toklas,* where Stein (in Toklas's voice) compares the act of reading to that of proofreading or dusting: "I always say that you cannot tell what a picture really is or what an object really is until you dust it every day and you cannot tell what a book is until you type it or proof-read it" (138–139). In these anecdotes, Stein pays attention to both form and its disruptions. Works are interesting, she is arguing, when their form is distorted, whether by isolation and magnification or by relentless daily attention to detail. It is probably true that Stein's ideal audience was middlebrow (she longed for acceptance by the New York publishing world), yet it is interesting to note who Stein's "ideal" readers are here: dusters, typists; women, basically, Toklas specifically. Her feminism, always a subject of some controversy and doubt, resonates in this passage not as essentialism but rather as a revision of women's domestic space and the repetitive task. For Stein, conventional reading misses the fragility and detail of the object, both its composition and its errors. What she offers instead is a sort of domestic reading of repetitive disruptions. While Stein's work is often seen as employing an aesthetic of brashness that knocks you over the head with its obviousness, understanding it frequently requires surrendering to caresses of consciousness.

I like to see Stein's emphasis here on distorted forms as not simply registering the difference of the form of her writing but as a concern for how readers experience its forms and a cultivation of readerly differences. Stein's work shifts emphasis away from the single, inherent meaning and toward the choices and possibilities of meaning that, to some extent, are encountered by any reader. She valorizes all those moments of reading that many theorists filter out as irrelevant or uncommon or mistaken. The question here shifts from how an author should represent the world to how readers are (or can be) engaged in continual acts of representation. Stein insists that readers take active roles in their relationship with the work. It is in her continual return to words (rather than an avant-garde breaking off) that the possibilities of reading are evident. Her polylingual grammars allow readers to connect with multiple meanings and thus to recognize multiple strategies of response. Stein's works allow a decentralized self-governance and autonomy on the part of the reader by giving the reading act as much authority as the authoring act.

Stein's attention to multiple, alternate grammars suggests an egalitarian theory of reading that is radical in its intent and form. Her works do not emphasize community but rather that which makes community work: communication. She does not give in to those policing and conservative worries about creating a Tower of Babel. Instead, she acknowledges that there will always be people who have trouble understanding each other and that it is the role of literature to demonstrate tolerance and respect for those moments. And her work provides readers with the tools to handle such situations by writing a tolerant literature of polylingual grammar that makes room for less smooth communication, for a slower and different discourse of possibility. This work questions literary criticism's emphasis on the desirability of fluent reading by always asking who controls reading, for what purpose. It undermines all easy assumptions about language, class, and ethnicity. It is not that Stein's fragmentation is in itself necessarily revolutionary, but rather that her alignment of it with immigrant and other nonstandard Englishes provides a new perspective on the ramifications of fragmentation. And most importantly, it points to the importance of linguistic patience and respect in a country where everyone might not be fully fluent.

"An Animal Enters Into Things"

To make use of the polylingualism of one's own language, to make a minor or intensive use of it, to oppose the oppressed quality of this language to its oppressive quality, to find points of nonculture or underdevelopment, linguistic Third World zones by which a language can escape, an animal enters into things, an assemblage comes into play.

—Gilles Deleuze and Félix Guattari, *Kafka: Towards a Minor Literature*

—Photograph of Gertrude Stein with Pablo Picasso's portrait (March 1930, copyright © UPI/Corbis-Bettmann)

—photograph of Stein and Baskett II with Marie Laurencin's portrait of Basket (ca. 1940–1946; The Yale Collection of American Literature, Beinecke Rare Book and Manuscript Library)

When suddenly you know that the geographical history of America has something to do with everything it may be like loving any man or any woman or even a little or a big dog.

—Stein, *Geographical History of America: Or, The Relation of Human Nature to the Human Mind*

Stein's work is many animals.[27] It turns populist speech patterns into art. It argues that this art which appears strange and unusual to some can have roots in the common, the everyday, can include everybody. It points to the polylingual roots of American speech and literature. I am well aware that I am in some sense candy-coating Stein's desires of bourgeois assimilation (her desire to be published in the *Saturday Evening Post*) and her complicated politics (her lack of respect for conventional feminism, her friendship with Bernard Fay). Yet if Stein's work is guilty of a bourgeois assimilation, it is a very peculiar manifestation of it. In part, the reception of her as "art," as divorced from culture, is indicative of a certain crisis in how avant-garde writing often gets read. But we cannot afford to ignore the avant-garde's engagements with culture. We cannot afford to overlook works that suggest alternate ways of speaking English. Or, in other words, if Stein is not the democrat that I am arguing her work suggests she could be, still there is much to be learned from the anarchic democracy of the works themselves.

I have begun with Stein's work because it provides a clear articulation and example of the relationship between nonstandard grammars and reader connection. In the chapters that follow, I look at writers that talk directly with and to Stein's work or its intent. I look at work by Bruce Andrews, Lyn Hejinian, Harryette Mullen, and Theresa Hak Kyung Cha, all writers in the United States from the 1970s to the present. I am interested in what reader autonomy has to add to discussions of subjectivity that happen at this time, in how language writers Hejinian and Andrews use Stein's multivalence to critique both the privileges of white subjectivity and the language that holds this privilege in place, and in how an African-American poet like Mullen responds to Stein with both critique and homage by taking advantage of Stein's mandate to "re letter and read her" (*Tender Buttons* 59). I conclude by looking at the work of Cha. While there is no evidence of any direct line of influence between Stein and Cha, Cha writes out of a late 1970s and early 1980s experimentalism and performance scene that is very much concerned with issues of audience/reader response and nonstandard language practices.

Despite their differences, these writers all represent some fulfillment of the egalitarian project that manifests itself in Stein's peculiar turn to avant-garde modernism in order to write a literature for "everybody." I am not suggesting that Stein's work is the only or even the pivotal influence on the work of Andrews, Hejinian, Mullen, and Cha. Rather, these works made my vision of Stein possible as much as her work makes my vision of these other works possible. The back and forth here is intricate, for when Stein abandons her authority her works become susceptible to all sorts of time and space distortions. This is what Nicholas Royle calls a reading method of "telepathy": an "uncanny reading-machine, a sort of reader-response criticism in reverse" (7). As much as Stein helps one to read Mullen, for instance, Mullen helps one to read Stein.

"Make It Go with a Single Word. We."

Bruce Andrews's "Confidence Trick" and Lyn Hejinian's *My Life*

Reading does not consist merely of decoding the written word or language; rather, it is preceded by and intertwined with knowledge of the world. Language and reality are dynamically interconnected. The understanding attained by critical reading of a text implies perceiving the relationship between text and context.

—Paulo Friere and Donaldo Macedo, *Literacy: Reading the Word and the World*

Literacy, here, suggests building a public in the old-fashioned sense—one where individuals are able to orient themselves to social life more broadly, rather than just rubber-stamping the existing agendas of the rich and the powerful. In a parallel way, this kind of writing might then seem like a part of public life—in the sense of the public sphere—an access point to totality, the underlying conditions for the construction of which are tied up with the social system of meaning. So that a totalizing poetic practice involves a kind of social denormalizing—at work on the structure of the sign but also on these larger shapes of meaning—that would allow for a revitalizing of the idea of a *public sphere* as more than a cheering section for the effects of capitalism.

The whole is unfinished.

—Bruce Andrews, *Paradise & Method: Poetics & Praxis*

After crossing the boundary which distinguishes the work from the rest of the universe, the reader is expected to recross the boundary with something in mind.

—Lyn Hejinian, *My Life*

"Building a Public in the Old-Fashioned Sense"

If, as Foucault so famously claimed, the author is dead, then language writing adds: long live readers.

"Language writing" is a term used to describe a school of experimental writing of the 1970s and 1980s that often looks at first glance like a disjunctive morass of phrases and sentences. This movement takes up Stein's emphasis on reader autonomy as a mandate. As Marjorie Perloff notes, language writing shows that "our words can no longer be our own but that it is in our power to represent them in new, imaginative ways" ("Can(n)on to the Right of Us" 654). In this context, reading gains a political possibility. The disjunctive morass that characterizes much language writing emphasizes the inversion of hierarchical models of reading. As with Stein's work, it is readers, not an author, that matter here. Yet as much as this writing is under the influence of Stein,[1] it is also under the influence of changing models of politics that come to prominence in the 1960s. Like that decade's model of grassroots organizing, language writing valorizes multiple and individual response. It tends to emphasize reading's social function and optimistically argue for its reconstructive possibilities. As Bruce Andrews argues, it wants to build "a public in the old-fashioned sense" (*Paradise & Method* 48).

In much language writing the clear, distinguished poetic voice of most political writing is replaced with fractured words and/or sentences that lack attribution. Quotation and bricolage are dominant compositional techniques. (Andrews's notes about his compositional style: "writing is editing, writing is a construction of previously generated materials, similar to what my filmmaker friends do—go out and shoot short chunks of footage, go to the flatbed, assemble films in the *editing* process. As opposed to writing out draft poems in notebooks" [*Paradise & Method* 103].) Phrases and sentences that avoid narrative's necessary hierarchies are preferred. Antihierarchical language is a value in its own right, as it refuses lineages and cultural privileges.

The focus of this chapter is this politicized model of reading. As I examine the claims this group of writers makes for reading's autonomous possibility, I concentrate on Bruce Andrews's "Confidence Trick" and Lyn Hejinian's *My Life*. Both of these works reach out and engage large, public worlds that are in turn shared with readers. Writing a work that encompasses the world is a modernist impulse, but if it is necessary to locate something in language writing that is distinct from modernism, it might be found in this pursuit of a work that is public and yet at the same time nonappropriative. In "Confidence Trick" and *My Life,* an attention to a larger world is accompanied by a move to share authority with readers and an accompanying abandoning of authorial privilege. My desire thus is to distinguish the public works of language writing (works that reflect and respect multiple places for engagement) from the global works of modernism or ethnopoetics (works that collect representative references to a wide range of cultures). As the public work is more multiply connective and less culturally referential, it is one that assumes reading is generative as well as interpretative. In this chapter, I begin with an overview of the theories of reading associated with language writing, concentrate on the attention to connective reading in these works, and then conclude by moving outward and arguing that this turn to reader autonomy that dominates avant-garde literature of the late twentieth century has much to add to discussions of identity and subjectivity.

"But Not Bitter"

We aim to involve people and use (unlike other movements locked in ideology) any weapon (prop) we can find. The aim is not to earn the respect, admiration, and love of everybody—it's to get people to do, to participate, whether positively or negatively.

—Free [Abbie Hoffman], *Revolution for the Hell of It*

Language-centered work resembles an active mythmaking. It resembles a creation of a community and of a worldview by a once-

divided-but-now-fused Reader and Writer. This creation is not in-
strumental. It is immanent, in plain sight (and plainsong), moving
along a surface with all the complications of a charter or town
meeting.

—Andrews, "Text & Context," in *Paradise & Method*

To follow the progress of ideas, or that particular line of reasoning, so full of surprises and unexpected correlations, was somehow to take a vacation.

—Hejinian, *My Life*

An extremely pleasant and often comic satisfaction comes from
conjunction, the fit, say, of comprehension in a reader's mind to
content in a writer's work. But not bitter.

—Hejinian, *My Life*

The theories of reading promulgated by language writing take up the multiplicity of meaning that deconstruction so successfully illuminated. And yet,
if deconstruction at times slides into a sort of fancy and apolitical form of
close reading in the American context,[2] in the theoretical work of language
writing its multiplicity remains resolutely and primarily political. This is most
evident in the writings of Andrews and Ron Silliman. Both these writers'
criticism is characterized by a utopian dogmatism that violates much of the
decorum of the traditional academic essay. Their writing is often attacked
for its bold optimism,[3] yet it is this optimism that makes it interesting, not
to mention a useful contribution to academic thinking in general, which
tends to privilege dystopic thinking. But more importantly, this theoretical
writing extends, politicizes, and radicalizes reading-orientated theories that
came to prominence in the 1980s. And while attention to reading has fallen
out of fashion with the rise of more culturally concerned methodologies,
much of this writing points to important reasons why reading and culture
should not be separate concerns in literary studies.

Andrews refuses to ever underestimate reading. In terms that resemble reader response theory, he argues in "Text & Context" for "[r]eading as a particular reading, an enactment, a co-production" (*Paradise & Method* 12). Similarly, he calls for works that emphasize the reader's productive role: "Altering textual roles might bring us closer to altering the larger social roles of which textual ones are a feature. READING: not the glazed gaze of the consumer, but the careful attention of a producer, or co-producer. The transformer. (capacitators? resistors?) Full of care. It's not a product that is produced, but a *production*, an event, a praxis, a model for future practice" (*Paradise & Method* 12). In "Poetry as Explanation, Poetry as Praxis" his vocabulary and attention extend beyond reader response theory's emphasis on decorous (or model) reading as he calls for wild reading:

> Define comprehension as something other than consumption. (*Other then.*) So it's politicizing: a radical *reading* embodied in writing. A writing that is itself a "wild reading" *solicits* wild reading. The reading is a response, is a *dialogue with* the paradigms of sense—with *rhetoric* (which is a misreading in the writing itself): "We've been misread!" The job is to go beyond these norms and limits, to *read them backward,* to offer up a different refraction of the circumstance. Let's let the status quo *read itself* being quarantined, scolded, frag'd, & interrupted. (*Paradise & Method* 54–55)

Wild reading here critiques the status quo because it disrupts schooled reading's conventions, its socialization. This is in contrast to much reading-orientated theory that is concerned mainly with expanding conventional reading's possibility within the institutional setting.

One's approach to reading, Andrews argues, defines how one engages the larger social apparatus. Language systems are continually presented as analogous governmental systems in his theoretical work. In "Constitution/ Writing, Politics, Language, the Body" Andrews portrays U.S.-supported tyranny as a social grammar: "*Pause to reflect on prevalence of U.S.-supported tyranny in Third World* (for certainly the world political economy also takes the shape of a *correctional* institution, of a disciplinary society, a social grammar)" (*Paradise & Method* 27). Conventional or schooled reading is a socializing and colonizing force in essays like "Revolution Only Fact Confected."

This faith in reading is not unique to Andrews. While I have concentrated on his work because of the intenseness of his rhetoric, it would be a mistake to suggest that these ideas are his alone. Language writing as a movement is a mix of agreement and disagreement. As Jed Rasula points out, there is no "unified or typical voice," but there is some consensus around the importance of "the restoration of the reader as coproducer of the text and an emphasis on the materiality of the signified" ("The Politics of, the Politics in" 319). Similar utopian rhetorics are in the essays and critical writing of Charles Bernstein (especially in *Artifice of Absorption*), Lyn Hejinian (especially "Rejection of Closure"), Steve McCaffery (especially in parts of *Rational Geomancy*, written with bpNichol), and Ron Silliman (especially in the essay collection *The New Sentence*).[4] The rhetoric of language writing points again and again to how language is bound up with a repressive governmental apparatus and also with capitalism in general. Silliman's "Disappearance of the Word, Appearance of the World," for instance, argues that language, beginning in 1557 with *Tottel's Miscellany,* "moves toward and passes into a capitalist stage of development" which "is an anesthetic transformation of the perceived tangibility of the word, with corresponding increases in its expository, descriptive and narrative capacities, preconditions for the invention of 'realism,' the illusion of reality in capitalist thought" (10).

If the theoretical aspects of language writing's call to arms seem reductive at times, it is nevertheless a productive reduction. This writing gets at something that is often ignored. Western languages support and are supported by the mercantile tendencies of society, which valorize that which can be counted: the grammatical subject/object. The subject of the sentence is always an object—a person, place, or thing—and is given hierarchical priority. Subserviently, the verb gives action to this subject. Its conjugation is dependent on the subject/object's numerical quality, and the adjective bestows qualities on this subject. These objects are represented in grammar as fixed, locatable, and countable. Even uncountable subjects, abstract nouns such as "freedom" or "love," for example, appear to be quantitatively manageable in the sentence. The emphasis on disjunction and the nonstandard grammatical economy that accompanies much language writing challenges the assumption that language is an individual affair, a segregated mode of expressive correspondence that is unconnected to larger social apparatuses. It follows, therefore, that reading has a primary shaping influence on modern consciousness. And, when reading is social, it has the potential to either transform or reinforce the status quo. The urgency of much of Andrews's and Silliman's theoretical writing can be traced back to a utopian desire to write social spaces where conversation, shifts of thinking's conventions, and exchanges of ideas can happen. Both argue that shifting writing's conventions will shift readers' understanding of the world as they become themselves authors.

It is this claim to refigure reading's politics that has come under contestation in recent years. In general these critiques have tended to reply to the utopian claims of those associated with language writing with a parallel dystopian dogmatism. (And also tend to ignore, or not engage, the more balanced investigation of critics like Alan Golding, George Hartley, Hank Lazer, Perloff, Rasula, and Andrew Ross.)[5] An editorial in the journal *Apex of the M,* for instance, polemically asserts without much analysis that "[l]anguage poetry, in reproducing and mimicking the methods and language of contemporary capitalism, ultimately commits itself to the same anonymity, alienation, and social atomization of the subject in history that underlie capitalist geo-politics" (5).[6] Fredric Jameson does a similarly cursory reading in *Postmodernism: Or the Cultural Logic of Late Capitalism,* where he calls language writing, using Bob Perelman's writing as example, "schizophrenic fragmentation" (28).[7] Jameson's argument is basically the opposite of many of the claims made by those associated with language writing who equate form with effect. To Jameson, because language writing appears to be fragmentary, it fragments the mind.

A lot of the resistance to language writing by otherwise skilled readers like the editors of *Apex of the M* and Jameson seems to have to do with how this writing questions not only conventional lyricism but also conventional politicism. Most critics of language writing tend to overlook how the writing creates sense on its own terms once readers switch over to being co-producers. Thus this work seems especially alienating or schizophrenic if one considers reading as an act that illuminates meaning's singularity.

But also, language writing often appears alienating to those concerned with the political possibilities of poetry because it challenges the conventions of American political yet experimental poetry that get defined in the 1960s with the publication of *The New American Poetry.*[8] The New American poetry speaks against the system, yet remains voice- and personality-centered. It values individualism and nonconformity. It sets the poet up as seer, guide, and shaman. Allen Ginsberg's "Wichita Vortex Sutra" is a stunning example of this poetry.[9] It is clearly ego-centered and easily recognized as political verse by its calling out to the system and its idiosyncratic engagement with the world. Ginsberg writes, for example,

> I lift my voice aloud,
>> make Mantra of American language now,
>>> I here declare the end of the War!
>>>> Ancient days' Illusion!—
> and pronounce words beginning my own millennium.
> Let the States tremble,
>> let the Nation weep,
>>> let Congress legislate its own delight
>>>> let the President execute his own desire—
> this Act done by my own voice. (407)

This piece, a sort of poetic *On the Road,* beautifully mixes American geography with Buddhist terminology with commentary on the Vietnam War.

But when language writing emphasizes reading's co-production, the forms of writing change. Individualism and its clear voice, even in its plural forms, are necessarily abandoned. And at the same time, the left's conviction that an uneducated populace needs to be educated by works written in as conventional (often called "clear") a manner as possible is challenged. While Jameson's readers encounter the fragment only as fragment, Andrews's readers move from fragment to wild forms of reading.

Of all the critics who have taken on language writing, Charles Altieri has questioned the claim of reader freedom and its political aims the most cogently. In an extended reply to a defense of language writing by Jerome McGann, he challenges the equation between "art as a mode of production and the psychic economies governing basic forms of social life" ("Without Consequences Is No Politics" 303). He points out that empty claims of reader freedom at times resemble "the free, pleasure-seeking consumer that L=A=N=G=U=A=G=E Writing's doctrines so pompously revile" (306).[10] In another article that covers similar territory, he worries that these works "risk trapping us in wordy prisons because they do not make sufficient demands that we try out identifications with how others construct meanings for situations" ("Some Problems about Agency" 215).

Many of Altieri's concerns are legitimate, especially his worry that freedom is being reduced to a slogan. There has been a tendency for those associated with language writing to privilege the form of manifesto in their theoretical writing and to pursue the rhetoric of readerly freedom without detailed analysis.[11] And his unease is also provocative because it so directly addresses what is crucial about reading: its role in community formation.

But while I share some of Altieri's concerns, many of them disappear when one turns to what is crucial about reading in the time of language writing. Freedom is, of course, impossible to even imagine as a concept related to reading (and even the most utopian rhetoric in language writing merely envisions form guiding toward a sort of localized emancipation for the individual reader; or the claims seem not as grand as Altieri fears they are). Instead of freedom, which tends to imply that readers are somehow freed from meaning's mandate, what interests me about this work is how connection becomes the crucial value. And the importance of the theoretical optimism that accompanies language writing is how the often narrowly conceived values of beauty or lyricism are replaced by the values of connection and generative thinking. This writing argues that one can have both a political and an aesthetic sensibility. A work that privileges the shareable, that encourages connection, is not only a more productive read but also a more rewarding one. As Hejinian realizes, it is the correlation, the conjunction, the fit of comprehension, that delights and stimulates.

"Make It Go with a Single Word. We."

We don't want to be shy about this—we want to be in contact with other writers whose work we think is worthwhile; we want to learn something from them. That is why we advocate freedom of association, and through that freedom, within the economy of means of any social process, comes the dynamics of a literary school. It's a part of a mutual, collective finding out not formally defined by abstract judgment. And, by extension, we assume that other writers and groups would pursue their ends in similar means.

—Ron Silliman, Carla Harryman, Lyn Hejinian, Steve Benson, Bob Perelman, Barrett Watten, "Aesthetic Tendency and the Politics of Poetry: A Manifesto"

Make it go with a single word. We.

—Hejinian, *My Life*

Class background is not landscape—still here and there in 1969
I could feel the scope of collectivity.

—Hejinian, *My Life*

Why diddle?

—Andrews, "Confidence Trick"

Think of yourself as a twin.

—Andrews, "Confidence Trick"

"Building a public in the old-fashioned sense"; the word "we";[12] "the scope of collectivity": these tend to be related but vague concepts in the work of Hejinian and Andrews. Yet these phrases point to what is crucial about the role of reading in twentieth-century avant-garde writing in general. They point to how this writing moves reading from a solitary act of complicity (of comprehension, say, in the most reductive sense of that term) to a shareable and social act of exchange. Most simply, works are created so that readers are encouraged to engage with them multiply. But this multiplicity of meaning extends beyond words themselves and into communal, social engagements. Reading here is an act of reciprocity. It is speculative and dynamic. It is a place to rethink the status quo or to learn new things because it is part of a communal attempt to shift discourse. This work insists that the politics of writing does not reside merely in content or in individual writers, as is often assumed, but in a collective and social attention to language. The aesthetic of these works is not individualistic (there are no genius writers or readers),[13] but rather anarchically communal.

The most obvious, and most often commented upon, emphasis on the shareable is the dominant role communal activities, such as collaboration, have played in language writing.[14] And while the grouping, and the term, "language writing" is often contested by those who are considered part of the scene, as Perelman notes, "language writing is best understood as a group phenomenon" (31). In *The Marginalization of Poetry: Language Writing and Literary History*, for instance, Perelman tells of a writing exercise he did with Kit Robinson and Steve Benson: one person would read from a book, and the other two would type in response (riffing off whatever was read).[15] This example is a good literal metaphor for the emphasis on shareable process and on the relation between reading and writing. Similarly, in the communally written "Aesthetic Tendency and the Politics of Poetry: A Manifesto," Silliman, Harryman, Hejinian, Benson, Perelman, and Barrett Watten refer to "our" work (but also avoid terms such as "language writing").[16] They note: "If there has been one premise of our group that approaches the status of a first principle, it has been not the 'self-sufficiency of language' or the 'materiality of the sign' but *the reciprocity of practice implied by a community of writers who read each other's work*" (271). There are also numerous co-authored works, such as *Legend* (authored by Andrews, Bernstein, Ray DiPalma, McCaffery, and Silliman) and *Leningrad* (authored by Michael Davidson, Hejinian, Silliman, and Watten).

Further, this emphasis on community building is accompanied by a do-it-yourself sensibility. Beginning in the 1970s, this group of writers created a parallel universe to the mainstream poetry establishment where they jointly controlled the production, distribution, and reception of their work.[17] This parallel universe differs in several important ways from the poetry establishment, or what Bernstein calls "official verse culture" (*Content's Dream* 247).[18] Most obviously, those who control the production are multiple and are also writers as well as publishers and editors. Also, this community never claims to be official, authorized, or dominant. And within this attention to production, the emphasis is on the permeable and the ephemeral. A different poet curates the New York City–based Ear/Double Happiness reading series each month. Language writing gets its name, the story goes, from *L=A=N=G=U=A=G=E*, edited by Andrews and Bernstein (a photocopied and stapled pamphlet that concentrated on poetics rather than poetry).

Undeniably, this do-it-yourself sensibility comes about because these writers felt that a mainstream dominated with a restrictive aesthetic. The appendixes to Jed Rasula's *American Poetry Wax Museum* lay this conspiracy theory out in statistical black and white.[19] Setting up an alternate aesthetic guided by communal concerns allows these writers to remove themselves from the domesticating imperatives inherent in the more mainstream poetry scene, although it seems also important to notice that one unfortunate limitation of this do-it-yourself sensibility was that it was not accompanied by much attention to alliances with other writers who were also investigating language's relation to systems of power, such as Kamau Brathwaite, Diane Glancy, and Nourbese Philip (all writers concerned with language and colonialism who were prominently writing at the same time and similarly avoiding an identity-centered lyric).

This alternate universe has not gone unnoticed by critics. Some critique it for establishing a new dominance. And as some language writers entered the university in the 1980s, it is not unusual to hear the complaint that the language writers have "sold out," or have been appropriated into the university, or have not been true to their anti-establishment ideals. Norman Finkelstein, for instance, writes, "In a paradoxically self-promoting move, they have lambasted the academy, which has been all too eager to lionize them and admit some of them into its ranks" (103). However, many of the writers associated with this movement have moved in and occupied the university on their own terms.[20] For example, Bernstein, in "A Blow Is Like an Instrument," published in *Daedalus,* the journal of the American Academy of Arts and Sciences, openly discusses his reader's reports for an article rejected from the *PMLA* (a breach of academic decorum). Susan Howe and Bob Perelman continue to publish poetry and criticism that defy dominant genres.[21] Hejinian, when she taught at the New College of California, was a pivotal influence on a number of younger writers who are now actively editing journals and publishing books of their own. And more importantly, this takeover of production is accompanied by an abandoning of both the rugged individualistic lone writer who is above marketplace concerns (yet welcomed by the marketplace) and all claims that it might, or should, be the authorized mainstream.[22] While various writers associated with this scene have at times been shrill in their demands for individual attention, there has never been a claim that language writing is or should be the single poetry at the expense of other poetries. The attention here is to poetries, not just one poetry, and to that "reciprocity of practice" to which Silliman, Harryman, Hejinian, Benson, Perelman, and Watten refer.

But the works themselves are as important as the social configurations I have been describing. I often use a simple classroom exercise to demonstrate how this work shares its authority with readers, encourages production of new works, and also blurs the lines between reading and writing. I choose a poem for the exercise that at first glance might be disconcerting to those new to this sort of writing.[23] I begin by having members of the class read the poem aloud a few times in different ways and then briefly discuss what might be disconcerting about this poem. Each of us then picks a phrase that struck us in some way and writes out of, in response to, or in dialogue with that phrase (using the chosen phrase as the opening words of our own piece) for about ten minutes. When ten minutes are up, someone reads the original poem aloud. Each person interrupts this reading by reading their new piece when the reader reaches "their" first line. What is created is a vocal hypertext (I have heard this technique also called "patchwork reading" or "exploded image") that dramatically demonstrates the richness of these works when approached with collective reading methods and which gives students a sense of the vast possibilities of the collective reading experience. This exercise often reminds us that reading is at its most useful when it brings people together.[24]

Similarly, when Andrews talks about reading's co-production, he moves from an assertion that equates indeterminacy with freedom to one that links reading to an autonomy that is firmly rooted in the social, that builds a public "in the old-fashioned sense." And, when reading is social, what is important about indeterminacy is not a mindless freedom of wordplay, but rather the ways it illuminates the old pun on word and world. In Andrews's work, this connection between word and world is a vexed one. To illustrate, here is the first paragraph from his "Confidence Trick":

Intentionally leaderless—Recite this alphabet; body never *ends*, little bits of plastic come-on, recite catatonia chic—Up anyway I Say Yes rewriting the body systematic sex cult thing; contrite—Don t give a shit *what* you think; it s all we do—Not to mention everyone is a bigot, wheels so good; how s your ambient buddy system?—If I understand these words, then I find them disgraceful —Camera obscura don t give a damn about my bad reputation—Capture the street severe machine we talk does loud fast is he rambling?—What rules are innocent, *enthusiate* me; we died pts 1 & 2, soul not really coordinated like an orientation for me, curtsy kineme like dirt—They re not developing my image

anymore, they re just operating it squeamish administrative relationships, this
is not one of the regular correction tape tricks, fortunately, more Americans
than I do; tendons as sugar, we can count (*Give Em Enough Rope* 142)

"Confidence Trick" appears in the 1987 collection *Give Em Enough Rope*.
The work in this collection is decisively anti-poetic and avoids any hint of
lyricism.[25] This passage, for instance, is built around disjunction. The work
has an uncensored (some would say unedited) quality. Intellectual and often politically inflected language ("Intentionally leaderless"; "rewriting the
body"; "Camera obscura"), accusations, insults, challenges ("Don t give a
shit *what* you think"), and rock and roll lyrics (Joan Jett's "I don't give a
damn about my bad reputation") are all given equal attention. Often, although not in this passage, racial or sexual slurs are mixed in. The address,
the audience, the subject position, and the narrator are all unclear. And it is
not unusual for slang and colloquialisms in English and in other languages
(especially Spanish) to enter into Andrews's mix.

Just as Stein's work reflects the language contacts occurring in cities in
the early parts of the century, Andrews's reflects the same contacts in the
late twentieth century (although with more attention to class divisions and
political analysis than Stein). Andrews's works often look like successful attempts to channel all the language that might run through the head of an
angry and confused seventeen-year-old boy. Peter Quartermain calls this "social language" ("Getting Ready" 164). And he is right if social language
means language about how individuals are in society. Andrews's works articulate what often goes unsaid in life's more decorous moments. And that,
in part, is what is valuable about his work. I would locate one connective
possibility in this attention to how language might appear in uncensored,
unregulated public spaces. Reading his work is in part a huge relief under
the theory that if everyone just said the idiotic things they feel but suppress
because of decorum, then at least they could be let out, maybe exorcised.

But also the structure of this work—phrases joined by dashes—is in itself
a shareable grammar. In "Confidence Trick" the textual role is altered by the
avoidance of standard punctuation, by the dashes, by the unrelated phrases,
by the conversational language that claims no unified narrative voice. Literally, it is hard to tell where one phrase ends or begins or how it relates to
what precedes or follows. Many different speech registers, quotations, lan-

guage tendencies, and language systems enter into this work. Writing's sorting principle—the way, say, a novel tends to guide readers to look at certain moments in a certain order—is abandoned. And similarly, the assumed distance between reader and work (the voice that says "it is not me that says everyone is a bigot to justify racism" in response to Andrews's line "Not to mention everyone is a bigot") is challenged.

With its avoidance of smooth aesthetics and slickness, Andrews's work is the poetic equivalent of the late 1970s and early 1980s punk and hardcore music. "Confidence Trick" heavily references this tradition in content. Throughout this piece are references to groups like the Pop Group ("How long do we tolerate mass murder" [144]), Richard Hell and the Voidoids ("blank generation" [145]), the Tubes and Nina Hagen ("white huskies on dope" [147]), Velvet Underground ("we don t perform *Heroin* anymore" [153]), Joy Division ("Joy division" [156]; "love will tear us" [161]), the Buzzcocks ("orgasmaddict" [157]), Teenage Jesus and the Jerks ("freud in flop" [161]), the Sex Pistols ("NO FUTURE" [166]), and the Clash ("radio free europe" [166]; the title of Andrews's book, *Give Em Enough Rope,* is the title of an album by the Clash).

But, more than content, there is a clear sensibility of influence. I think it is difficult to understand Andrews's work without seeing it as similarly attacking decorum and reigning apolitical systems of aesthetics. Punk (and/or hard-core) abandoned studio slickness. At the same time, it attacked the passivity of the audience (often literally: screaming, spitting, punching, kicking). At its conception, it was also one of the more profoundly political white working-class movements (despite the fact that it often attacked traditional leftist values and music). When Malcolm McLaren talks about the Sex Pistols's "Anarchy in the U.K.," he calls it a statement of "do-it-yourself" (qtd. in Marcus 9). Punk is a denial of craft, of practice, of studio space, of quality in instruments, of the public relations machine, and of musical tonality. This denial partially rises in response to a dramatically corrupt and hierarchized music industry. And this do-it-yourself aesthetic spawns thousands of garage bands as they realize the possibilities in making low fi into an aesthetic. Bernard Sumner of Joy Division puts it like this: "I saw the Sex Pistols. They were terrible. I thought they were great. I wanted to get up and be terrible too" (qtd. in Marcus 7). There is here a similar interesting tension in punk and in Andrews's writing. On the one hand, Andrews is one of the more strident theorists of reader autonomy. On the other, as Hank Lazer notes, "there is very little poetry that is truly disconcerting. Much of Andrews's is" (*Opposing Poetries* 89). Often critics feel that works of autonomy should not be so disconcerting. Yet Lazer explains this away by quoting Andrews and noting that within breakage "a utopianism remains, a hopefulness, for we are in the midst of an investigation of 'the arrangements that make knowledge possible'" (93). Similarly, Rod Smith ties this all together when he writes, "Clearly Andrews belongs to a tradition of Avant-Garde interactivity. If it began with the Paris Commune it carries on through Dada, the Situationists, Punk, & Rap. Negation of tradition is not the point. There is no point that we do not collectively create is the point" (v). Smith points to an anarchist, collective avant-garde in Andrews's uncensored, indecorous, and raw writings.[26] I might point to a narrower, more specific lineage: that the word "free" that Abbie Hoffman would paint on his head at protests mutates into the anarchy of the Sex Pistols ten years later which mutates into the word spew of Andrews's *Give Em Enough Rope*.

In contrast is Hejinian's *My Life*. It is in no way indecorous or raw. Here, as example, is the first section of Lyn Hejinian's *My Life:*

A pause, a rose,
something on paper

A moment yellow, just as four years later, when my father returned home from the war, the moment of greeting him, as he stood at the bottom of the stairs, younger, thinner than when we had left, was purple—though moments are no longer so colored. Somewhere, in the background, rooms share a pattern of small roses. Pretty is as pretty does. In certain families, the meaning of necessity is at one with the sentiment of prenecessity. The better things were gathered in a pen. The windows were narrowed by white gauze curtains which were never loosened. Here I refer to irrelevance, that rigidity which never intrudes. Hence, repetitions, free from all ambition. The shadow of the redwood trees, she said, was oppressive. The plush must be worn away. On her walks she stepped into people's gardens to pinch off cuttings from their geraniums and succulents. An occasional sunset is reflected in the window. A little puddle is overcast. If only you could touch, or, even, catch those gray great creatures. I was afraid of my uncle with the wart on his nose, or of his jokes at our expense which were beyond me, and I was shy of my aunt's deafness who was his sister-in-law and who had years earlier fallen into the habit of nodding, agreeably. Wool station. See lightning, wait for thunder. Quite mistakenly, as it happened. Long time lines trail behind every idea, object, person, pet, vehicle, and event. The afternoon happens, crowded and therefore endless. Thicker, she agreed. It was a tic, she had the habit, and now she bobbed like my toy plastic bird on the edge of its glass, dipping into and recoiling from the water. But a word is a bottomless pit. It became magically pregnant and one day split open, giving birth to a stone egg, about as big as a football. In May when the lizards emerge from the stones, the stones turn gray, from green. When daylight moves, we delight in distance. The waves rolled over our stomachs, like spring rain over an orchard slope. Rubber bumpers on rubber cars. The resistance on sleeping to being asleep. In every country is a word which attempts the sound of cats, to match an insoluble portrait in the clouds to a din in the air. But the constant noise is not an omen of music to come. "Everything is a question of sleep," says Cocteau, but he forgets the shark, which does not. Anxiety is vigilant. Perhaps initially, even before one can talk, restlessness is already conventional, establishing an incoherent border which will later separate events from experience. Find a drawer that's not filled up. That we sleep plunges our work into the dark. The ball was lost in a bank of myrtle. I was in a room with the particulars of which a later nostalgia might be formed, an indulged childhood. They are sitting in wicker chairs, the legs of which have sunk unevenly into the ground, so that each is sitting slightly tilted and their postures make adjustment for that. The cows warm their own barn. I look at them fast and it gives the illusion that they're moving. An "oral history" on paper. *That* morning this morning. I say it about the psyche because it is not optional. The overtones are a denser shadow in the room characterized by its habitual readiness, a form of charged waiting, a perpetual attendance, of which I was thinking when I began the paragraph, "So much of childhood is spent in a manner of waiting." (7–8)

My Life, written in the late 1970s and rewritten in the early 1980s, is one of the more prominent works of the language movement.[27] It is an autobiography, but not a conventional one. There are, for instance, two editions of *My Life*. The first (Burning Deck) edition of 1980 was written when Hejinian was thirty-seven (it was first written in 1978) and is composed of thirty-seven sections of thirty-seven sentences each. In the revised edition of 1987 by Sun & Moon, there are forty-five sections of forty-five sentences.[28]

My Life explores the ramifications of reader autonomy within autobiography, a genre of the personal with a tendency to self-aggrandize. It is written as a nonpersonal mix of confession and everyday observation. It moves non-synchronically through the past and the present. The first full sentence in the book locates, from an unspecified future, the beginning of this autobiography as a remembrance "four years later." And the color yellow is itself a remembrance of something shared with Henry Adams's *The Education of Henry Adams*.[29] Hejinian continually breaks the absorptive flow of narrative convention by inserting references that interrupt the insistent and mesmerizing tug of narrative that characterizes autobiography. The words "wool station" in the first page, for example, are an independent syntactical unit without easy reference (7). She also frequently uses repetition, which can be antithetical to autobiography's linear progress.[30] Certain key phrases, such as the beginning "a pause, a rose, something on paper," appear over and over throughout the book.

In *My Life* Hejinian places sentences and readers' connections with them as central to the reading process. Perloff notes this when she writes that "Hejinian's strategy is to create a language field that could be anybody's autobiography, a kind of collective unconscious whose language we all recognize. . . . At the same time, *My Life* conveys what the archetypal life of a young American girl is like" (*The Dance of the Intellect* 225). In contrast, Lisa Samuels points to the dangers of reading this book as "generic, fully identified with known language or known cultural habits," and goes so far as to state that "this is a story of Americans who make good emotionally on the backs of their less happy progenitors" (107, 114).[31] Samuels's warning about the dangers of reading this as a generic girlhood are legitimate (although I am not sure that this is exactly what Perloff, or other critics, are doing). This book is written in a standard English and presents uneventful (which some might associate as bourgeois) events. It is not the rags to riches or the obscure to famous or the overcoming abuse, disease, or other trauma plot that usually justifies autobiographical attention.

The key word in Perloff's observation is "strategy." For this autobiography never claims to be unconstructed (its very numeric form points this out). And it is crucial to read this book as one that deliberately avoids big events and instead embraces observations.[32] As Marnie Parsons points out, Hejinian "produces not a chronology of significant events, but a sonal and visual dramatization of how language constructs one's 'reality' and one's memories. She presents an intuition of the 'pure duration,' the ongoingness, the presentness of time, and simultaneously the wonderful plasticity, the expansive, procreative embrace of both memory and language" (207).[33] When Samuels critiques *My Life* for being "too happy" because nothing bad happens, she misses how this work is neither happy nor sad, how it is avoiding the significant events that make autobiography into one of the more narcissistic genres. The statements in *My Life* engage rather than perpetuate the clichés of a generic girlhood. Hejinian continually draws attention to the tension between the conventional cliché and the actual individual complexities of life. She writes, for instance, "It was hard to know this as politics, because it plays like the work of one person, but nothing is isolated in history—certain humans are situations" (10). Further, Hejinian's switch of autobiography from narcissistic and individualistic to the constructed nature of collective memory is a deliberate reinterpretation of the privileged history of the autobiography. The twist of *My Life* is to show how even the most narcissistic of genres, the most self-privileging, has possibilities for outward connection.

Hejinian explains how this connection happens in her essay "The Rejection of Closure." Here she, like Andrews and Silliman, figures reading as a sharing rather than a conquering, as exchanging rather than fixing. A work that "is open to the world and particularly to the reader," she writes, "invites participation, rejects the authority of the writer over the reader and thus, by analogy, the authority implicit in other (social, economic, cultural) hierarchies" (134). It is separation (the separations between the sentences of *My Life*, for example, that lack conventional narrative structure) but also the separation between *My Life*'s observations and readers' own lives that invites the reader to connect their life with the autobiographical moment: "The reader (and I can say also the writer) must overleap the end stop, the period and cover the distance to the next sentence. . . . Meanwhile, what stays in the gaps, so to speak, remains crucial and informative. Part of the reading occurs as the recovery of that information (looking behind) and the discovery of newly structured ideas" (136).[34]

The beginning of *My Life*, similarly, guides its readers to moments when they are required to enter into an exchange with the work. While there are themes in the earlier-quoted opening section—writing, nature, and windows, for instance—these are left unconnected. When the rose of the title phrase returns ("a pause, a rose, something on paper"), it is "in the background" and merely present in rooms "that share a pattern" (7). Even the possibility that this might flower into an elaborate horticultural metaphor is cut short by the oppressive redwoods and the woman pinching off cuttings in others' gardens. Instead the emphasis in this beginning section is on trespassing. The woman's stepping into others' gardens to pinch off cuttings is analogous to readers' stepping into the work to break off pieces of the work to take away into their own lives. Even the sentiment of the sunset is connective, as it is not encountered directly but rather occasionally "reflected on the window" (7).

So instead of reading the generic qualities of this work as moments that cover over America's troubled politics, I read these moments as deliberate blanks, as templates that provide numerous points of entry into the work. Early in *My Life,* Hejinian tells of how a highway had been tunneled through a living redwood tree and how "in so doing they had changed the tree into the tunnel, made it something it had not been before, and separated it forever from any other tree" (28). This is an apt metaphor. Her autobiography is one that readers pass through. But as readers enter and are surrounded by the tree-turned-tunnel, they realize that the tree is something different, that the life they have entered leads them out through the autobiography's concern with the self. As a result, the tree (the self) is not merely a tree, but something that opens up for people to walk through.

The tree-turned-tunnel vividly demonstrates that the structural point of this work is not to assert personal power or identity, but to activate readers' minds. The discontinuous sentences of *My Life* contain many possible intricate narratives. Readers are invited to recognize webs of relations, to feel lost in the life and to feel numerous moments of connection. *My Life* avoids self-affirmation and puts in its place reciprocity and exchange. To read Hejinian's work is not to read a copy of her life, but rather to shape her life and one's own with and/or against her work. There are, undeniably, boundaries to this experience. *My Life* is but a limited template for possible readerly encounters. But within this limitation, the genius of this work is how it manages to use the self of autobiography and yet avoid the self-prioritizing rhetoric of identity, all the while keeping open possibly intimate connections. This attention to the collective definition of self is not to demonize or trivialize identity's more essentialist moments, but rather points to how the personal can also be a way of cohabitating with others.

"How Can Anyone Represent Anyone Else?"

How can anyone represent anyone else?

—Daniel and Gabriel Cohn-Bendit, *Obsolete Communism: The Left Wing Alternative*

How do we position my body while white is not right?

—Andrews, "Confidence Trick"

My life is as permeable constructedness.

—Hejinian, *My Life*

One could, I think, end with the observation that these works are ones of connection. For connection has its own values. It points out that to see anything clearly (in this instance the self or language), we need to see its points of contact with other things. And the work of connection encourages readers to come together and points to how it is right to be interested in works that have meanings that lie beyond one's control. Yet it also respects individualism. In works of connection, readers mix with a (textual) space that is multifaceted, a space where separateness and difference are not neglected but are made to play themselves out within and against a model of collectivity.

This desire to have it all, to be both autonomous and related (also a central concern of anarchism), is a useful one for discussions of identity. In current debates on the topic, identity is generally framed as either essentialist or constructivist. It is unfortunate that literary works of connection have not been given more attention in these discussions, because the outward turn to readers that happens in this writing has much to add to how we think of identity. Many critics assume that language writing has disavowed absolutes of identity. But it is, I think, more productive to see this writing as a dialogue that negotiates between these positions of pluralist inclusion and respectful, categorical separation. And to continue the dialogue with Altieri, I think language writing often does demand, as he wishes it would, that "we try out identification"; but the nature of this identification is not formulated in a conventional manner ("Some Problems about Agency" 215). The identities proposed by these works are ones that reject theories of identification based on sameness. Hejinian, for instance, uses identification to move her readers in, through, and out of her autobiographical "I."

Works of connection do not simply widen readers' fields of engagement. These works pursue connection so as to challenge the assumptions and complacency of dominant identity positions. Much of language writing arises in response to and in dialogue with the discussions around identity that began in the 1960s and continue today. This is not to say that the work of connection is a new thing, a unique and decisive break with other traditions.[35] Concerns of reader autonomy take on a certain prominence in avant-garde literature in the second half of the twentieth century. Creating works that invoke autonomy becomes a priority, not only for language writers, but also for those who use chance methods like John Cage and Jackson Mac Low, for American independence cinema, and also for performance art. Further, many language writers point to a tradition in rereadings they do of various works. Stein, for instance, becomes a major figure.[36] But also Susan Howe's essays— which argue that Emily Dickinson's alternates are integral to any reading of Dickinson's poems—are one of the best examples of the critical interventions created by language writing's emphasis on what Andrews calls wild reading.[37]

Crucial to understanding the ramifications of this autonomous turn and its relation to identity is realizing that language writing emerges in the late 1970s and is as much a child of the previous two decades as anything else. Much has been made of these years, especially the 1960s.[38] Unfortunately, these years often get categorized as an independent moment and fetishized as a brief, failed possibility in popular commentary. But as Jameson argues, as a result of Vietnam War protests and various decolonization movements throughout the world, the 1960s exemplify a seismic switch in how Western society thinks of subjectivity. "The 60s," he writes, "was, then, the period in which all these 'natives' became human beings, and this internally as well as externally: those inner colonized of the first world—'minorities,' marginals, and women—fully as much as its external subjects and official 'natives'"

("Periodizing the Sixties" 181). In addition to some civil rights gains, the dominant cultural values of the time are challenged, diversity is valued over totalization, patriotism is questioned, and grassroots political organizing challenges the command structures of traditional leftist movements. And although both academic and popular commentators on the 1960s point to how the reforms of this period have been uneven (and seem to be eroding today), the civil rights reforms that began at this time continue to have major cultural and political impacts. Or, if the 1960s did anything, they at least got issues of race and gender on the table.

In the more specific arena of experimental or avant-garde poetry, the 1960s begin with Donald Allen's *The New American Poetry* (published in 1960; the first student sit-ins in North Carolina were the same year). This anthology basically defines American protest poetry and its pluralist "I." This "I" that the New American poets use lets everyone into the privileged position, says that all can speak together.[39] It is a utopian poetics that has its roots in Walt Whitman's claim to contain multitudes. Lawrence Ferlinghetti, Allen Ginsberg, Jerome Rothenberg, and Gary Snyder again and again sample and riff Whitman's pluralism. They not only use inclusive "I"s, but they also extensively and heroically catalog. And the New American poetry is at its most convincing (and interestingly remains convincing today to a great number of people otherwise uninterested in poetry) in its use of this inclusive catalog.

As the 1960s develop, identity concerns come to the forefront. In 1962, the Students for a Democratic Society issue the *Port Huron Statement* and Algerian independence is realized. In 1963, there is a large civil rights march on Washington and John F. Kennedy is assassinated. In 1965, U.S. combat troops enter Vietnam and large-scale bombings begin. Protests against the war accelerate. In 1966, NOW and the Black Panther Party are founded. In May 1968, students protest in Paris. In 1971, prisoners in Attica rebel. In 1975, Saigon is liberated.[40] As concerns language writing, *This* begins publication in 1971 and *L=A=N=G=U=A=G=E* magazine begins in 1978 (1978 is also the year the Clash releases *Give 'Em Enough Rope*).

The differences between the New American poetry (loosely individualistic and ego-centered) and language writing (loosely anti-individualistic and anti-ego-centered) resemble the differences between early 1960s politics and late-1970s politics. Basically, by the mid-1960s the possibility of a pluralist "I" has come under critique. Race and gender separatism more or less begins to dominate American politics in the second half of the 1960s. Pluralism becomes suspect because it leaves the dominant subject and all its privileges intact, reinforces hierarchy with its individualism, and gives no credence to a multitude of power differentials. Or, in other words, while the pluralist "I" claims to be everyone's, it does not allow room for the "I" of the separatist or the nationalist. Nor is it the "I" of those who meekly want to drop out of affiliation altogether.

In terms of poetry, the faith in language and the self as under one's control (a faith that lets Ginsberg claim he can "make Mantra of American language now" even as he admits "the war is language" in "Wichita Vortex Sutra" [407, 401]) has faded for numerous writers by the 1970s. Some critics have located this lack of faith in a revival of interest in early modernism or in the rise of theories of reading such as deconstruction.[41] But following Jameson's observation, once the "native" becomes human, questions of how to represent others and selves in literature change. The dominant subject suddenly has to recognize itself as such and as not necessarily natural. Questions further change as the war in Vietnam continues. The issue seems not so much how to save one's self by looking to the other, but rather how to save the other as well as one's self from being killed by the U.S. government.

This is Silliman's argument: language writing is a response and necessary challenge to the government's misuse of language in the Vietnam War. He writes: "One of the things I think is a real characteristic phenomenon of the 'language poets,' so-called, is the Vietnam War experience. Every one of the males in the U.S. had some kind of intense relationship with the draft. When the government's trying to kill you for five or six consecutive years, it gets your attention. It was a really shaping experience. I don't think one can even *imagine* 'language poetry' without that experience" ("Post-Reading Discussion" 13).

Vietnam certainly was very much a part of Andrews's consciousness. Andrews got his Ph.D. from Harvard in political science in 1975. His dissertation was on the Vietnam War, and he published several crucial articles on the war in the early 1970s. This early work investigates and critiques the argument made by policy elites at the time that resistance to the war was something limited to college students and other radicals and that the general public, frightened of communism, demanded the war in Vietnam. Instead,

Andrews argues, "Domestic opinion was one of the *hurdles* that had to be overcome in this period before the escalation could proceed, not one of the immediate factors pressuring it along" (*Public Constraint* 52). His argument here—that a political elite uses the rhetoric of public demand that is often unreflective of actual public desires to justify its decisions—challenged the conventional analysis of the war.[42]

And while this might be too easy a connection, I wish to argue that as Andrews points out the claims that get made in the name of the public, so much language writing contests the claims that get made in the name of the reader. How to represent subjectivity's social language without reifying dominance is, for instance, a concern of Hejinian's *My Life*. As Hejinian is well aware, autobiography tends to be a popular genre not necessarily because readers are concerned with the subject, but because they might identify with the subject. And her autobiography is constructed to expand on this identi-fication to such an extent that the work is no longer her own autobiography. While this revision of the identification patterns of autobiography is just one way that this work fails to uphold the traditional representational practices of the genre, it is still of the genre. I want to insist on this because the criticism of autobiography has had a tendency to limit itself by ignoring much work that challenges individualism. Philippe Lejeune's equation of autobi-ography with a "retrospective prose narrative written by a real person con-cerning his own existence, where the focus is his individual life, in particular the story of his personality" still remains (this despite a huge amount of definitional discussion in the criticism around autobiography) in many ways an insufficiently challenged norm that defines the genre in much writing about autobiography (4). While it is not uncommon to talk about autobiog-raphy as the space for multiple selves, or as the space for self-invention, or even as a space for the investigation of hybrid and complex identities, there has been a continuing reliance on the basic, and very limiting, precepts of Lejeune's definition, words such as "retrospective," "prose narrative," and "individual." The critical discourse that surrounds autobiography has been caught between a desire to bring forward life writing by marginalized sub-jects and an unwillingness to abandon much of its generic conventions and an emphasis on individualism.[43] For example, Stein's *Autobiography of Alice B. Toklas* (which is retrospective, prose narrative, and individual-centered, even though this is, of course, complicated in this work) has been a canonical example of innovation in autobiography, yet autobiography criticism does not turn to the poetic "Stanzas in Meditation" which Ulla Dydo has called "the other autobiography."[44] These issues have also come to the forefront in the controversy surrounding David Stoll's accusations that Rigoberta Menchú in *I, Rigoberta Menchú: An Indian Woman in Guatemala* misrepresents her life. But clearly another way of looking at Menchú's story would be as a collective (cultural) story that calls into question the reading assumptions that surround autobiography. In other words, the contested truth of Menchú's work comes to the forefront because of attempts to place it in the genre of autobiography (or in this case, when testimonial is defined as an autobiography by a less privileged subject) with its accompanying individualism.

These examples, especially Menchú's, are telling. Many have accused autobiography of not transcending its beginnings in narratives of bourgeois white individualism such as work by Rousseau and Adams. In the late 1970s and early 1980s (the years when the two editions of *My Life* were written), autobiography is critiqued for perpetuating and not investigating these privileged beginnings. In response, critics importantly turn their emphasis to racially and ethnically diverse writers. Many of these works challenge the conventions of the genre. Some, such as Gloria Anzaldúa's *Borderlands: La Frontera: The New Mestiza*, are written in a mix of poetry and prose. Others, like Maxine Hong Kingston's *The Woman Warrior*, mix fiction and nonfiction, confession and myth. The response by critics was to discuss these works, especially in the context of women's autobiography, as ones that propose "multiple subjectivity." It was argued that a multiply constructed subjectivity both preserved the autobiographical subject and also diversified it. Anzaldúa herself presents her subjectivity, as is written on the back cover of the first edition, from the varied positions of "Chicana *tejana* feminist-dyke-*patlache* poet, fiction writer, and cultural theorist." In Kingston's work, subjectivity becomes tied up with myth that allows her, like Anzaldúa, to occupy multiple subject positions.[45] This has been a politically significant move for critics interested in socially marginal writers who have not had Rousseau's or Adams's authority to throw away. It avoids limiting definitions of singular authority and yet retains essentialisms.

In this context, I read *My Life* as aligned with works of multiple subjectivity because it wants to use the personal language of the self to point to the complicated language of the social. Yet unlike these works of multiple subjectivity, it avoids an arithmetical alternative to dominant subjectivity and the individualism that remains even in a multiplied subject. In fact, it provides a pointed critique of privilege. Hejinian's move is not to completely deny the subject; *My Life* is still an autobiography. Instead, *My Life* mutates auto-biography from an ego-centered exploration of the self to a form of cultural critique. This is the tree-turned-tunnel that is also the self-turned-public.

Many would argue that this is another example of the postmodern dissolution of the subject, and that this dissolution is in itself exclusionary. Barbara Christian, for instance, makes a common complaint when she writes that critiques of subjectivity "surfaced, interestingly enough, just when the literature of peoples of color, black women, Latin Americans, and Africans began to move to 'the center'" (71). Following this, one might argue that because those associated with the language movement have been predomi-nantly white and educated, they are yet another example of those who want to deny subjectivity out of an insensitivity to subjectivities other than their own.

And Christian's suspicions are valid; it is crucial that discussions of sub-jectivity not prevent or discredit the strategic moves of ethnic and race stud-ies to put marginalized identities to the forefront. Yet at the same time, I want to twist this argument. Christian is right to notice that dissolute and performative models of subjectivity and ethnically and racially essentialist models of subjectivity gain prominence at the same time. But these positions might be less antithetical than is often assumed. Rather than reading the dissolute subject as something that wants to take away the strategic moves made by essentialisms, one could instead read it as a move that similarly wants to challenge the privileges of dominant models of subjectivity. While it is often argued that the turn to reader autonomy is a denial of subjectivity, I want to suggest that this denial is more specific. Rather than being a post-modern call for the end of subjectivity, the turn to reader connection in works like *My Life* or "Confidence Trick" is a more specific critique of the dominant subject. The turn to readers is, after all, a turn to a certain type of subject. Or I think both these moves can be read as related strategies in the same game plan to critique an unexamined subjectivity that denies power differentials. One move puts forward a marginalized subject in essentialist

terms, while another pulls back from the essentialism of dominant subjectivities. And not only can these moves be aligned, but both are necessary
moves in the pursuit of equality.

At the same time, though, I am well aware that these two sides are not
always aligned. Rather, it seems crucial that there be more examination of
how and where these two positions might do related work. And thus, these
connections are crucial for current concerns. I think it is important to avoid
dismissing out of hand the complicated nature of the postmodern critique
of subjectivity, because that critique does much to counter the privileges of
dominant subjectivity. And I also want to avoid setting up the subject of a
work like *My Life* or "Confidence Trick" as one that is a negation, an emptiness.[46] Language writing does focus on the human, but in a social context
(rather than an individualistic one). Andrews's turn to the heterogeneous
and indeterminable subjectivity of readers avoids an author's complicity with
appropriation while constructing a subject that is necessarily variable. The
move here is from a subject that is individualistic to one that is cultural and
social. (One way to read Hejinian's and Andrews's work is as the literary
translation of the photograph in *Everybody's Autobiography* of Stein surrounded by a crowd.)

Instead of establishing a series of full, coherent identities, Hejinian turns
to mapping the networks of power and meaning that link her inner life to a
politically suspect outer world of representational authority. Or while *My Life*
rejects rigorous self-definition, this work is still about the self.[47] For example,
in the early years of the book, Hejinian frequently repeats the phrase "I
wanted to be . . . ," a phrase that concentrates on what the "I" is not. "I
wanted to be . . . " takes many forms in the "early years" of the book: "In
any case, I wanted to be both the farmer and his horse when I was a child,
and I tossed my head and stamped with one foot as if I were pawing the
ground before a long gallop" (22). Or "I wanted to be a brave child, a girl
with guts" (25). Or "If I couldn't be a cowboy, then I wanted to be a sailor"
(35). Or "she pretends she is a blacksmith. . . . Now she's a violinist" (37).
The listing here of things the narrator wanted to be wonderfully crosses gender, class, and even the human/animal divide.

While this book begins with an investigation of what the "I" wants to
be, at a certain point the declaration of "I wanted to be . . . " changes into
"I am . . . " This change, if one was doing a straightforward developmental

reading of this work (a possibility that is often overlooked by critics who celebrate *My Life*'s postmodern impulse), could be read as emblematic of the transition from childhood to adulthood. But Hejinian's "I am" statements differ radically from "I am" statements that speak to a grammatical connection between the subject and the object of identity. Or what the "I" is in these statements is often variable. Instead, Hejinian writes, "I am a shard, signifying isolation—here I am thinking aloud of my affinity for the separate fragment taken under scrutiny" (52). At other points, the syntax of the sentence becomes confused and shard-like, as when Hejinian writes, "I remind myself, I don't exactly remember my name, of a person, we'll call it Asylum, a woman who, and I've done this myself, has for good reasons renounced some point, say the window in the corner of the room, and then accepts it again" (69–70). Here the pronoun confusion is deliberate, the "I" reminds itself of something else and forgets its reference ("I don't exactly remember my name") to suggest with the reader "*we*'ll call it Asylum" that the woman also be considered an "it," a nongendered pronoun. The syntax here, with its confusion of first and third person, is a deliberate complicating not only of gendered identity but also of the relation between this identity and grammar. This occurs in several other places in *My Life*, especially in the last quarter of the work. Hejinian writes, for instance, "And if I feel like a book, a person on paper, I will continue. What is the gender on paper," and "The postman became a mailman and now it is a carrier," and also "The musician has a spouse and it attends" (76, 89, 90).

Hejinian's subjectivity thus moves away from a capitalized "Self." Her adult subjectivity, more empty than full, concentrates on the "separate fragment under scrutiny." It is defined by fluctuation, by the move from "I wanted to be . . . " to the lack of fixity that characterizes a statement like "I am a shard." In *My Life*, gender is neither stable nor absolute. "As such," Hejinian writes, "a person on paper, I am androgynous" (105). Or as she writes, referencing the title, "My life is as permeable constructedness" (93).

Similarly, Hejinian willfully refuses to indulge in rhetoric of self-propaganda or self-restoration. There are no photo-like descriptions of her body, of her physical "self," no photographs documenting her life collected in the center of the book as is so common in the mass-market autobiography.[48] In *My Life*, mirrors do not reflect the authorly self, but rather a hole, an opening in the work: "A mirror set in the crotch of the tree was like a hole in the out-of-doors" (12). In this image, the mirror (the autobiography) is no longer the reflection of an authorly self, but instead is one of a hole, a space for readerly response. As *My Life* refuses to reflect the image of the autobiographical subject, it encourages readers to take on agency and to question the changes in perception, knowledge, and thinking that they undergo in this autobiographical encounter. Thus *My Life* is written by an author who claims, "I've been a blind camera all day in preparation for this dream" (115). The book, too, is a blind camera, directing readers' attentions to the symbolically constructed nature of reflection (thus the book's continual concern with and discussion of language) and away from any "actual" reflection itself. With a blind camera, Hejinian is always defining herself against her "self" and switching the emphasis from a stable, physical "self" to the language of the "self." Yet the subject here is not empty, is not nihilistic. It just does not claim anything that resembles the representational conventions of autobiography and deliberately plays against them.

While the rhetoric around Hejinian's "open text" is common to the language writing movement, her application of this rhetoric to the genre of autobiography is an interesting turn. Theories of autobiography have always been confused about the place of readers, and as Nancy Miller notes, have consigned "autobiography as a genre to a realm of impossibility and then— nothing daunted—displac[ed] the problem of definition from the writing of autobiography to its reading—in other words, to autobiography's effects" ("Facts, Pacts, Acts" 11). But what is unique about Hejinian's work is that the role of readers extends beyond the argument, as presented by Lejeune that the autobiographical moment is reader-centered and reader-recognized. Instead, the autobiography is, in Stein's words, everybody's autobiography as it is also reader-created.

With its self-conscious exposure and revision of the role of the reader, Hejinian's autobiography can help us also through its example to be better readers of the non-normative autobiography and other forms of life writing. Critical avoidance of readers' potential for resistant reading of autobiography plays into the reductive cliché that autobiographies are primarily about the subjectivity of the author. Yet *My Life* points to how the question of the personal is responsible to the larger question of the collective. I like to think of *My Life*, with its almost unprecedented attention to the act of reading autobiography, as a sort of primer for how to read the genre expansively.[49]

Yet at the same time, if I had to point to a limitation in this work, it would be that while Hejinian constructs an autobiography that investigates and challenges much that is taken for granted about subjectivity as concerns gender (and also, but less so, class), she avoids doing similar work for race. References to race are few and far between. She approaches critique when she writes, "The lace curtain Irish hate neighborhood Blacks" (56), but then avoids investigating the larger issues that surround race when she writes, "White and black are not colors they are inks and paints" (63). Similarly, in the "If I couldn't be a cowboy, then I wanted to be a sailor" statement the obvious move of racial crossing (which would be: if I couldn't be a cowboy, then I wanted to be an Indian) is avoided (35).

It is not that every work has to address every issue. *My Life*'s investigation of gender and autobiographical form is a profound one that I do not wish to belittle through complaint. And also, it seems important to note that *My Life* has been an interesting influence on younger writers who are using its concerns and intents to discuss race more directly, such as Pamela Lu in *Pamela: A Novel*, Renee Gladman in *Arlem* and *Not Right Now*, and Summi Kaipa in *The Epics*.[50] But because *My Life* is so concerned with avoiding and critiquing the ego dominance of autobiography, I cannot help but wish for a more investigatory position on whiteness. This is a complaint I have of much of the scene around language writing in the late 1970s and mid-1980s. While this scene at that time was doing much to investigate privilege, to politicize writing and break down hierarchies between readers and authors, while time was spent on gender, sexuality, and class (and various authors' relation to privilege in these categories), much of this work has acted as if it was an option to avoid talking about race (rather than a necessary part of any investigation of privilege). My argument here is not that language writing or writers have been racist, but rather that they have been guilty, at moments of inattention, of missing an ideal opportunity to investigate further racial privilege.[51]

One exception to this is Andrews's work, which is all over race. And one of the things I want to argue in this chapter is that if we take language writing as valuable because it investigates privilege, then Andrews's work is perhaps uniquely valuable. Like much language writing, just a quick glance shows that as the "I" of Andrews's work is notably different than the "I" of the New American poets, it is also different from the "I" of many of the works in the ethnic and race studies canon. Andrews's "I" is ever present but not stable. And it has no clearly locatable voice. The term "narrator" here makes no sense. "Confidence Trick" begins with the words "Intentionally leaderless" and then goes on to demonstrate this by avoiding both decorum and linear development. While the "I" is prominent, it is clustered around negations: "If I understand these words, then I find them disgraceful—Camera obscura don t give a damn about my bad reputation" and "They re not developing my image anymore." "Confidence Trick" twists this "I" into a mess of assertion and denial to create multiple points for contact. There is an emphasis on polyvocality: "These I," as is written in "Give Em Enough Rope" (*Give Em Enough Rope* 55). Yet importantly, the "I" in Andrews's work is never allowed to resemble or make the claims of inclusive pluralism. Even while these "I"s are not implicitly raced or gendered, throughout "Confidence Trick" inclusion is continually troubled and denied. "I m so hollow" this work claims (142). And, as if to prove this, the "I"s in this poem are ones that readers, especially the liberal readers of the political poem, would not want to have anything to do with. "I believe in homicide," one ambiguously claims (143). And also, "what I use is Nestle baby formula to irritate the rodents before they expire" (144). And "I m nobody s fat smart darling anymore" (144). And "I am learning the language earnest" (145). And "I hate humans" (146).

To return to Christian's earlier comments, Perelman notes (as he compares Andrews's work to Maya Angelou's inauguration poem "On the Pulse of Morning"), "There are many reasons why Andrews will not be invited to read at any foreseeable inauguration, but high on the list would be the intensity of his aggression toward the range of ethnic and cultural identities that Angelou's poem celebrates" (*Marginalization of Poetry* 102). Perelman is correct that Andrews attacks subjectivity. Following this through Christian's argument, this would be a reason to be suspect. But in Andrews's work it is also important to look beyond what the dominant subject is in the generic and to look more specifically at what this subject does, how it represents and is represented, how it acts in literary works. bell hooks and Toni Morrison have already argued for more investigation of dominant subjectivities. They point out that while it has not been unusual to look at representations of marginalized subjectivities in literature, it has been unusual to do the same work on dominant subjectivities. hooks notes that "Critically examining the association of whiteness as terror in the black imagination, deconstructing it, we both name racism's impact and help break its hold. We decolonize our minds and our imaginations" (*Black Looks: Race and Representation* 178). And Morrison urges more study of the influence of Africanism in American literature by white writers in *Playing in the Dark: Whiteness and the Literary Imagination*.[52]

The studies of whiteness that follow their work and reach popular momentum in the 1980s and 1990s no longer present whiteness as an invisible neutrality that escapes comment.[53] Much that is valuable in these studies disrupts a monolithic and naturalized whiteness and attends to how assumptions of white collectivity perpetuate racism. And some recent work on whiteness in literary studies follows Morrison's advice and points to Africanist influence on white writers and examines the ramifications of this influence.[54] Yet not all of this work has been as liberatory as one might hope. One colleague of mine calls this work "studies in the cracker diaspora." He is guilty of being too easily dismissive, but his joke points to the ever present danger of white studies: that studies of white ethnicities such as Irishness or Italianness will appropriate the rhetoric of ethnic studies for personal ends while ignoring the larger dominance of whiteness in U.S. society.[55]

Yet what interests me about Andrews's "Confidence Trick" in the context of white studies is its continual mocking exposure of dominant identities. (But I should specify here that I am talking about one specific work and not about Andrews's oeuvre as a whole.)[56] In "Confidence Trick," Andrews does not allow white ethnicities any sense of their marginalization. What makes more sense as a critical frame for Andrews's work is Noel Ignatiev and John Garvey's urging that white people be traitors to whiteness. Pointing out that "[t]he white race is a historically constructed social formation," Ignatiev and Garvey argue that "[t]he key to solving the social problems of our age is to abolish the white race" (9, 10).

Ignatiev and Garvey are, unfortunately, often vague as to how exactly to renounce the privileges of the white race in literature. Yet "Confidence Trick" gives this a try in several different ways. Most obviously, the work points to how one way to abolish the white club that Ignatiev and Garvey point to would be to renounce years of literary decorum and the individualism of character and voice that upholds whiteness as a confidence trick in itself. Further, as many critics have pointed out, whiteness secures power in literature and other arts by being dominantly invisible and inclusive of a large number of people while maintaining a supposedly clear exclusion at the same time. So as challenging dominant subjectivity means also addressing the dominant positions of the generic subject, throughout "Confidence Trick" the "I" is often racially inflected. And whiteness, whenever it appears, is never allowed to be neutral in this poem. "I m Dracula," the poem declares, and the resonance between bloodsucking and paleness is clear (149). "How do we position my body while white is not right?" the poem asks (149). And as if investigating how to write out of a white space without perpetuating a system of privilege, whiteness gets continually associated with privilege: "I don t need to want to remind you of white ambition right now" (150); "The white suburban kids couldn t handle it" (153); "you want MX missile systems up your ass, a white judge has said so" (156); "Caucasians swore by the factory system" (158); "America has all these commodities to cooperate what whites think about birth control" (176).

Further, and as I mentioned earlier, because the "I" in this work is not something that most people would want to identify with, the New American poetry's inclusive pluralism is rejected as an inadequate method of challenging privilege. Rather than inviting "everyone" into a space of privilege they cannot possibly be included into, Andrews's work does not allow this space to exist with any solidity, as anything useful. Most obviously, to have an "I" that irritates the rodents with Nestle baby formula is to question the identificatory pleasures that readers might possess with dominant subjectivities. As Sianne Ngai writes in "Raw Matter: A Poetics of Disgust" (an article which argues that Andrews is a poet of disgust), "the possibility of disgust as a poetics resides in its resistance to pluralism and its ideology of all-inclusiveness which allows it to recuperate and neutralize any critical discourse emphasizing conflict, dissent, or discontinuity" (102).[57] Andrews's work, as Ngai realizes, points to how self-alienation is one possible configuration of reader relations (something that reader-orientated theory tends to avoid as a possibility). And this self-alienation in "Confidence Trick" is continually insisting that readers question their relation to dominance.

But at the same time, it is not that Andrews's work empties or denies subjectivity. The quotes Perelman uses to suggest that Andrews's work is aggressive toward a range of ethnic and cultural identities and that this aggressivity leaves only a "narrow margin for readers" have potency as attack only out of context (nor should one assume them to be the position of an author or a narrator—which Perelman does not) (*Marginalization of Poetry* 108). In context, they clearly have no supportive authorship. And also it would be difficult to read them as anything but a series of statements that want to get at the endlessly complicated and messy construction of subjectivity in contemporary society. His work also avoids cultural appropriation by openly using others' words and yet not claiming ownership over any words. Statements of race and ethnicity are presented in this work as raw social materials. The channeled bricolage quality of Andrews's work is one reason it continually violates the decorum that surrounds discussions of race and ethnicity in leftist literature which privilege a clear position as a political necessity. Similarly, the move to reader autonomy in Andrews's work is a move from the singular reading practices that uphold systems of power to a multiplicity that challenges privilege's singularity.

"Anyone As They Are in the Modern Context"

Dear Ron,

I interpreted the (original *Socialist Review*) argument to be that white (and by implication "elite" or avant-garde) males (having perceived the split between themselves and experiences—i.e. the dismantling of narrative) were *more* inclined to question their own subjectivity than the others mentioned, who are thus thought of as "marginal," as "interest groups."

The basis of my argument was that anyone as they are in the modern context could perceive the split between themselves and experiences (this would actually be a *traditionally* held view in Asian, Buddhist cultures).

But "conventional narrative" does not express this.

For example, one is taught a definition of one's humanness when a small female child which is immediately unbelievable to that child—one knows that is not the self.

—Leslie Scalapino, "What/Person: From an Exchange"

In an e-mail, Ron Silliman writes that the avant-garde tradition came into existence "precisely because it was a mechanism for the privileged to question their own 'natural' position." He makes a similar point in "Poetry and the Politics of the Subject": "Progressive poets who identify as members of groups that have been the subject of history—many white male heterosexuals, for example—are apt to challenge all that is supposedly 'natural' about the formation of their own subjectivity" (63). I have kept this comment in the back of my head while writing this chapter. Silliman correctly notices the investigation of privilege that often gets overlooked in discussions of experimental works and language writing. It is this rejection of privilege that interests me about Hejinian's inclusive autobiographical "I" and Andrews's attack on white collectivity. One of language writing's more valuable attentions has been this willingness to turn away from the self that has so dominated U.S. poetry and instead look hard at the collective.

And yet he goes on to write in "Poetry and the Politics of the Subject" that "women, people of color, sexual minorities, the entire spectrum of the 'marginal'—have a manifest political need to *have their stories told*. That their writing should often appear much more conventional, with the notable difference as to whom is the subject of these conventions, illuminates the relationship between form and audience" (63). And this is where I want to separate from his argument. The avant-garde is often assumed to be a white, educated-class phenomenon. And undeniably the major figures of language writing have tended to be white and educated (and if one were to just read the criticism, one would think mainly male, but this is unrepresentative of the actual scene). Yet to extend this observation too far is to ignore a number of important language and language-influenced writers who do not identify as white and/or male. And further, Silliman's statement that the marginal need to have their stories told shuts down options for those who most need all the tools of the trade.

Leslie Scalapino, in response to Silliman's article, points out that "[t]hose in social power and those without it might be equally capable of questioning their subjectivity. But those who are without social power are less inclined to see reality as orderly; for example, less inclined to see the social construction as unified" (52). Scalapino's argument that reality as it is constructed is not necessarily more representational for those who are not dominant subjects is just one possible argument that can be made against Silliman's overly simplistic equation between experimentalism and dominant subjectivities.

I wrote this book in part because I wanted to argue that avant-garde forms are not at all divorced from cultural concerns, but are actually often used to critique dominant cultures. And I had heard it said once too often by supporters and detractors that the avant-garde is white and middle class and therefore has nothing to say about identity. I wanted to look at works that avoid patronizing attempts to write down for readers in their respect for reading's connective possibilities. And I wanted to also argue how crucial it is to not overlook the valuable work that is being done on issues of race and ethnicity in more experimental forms both by those who identify as white and those who identify as of color. In the chapters that follow I look at the work of Harryette Mullen and Theresa Hak Kyung Cha, both of whom use what might get called avant-garde techniques to suggest new configurations of reading that are concerned with community.

"What Stray Companion"

Harryette Mullen's Communities of Reading

proceed with abandon
finding yourself where you are
and who you're playing for
what stray companion

—Harryette Mullen, *Muse & Drudge*

I write for myself and others. An other is anyone who is not me. Anyone who is not me is like me in some ways and unlike me in other ways. I write, optimistically, for an imagined audience of known and unknown readers. Many of my imagined readers have yet to encounter my work. Most of them are not even born yet. . . . When I read the words of African Americans who were slaves, I feel at once my similarity and difference. I experience simultaneously a continuity and a discontinuity with the past, which I imagine is similar to that of the unborn reader who might encounter my work in some possible future. There is another kind of experience I sometimes have when reading the words of authors who never imagined that someone like me might be included in the potential audience for their work, as when I read in Cirlot's *Dictionary of Symbols* that a "Negro" symbolizes the beast in the human. When I read words never meant for me, or anyone like me—words that exclude me, or anyone like me, as a possible reader—then I feel simultaneously my exclusion and my inclusion as a literate black woman, the unimagined reader of the text.

—Mullen, "Imagining the Unimagined Reader: Writing to the Unborn and Including the Excluded"

Following the model of the Black diaspora traditions of music, athletics and rhetoric, Black cultural workers must constitute and sustain discursive and institutional networks that deconstruct earlier modern Black strategies for identity-formation, demystify power relations that incorporate class, patriarchal and homophobic biases, and construct more multi-valent and multi-dimensional responses that articulate the complexity and diversity of Black practices in the modern and postmodern world.

—Cornel West, "The New Cultural Politics of Difference"

"Proceed with Abandon"

In recent years, there has been much discussion of how subjectivity and identity are made manifest not only through assumptive readings of the body but also by the conventions of grammar and narrative. This is what Edward Said calls the "epistemology of imperialism" (309). And it is the racial *longue durée* that Michael Omi and Howard Winant notice as "the slow inscription of phenotypical signification [which] took place upon the human body, in and through conquest and enslavement to be sure, but also as an enormous act of expression, of narration" (8). And what Hortense Spillers calls "an American grammar" of subjectivity (68). As these critics are well aware, language and narration are not by themselves responsible for categorical oppression; rather, they at times walk hand in hand with the forces of oppression, enabling and justifying these practices by providing a grammar of categorization and hierarchy. A. L. Nielsen gives several succinct examples of how the language of race and ethnicity is written so as to perpetuate boundaries of oppression in *Writing between the Lines:* "Our news reporters tell us of 'ethnic strife' in Eastern Europe; they tell us of 'tribal conflicts' in Africa.

In our media 'black on black violence' is a problem within a race; 'white on white violence' is a meaningless signifier. Such modes of discourse reveal simultaneously the instability of race as a concept and the persistence of race as an oppressive defining trope in American culture" (3–4).

As these examples make clear, and as Spillers's article points out in greater detail, race is made absolute in linguistic reality in a way that it can never be in bodily reality. It is grammar that grants subjectivity. The "I" with its place as subject of the sentence can claim as a result of grammar's authorizing powers a substantive existence. This is not to deny the very real nonlinguistic results of oppression—bodily pain, for instance—but rather to suggest that attempts to counter oppression must also concentrate on the claims made by linguistic authority. In response, Spillers calls for a "project of liberation" which aims to break down an "American grammar" of exclusion and racism, and points to "two passionate motivations that are twinned—1) to break apart, to rupture violently the laws of American behavior that make such *syntax* possible; 2) to introduce a new *semantic* field/fold more appropriate to his/her own historic movement" (79). This is a project similar to what Paul Gilroy calls, in his study of the black Atlantic, "[t]he extreme patterns of communication defined by the institution of plantation slavery [which] dictate that we recognize the anti-discursive and extra-linguistic ramifications of power at work in shaping communicative acts" (57).

There has been, though, a disturbing gap between, on the one hand, these theoretical positions that posit linguistic and syntactical conventions and familiar narrative structures as enforcing racial divisions and unnecessarily inflexible models of identity, and, on the other hand, the literary canon that includes precisely those works that follow language's dominant formal conventions. The criticism around identity issues in literature tends to concentrate on novels and other sorts of narratives such as autobiographies or testimonials. In part, this attention to narrative structures seems an obvious response to the apolitical and culturally divorced reading methods of the past. Many models of reading that prioritized close readings without reference to cultural concerns as a whole falsely upheld poetry, with its language of artifice, as a model for all that was independent of cultural politics. And in part because narrative makes for easily recognizable identities. This is despite theoretical perspectives such as Spillers's and Gilroy's which indicate that works that break apart the syntax of race, that introduce new fields/folds, and that are written so as to prioritize anti-discursive and extra-linguistic techniques should have a crucial role in this discussion. And this is despite the growth of various sorts of culturally concerned and grassroots-organized forms of writing such as those represented by various experimental writing communities.

For this reason, I have chosen to concentrate on the work of Harryette Mullen, an African-American writer whose work is concerned with the relation between liberatory reading and the vectors of race, class, and gender. Mullen's later works—and these are the ones I concentrate on in this essay—turn to puns, samplings, and other sorts of wordplay to examine and challenge overly limiting constructions of race, ethnicity, class, and gender. As her work illustrates, the difficult and necessary work of challenging limiting subjectivities requires also that one challenge the strictures of grammar and rigorous narrative.

As many critics have noted, Mullen is clearly talking with Gertrude Stein and Anglo-American modernism on issues of race and class (which modernism, even if one looks at its more democratic tendencies, tends to overlook). Yet it is a mistake to consider Mullen's work only within the context of Stein's. Her work has diverse, and more direct, influences. It is clearly rooted in an African-American tradition, a tradition that Henry Louis Gates, Jr., has argued is deeply involved in rereading, or signifyin(g): "repetition with a signal difference" (xxiv).[1] The blues and the Black Arts movement richly influence Mullen's work. And, just as easily, one could call her work language writing. Her social and publishing history points to both influences—she has been influenced by Umbra poet Lorenzo Thomas,[2] yet it is not unusual to read her work in language writing–orientated journals, and her last three books have been published by independent, and experimental, small presses. This categorical difficulty is one way Mullen's work joins social and formal critique.[3]

Similarly, her oeuvre as a whole participates simultaneously in many categories. I am, therefore, reluctant to use the words "prose," "poetry," or even "prose poem" to describe it. Mullen's first book, *Tree Tall Woman*, is written in more conventional verse forms, even though these poems still clearly have the teasing puns and attention to colloquial language that dominate her later works. The differences between *Tree Tall Woman* and the three later works I will be discussing are obvious. While Mullen emphasizes a playful signifyin(g) in the later works, *Tree Tall Woman* shows her writing poems in the forms of conventionally liberatory poetics. It is not that *Tree Tall Woman* is a lesser work. The book shows Mullen in poems like "Painting Myself a New Mirror" skillfully negotiating themes that remain of concern in her later works, such as color and its relation to race (the poem begins, "I'd change the colors I see / to some that aren't invented yet" [65]), women's self-image ("I'd like to forget how we learn to measure ourselves / in mirrors that always showed us less than whole" [66]), and women's accessories (pocket mirrors, pocketbooks, brushes, and combs all appear in the poem). The language here has conventional syntax; the poem is confessional and developmental, moving from complaint to liberation. The poem begins with the narrator desiring a darker mirror, moves to an examination of the way women look at themselves in mirrors, has a list of things the narrator would like to reject about this act, then has the narrator remembering once looking at herself in the mirror and feeling pleased, and continues remembering to end with the narrator recalling using the mirror with her friends to "flash each other signals in the sun" (66). The poem clearly indicates that Mullen has a mastery of the discourse of liberatory, feminist poetics in the tradition of Gwendolyn Brooks, Adrienne Rich, and Sonia Sanchez. There is a clear "I" in this poem who is actively rereading herself out of oppressive social narratives. This "I" is an individual who has feelings, who is self-sufficient, who is whole and complete in the mirror by the end (the poem literally paints the self in the mirror into a sort of, although not simple, representative completion: "a silent mimic" [66]). This poem could easily appear in anthologies such as *No More Masks, This Bridge Called My Back,* or *Black Fire.*

But Mullen's next three books—*Trimmings, S*PeR M**K*T,* and *Muse & Drudge*—are all less conventional and more disjunctive. Compare, for instance, the beginning sections of each of these books:

Becoming, for a song. A belt becomes such a small waist. Snakes around her, wrapping. Add waist to any figure, subtract, divide. Accessories multiply a look. Just the thing, a handy belt suggests embrace. Sucks her in. She buckles. Smiles, tighter. Quick to spot a bulge below the belt. (*Trimmings* 7)

Lines assemble gutter and margin. Outside and in, they straighten a place. Organize a stand. Shelve space. Square footage. Align your list or listlessness.

Pushing oddly evening aisle catches the tail of an eye. Displays the cherished share. Individually wrapped singles, frozen divorced compartments, six-pack windows express themselves while women wait in family ways, all bulging baskets, squirming young. More on line incites the eyes. Bold names label familiar type faces. Her hand scanning throwaway lines. (*S*PeR M**K*T*, n.p.)

Sapphire's lyre styles
plucked eyebrows
bow lips and legs
whose lives are lonely too (*Muse & Drudge* 1)

This transition, from poems that are narratives about the self to ones more investigatory of a larger community, Mullen locates in interviews as a result of association with the California language writing community of the 1980s.[4] As is obvious from these passages, these works tend to be composed around phrases and lack a narrative structure. In place of narrative's causal flow, the works are loosely gathered around themes such as women's bodies, clothing, and accessories in *Trimmings;* supermarket products and their marketing and packaging in *S*PeR M**K*T;* and the blues and other forms of African-based culture in *Muse & Drudge*. The language is highly poetic, assonant, and rhythmical, but not in predictable ways. Words tend to resonate, pun, and repeat. This is evident in how the word "becoming" in the passage from *Trimmings* begins by alluding to the process of coming to be, but then shifts to the meaning of "unsuitable to the wearer."

While these later three works are playful, irreverent, and highly allusional, their attention is to individual and communal resistance and response. They allude to and engage many traditions, critique and pay homage to the blues, voodoo, modernism, psychoanalysis, Hollywood, homilies, and more to draw together diverse and divergent sources. This relentless, diverse allusion is what is most obvious about these later works. For instance, Mullen scratches and samples the Christmas carol "Joy to the World": "dead to the world / let earth receive her piece / let every dark room repair her heart / let nature and heaven give her release" (*Muse & Drudge* 39).[5] Or the song "My Favorite Things" from the musical *The Sound of Music* (a song also riffed and revised by John Coltrane): "Girls in white sat in with blues-saddened slashers" (*Trimmings* 38).[6] Or the spiritual "Swing Low, Sweet Chariot": "I didn't went to go / swing low zydeco / so those green chariots / light your eyes up" (*Muse*

& Drudge 57).[7] Or the writings of Booker T. Washington and W. E. B. Du Bois: "up from slobbery / hip hyperbole / the soles of black feet / beat down black streets" (*Muse & Drudge* 46).[8] Or Harriet Beecher Stowe's *Uncle Tom's Cabin; Or, Life among the Lowly:* "today's dread would awe / Topsy undead her missionary / exposition in what Liberia / could she find freedom to study her story" (*Muse & Drudge* 45).[9] She alludes to Lady Godiva as "thin-skinned Godiva with a wig on a horseback, body cast in a sit calm" (*Trimmings* 16).[10] Sigmund Freud's Dora appears "between the lines, in the spaces where nothing is written. . . . A name adores a Freudian slip" (*Trimmings* 22).[11] Popular African-American performer Josephine Baker appears "In feathers, in bananas, in her own skin, intelligent body attached to a gaze. Stripped down model, posing for a savage art, brought color to a primitive stage" (*Trimmings* 47).[12] Mullen transforms the instructions on frozen food or the pursuit of clean laundry into statements on race and class when she writes "Brown and serve, a slice of life whose side's your butter on" (*S*PeRM**K*T* n.p.) or "Ivory says pure nuff and snowflakes be white enough to do the dirty work. Step and fetch laundry tumbles out shuffling into sorted colored stacks" (*S*PeRM**K*T* n.p.).[13]

It would be tempting to end this discussion with the observation that Mullen's work is clearly signifyin(g). Mullen's work—at least all of it written after Gates's 1988 work—seems clearly and self-referentially to fit into this tradition of Esu, a tradition of "individuality, satire, parody, irony, magic, indeterminacy, open-endedness, ambiguity, sexuality, chance, uncertainty, disruption and reconciliation, betrayal and loyalty, closure and disclosure, encasement and rupture" (Gates 6). In *The Signifying Monkey*, Gates locates four types of signifyin(g): tropological revision (repeated tropes, such as the talking book), the speakerly text (self-conscious representation of a speaking black voice), talking texts (intertextual works or "black texts [which] 'talk' to other black texts" [xxvi]), and rewriting the speakerly (black dialect as pastiche). His concentration, like Mullen's, is on the vernacular tradition and its attention to intertextuality. Gates's study is richly revisionary. He does a confident tightrope walk in *The Signifying Monkey* by reading African-American literature as a separate category that is always in dialogue with others in its category (and without, for while Gates concentrates on African-American signifyin[g] on other African-American texts, he does point to the influence of non-African-based traditions).

Gates's attention throughout *The Signifying Monkey* is on production. He emphasizes writers, textuality, and literature. Yet signifyin(g)'s practices, as Gates also notes, are rooted in the provisional, in jazz performances, and in language games like the dirty dozens. And while Gates does not do a disservice to recognize signifyin(g)'s importance to the production of novels, his work ends there. It is as if one could validate formal revision or polysemy or dissonance or whatever word one wants to use simply because these forms are representative of the complexity of black experience. Gates's study is useful as a study of intertextuality, as a study of tradition, but less useful on the consequences of this work. Or as Wahneema Lubiano notes, "Gates's study glosses over the politics of the vernacular both between African- and Euro-American cultures and within African-American culture—across gender lines, for example" (227).

Joyce Joyce, in her infamous exchange with Gates and Houston Baker in *New Literary History,* has a similar critique. She argues that Gates ends his study at complexity and does not consider audience. Her essay opens with a student who complains that a James Baldwin essay is unclear. This student/reader reminds Joyce of "all those times when I cajoled and coerced her away from narrow and provincial interpretations of the literary work and preached of the responsibility of the writer to his or her audience" (335). Joyce notes also how "[t]his concentration [on audience,] on the relationship of Black Americans to the hegemony, to mainstream society, continues to this day to be the predominant issue in Black American literature" (336).

Joyce's critique has already been accused of being anti-intellectual by Gates and Baker (and numerous other critics).[14] I do not wish to retread this ground or join in the difficult and ugly gender politics that characterize this debate. Regarding Joyce's argument, I find myself in the difficult position of wanting to critically distance myself from parts of it while acknowledging at the same time that I find crucially useful her attention to the reader and her observation that readers tend to be ignored by the criticism that aligns itself with the tradition of Esu. Her article's attention to the reader moves the debate about a politically responsive African-American tradition away from realism (and which representation of it is more "real" or more reflective of black experience) to questions of what such a literature does for those it claims to represent.

But at the same time, I want to be very clear that I do not wish to join Joyce in a rhetoric that uses clarity and readers as a policing force. One reason

I feel that the critical language of the real, or of the complexity of the real, needs to be abandoned is to allow us to consider a wider range of works apart from a rhetoric of clarity. It is not representative to see works by African-American writers, and other ethnically or racially defined writers, that use "postmodern" or "poststructuralist" techniques as written under the sway of white, male critical establishments. And what has been so crucial about Gates's work has been his pointing out that what might look to be postmodern might be upon closer examination African-based.[15] More recent work by critics such as Nathaniel Mackey, Paul Gilroy, and Aldon Lynn Nielsen extended Gates's emphasis on this tradition beyond the colloquial. Mackey, for instance, looks to a diverse tradition that he calls "[d]iscrepant engagement, [which] rather than suppressing resonance, dissonance, noise, seeks to remain open to them" (20). Gilroy documents interconnections among "the stereophonic, bilingual, or bifocal cultural forms" of what he calls the "black Atlantic" (3). And Nielsen points to "multiplying free stories of ever more complex black modernities" in his study of the Black Arts and related movements (*Black Chant* 115).[16]

Further, Joyce, almost counterintuitively, argues that African-American critics are currently biased toward poststructuralist methodologies because of their emphasis on prose: "It is no accident that the Black poststructuralist methodology has so far been applied to fiction, the trickster tale, and the slave narrative. Black poetry—particularly that written during and after the 1960s—defies both linguistically and ideologically the 'poststructuralist sensibility'" (342). She mentions only Gwendolyn Brooks and Sonia Sanchez by name as poets who directly address the issue of audience (her reasoning: they publish exclusively with black presses), so it is hard to tell what exactly she might consider poetry that avoids this tendency. But it is important to remember that African-American writing is richly various. Its very strength is evident in how it has manifested issues of audience, or consciousness-raising, in various ways in various forms. Numerous writers of the 1960s and 1970s wrote linguistically nonstandard, diverse, and political works, as is evident in the work of Amiri Baraka, Julia Fields, Stephen Jonas, Elouise Loftin, Gloria Oden, Oliver Pitcher, Tom Postell, A. B. Spellman, and Lorenzo Thomas.[17] More recent writing by younger African-American poets, such as Will Alexander, Paul Beatty, Tisa Bryant, Thomas Sayers Ellis, C. S. Giscombe, Renee Gladman, Erica Hunt, Mackey, Tracie Morris, Akilah Oliver, Julie Patton,

Wanda Phipps, Claudia Rankine, Kate Rushin, giovanni singleton, and Patricia Smith, continues to engage, reformulate, and extend this tradition. This split between a thriving African-American experimentalism and a critical insistence on and validation of more traditional forms is, unfortunately, not unusual.[18]

But issues that remain important, post-signifyin(g)'s emphasis on innovation, are how works mobilize desire in empowering traditions, how they negotiate and recirculate individual and collective desire for emancipatory purposes. As Joyce points out, because there is a tradition or a tendency (and I would prefer to use these words rather than Joyce's "responsibility") of liberatory politics in African-American literature, this literature is an excellent place to consider how works engage the reader in pursuit of liberation. Mullen's work, for instance, is deeply engaged in this liberatory tradition as she signifies on signifyin(g) by writing a readerly work. Mullen's work (creative and critical—she writes both) is clearly in dialogue with these studies, these affiliations, but what I find crucial about her work is how she connects this polysemy to its larger politics of reading. In this article, I locate three different types of signifyin(g), ones that are concerned less with Gates's paradigm of how texts talk to other texts and more with how works talk to readers.

It is clear in this context that reading is no longer envisioned as an individual sitting down with a good book in a well-lit room (or a well-cultivated garden) for an afternoon's leisure. Rather, one way works are political is in the sorts of readings they encourage, in the sorts of alignments they pursue. In an interview with Farah Griffin, Michael Magee, and Kristen Gallagher, Mullen states how in *Muse & Drudge* she wanted to "encompass a generous, inclusive view, of what African tradition, Diaspora culture tradition, language, languages, might be. I tried to think about language and culture through the lens of a black woman who's not necessarily myself, but a representation of our diversity and our possibility" (n.p.). But even more interestingly, she describes very literally the connective intent in her work:

[O]ne reason I wrote *Muse and Drudge* is because having written *Tree Tall Woman,* when I went around reading from that book there were a lot of black people in my audience. There would be white people and brown people and maybe other people of color as well. Suddenly, when I went around to do readings of *Trimmings* and "Spermkit," I would be the one black person in the room, reading my poetry. I mean I'd find myself in a room that typically had no other people of color in it—which, you know, I could do, and . . . it was interesting. But that's not necessarily what I wanted, and I thought, "How am I going to get all these folks to sit down together in the same room?" *Muse and Drudge* was my attempt to create that audience. I wanted the different audiences for my various works to come together. I was happy to see those people who were interested in the formal innovation that I . . . that emerged when I was writing *Trimmings* and "Spermkit," partly because I was responding, in those books, to the work of Gertrude Stein, while dealing with my own concerns around race, gender, and culture. I had been hanging out with the language writers in the Bay Area, and listening to them and reading their work, so there was all of that influence as well. And then I thought, okay, well, I'm going to need to do something to integrate this audience, because it felt uncomfortable to be the only black person in the room reading my work to this audience. I mean, it was something that I could do up to a certain point with pure gratitude that an audience existed for my new work. I felt, "Well, this is interesting. This tells me something about the way that I'm writing now," although I didn't think I was any less black in those two books or any more black in *Tree Tall Woman*. But I think that the way that these things get defined in the public domain is that, yeah, people saw "Spermkit" as being not a black book but an innovative book. And this idea that you can be black or innovative, you know, is what I was really trying to struggle against. And *Muse and Drudge* was my attempt to show that I can do both at the same time. (n.p., ellipses in original)

In this anecdote, Mullen points to how her work shares with works by other African-American writers a self-aware investigation of her own relationship to issues of race, class, and gender, to dominant and subordinate cultures, to her role as spokesperson for "minority experience." Yet at the same time, she points to how the form of the work can change the construction of a segregated social space. Similarly, in "Imagining the Unimagined Reader" Mullen points to the possibilities of writing in a world of expanding illiteracy (she means both the illiteracy of not being able to read and the growing nominally educated who cannot read critically). Here, while acknowledging the limitations of her work—its limited distribution and its nonstandard forms—she writes that her future (ideal?) reader is "the offspring of an illiterate woman" and that she writes (echoing Stein) "for myself and others" (199).

While one cannot, and Mullen does not, claim even the most progressive writing as an antidote to illiteracy and the economic disadvantages that accompany it in Western society, Mullen's interest in reading and her alignment with those skilled in it is valuable. Her works investigate the privileges of education and the relationship between her work and the dominant canon she was taught, and at the same time it claims an African-American tradition of reading. This dual investigation counters years of denial of literacy and then, once literacy must no longer be kept under wraps or learned through trickery, years of unequal schooling in the United States. As Lubiano notes, "An old African-American truism runs thusly: being where they give out education must mean something or they (whites) wouldn't try so hard to keep us out" (206). While not answering reading's elitism with anti-intellectualism, Mullen's work does complicate the relation between reading and elitism by establishing multiple alliances between the dominant and the minority without abandoning the challenge of intellectual content.

Mullen's attention to the politics of reading extends beyond mere formal or representational issues. As Mullen signifies on signifyin(g), instead of emphasizing the way texts talk to texts, she privileges also the way they talk differently, talk back, and talk with readers.[19] While the differences between Gates's emphasis on how texts talk to texts and how Mullen's works talk differently, with, or back with readers may seem minor, it is nonetheless crucial for any consideration of a politics of textuality. Mullen's work presents a two-pronged engagement with reading: her work models reading as it refers, and as it manipulates these works, it reads.

I use the terms "read" and "talk" here as almost synonymous so I can say that Mullen reads blues singer Bessie Smith as a black, feminist innovator in the tradition of Sappho (or Smith talks with Sappho). In other words, Mullen both reads/talks with another work in the sense of passively ingesting, and she reads/talks back in the sense of providing an interpretation of. Configuring talking with reading, Mullen's work, instead of glossing over reading by seeing it as preparatory for writing, privileges reading's provisional, improvisational, and flexible possibilities. Like orality, reading is full of nonstandard and stigmatized ways of thinking. Reading can be a communal, resistant, and provisional act. And reading and talking are both ephemeral acts and thus have possibilities for being less policed. Reading here is figured in Mullen's work not as the ingestion of writing, a transcription of speech, but as a speech itself.

Critics have tended to privilege the orality of African-American literature, but I think also that by aligning reading with orality, one can realize an added dimension to orality. To see Mullen's work, and that of a good many other African-American writers, as simply, or even primarily, oral is to miss an African-American tradition of engagement with reading that complicates the oral.[20] The way that Mullen will pun both with sight ("buy 'n' buy pie chart" [*Muse & Drudge* 37]) and with sound ("hooked on phonemes imbued with exuberance" [49]) points to a desire to have both oral and written dimensions interacting in a continuum of alliances.[21]

Finally, Mullen's work points to how the complexity of black practices that West notes is directly related to a desire to break down restrictive hierarchies of who can speak and when. As Mullen writes in her critical article, "Runaway Tongue: Resistant Orality in *Uncle Tom's Cabin, Our Nig, Incidents in the Life of a Slave Girl,* and *Beloved*": "[S]laves countered institutional illiteracy with a resistant orality. Not everyone found opportunities to steal literacy or successfully escape slavery as a fugitive, but oral transmission passed on the verbal skills of runaway tongues: the sass, spunk, and infuriating impudence of slaves who individually and collectively refused to know their place" (245).

Talk Differently

. . . a talent for speaking differently, rather than for arguing well,
is the chief instrument of cultural change.

—Richard Rorty, *Contingency, Irony, and Solidarity*

Tender white kid, off white tan. Snug black leather, second skin.
Fits like a love, an utter other uttered. Bag of tricks, slight hand
preserved, a dainty.

—Mullen, *Trimmings*

To talk differently Mullen-style is to write in a language of colloquialisms, fractured words, games, homonyms, jests, joined words, jokes, nonsense, puns, repetition. Her work uses many different nonstandard language practices and joins them together in a continuum that reads at times like Black English meets Gertrude Stein. In *Muse & Drudge*, for instance, Mullen puns "mutter patter simper blubber / murmur prattle smatter blather / mumble chatter whisper bubble / mumbo-jumbo palaver gibber blunder" (57). Here, words used to demean other, nonstandard forms of speaking are gathered into a meaning of alliance (remember also that *Mumbo Jumbo* is the title of an Ishmael Reed novel). Throughout her works, she engages what is often constructed as other and, as she puns, of the "utter other uttered" (*Trimmings* 9).

Further, her work, in a move that mixes Du Bois's double consciousness with Richard Wright's double vision with Jacques Derrida's deconstruction, frequently points to the violence and inadequacy of language's attempts to be faithful. For example, the pun—the device that with its two-headed approach to meaning speaks concisely to the possibilities within reading—figures prominently. Mullen writes: "Polly and Esther living modern with better chemistry" (*Trimmings* 21) or "antistepton disinfunktant unknownabrasives" (*S*PeR M**K*T* n.p.) or "last chance apocalypso" (*Muse & Drudge* 65). In *Trimmings* there is an even further emphasis on things that talk differently by meaning doubly. The title itself means to add or to take away (and also is a euphemism for a woman's vagina or sexuality). And "Bareness," for example, "comes with coverage" and "[h]oles breathe, and swallow. Openings, hem, sleeve. Borders on edges where skin stops, or begins" (*Trimmings* 63, 53). This emphasis on the duality of the line—"skin stops, or begins"—is the crucial aspect of *Trimmings*'s resistance to systems that want to limit both race and reading. Mullen concentrates on the syncretism of things—holes both breathe and swallow, sleeves are both opened and hemmed, and trimmings are things both added and taken away—and thus presents an example of Spillers's call for a semantic field/fold that is not absolute. Her emphasis is, as she writes in *Trimmings*, on "cleavage[s] in language" (54). The pun here is telling: cleavages meaning breasts (referring to Mullen's emphasis on the relation between femininity and language in *Trimmings*) and spaces (referring to where language opens and many meanings enter).

Further emphasizing the unfaithful and unowned practices of reading is

Mullen's use of sampling, a technique used extensively and popularized by rap and hip-hop musicians. In sampling, musicians take snippets from other recorded songs and incorporate them directly into their own. The theft is deliberately self-aware and allusive. At times it functions in the song as ironic critique, but often it is used in homage, as an acknowledgment of influence or of the power of someone else's work. Either way, it points to how meaning is tied to community and is necessarily collective. The creative economy here emphasizes talking differently through reuse and recombination. This form of "talking different" is similar to Walter Ong's theory of orality in which originality is in the reshuffling of previous themes and formulas. In rap, the sample points to collective cultures, group identities, and community reading practices.[22] Mullen's use of sampling works similarly. When, as I examine in greater detail later, Mullen samples Sappho and overlays Bessie Smith, the sample functions as a reference with an emphasis on recontextualization that rewrites history. I call Mullen's use here "sampling" because it differs from modernism's intertextuality, which tends to function as a sort of tale of the tribe that often reinforces dominant canonical groups. But while Mullen's move here is highly literate, her work charts different sorts of cultural literacy and suggests alternative canons with its emphasis on oral traditions, contemporary oral forms like advertising jingles, popular culture, and high modernism. The allusions of her work function more as preservation of often overlooked works and traditions.

It is also crucial to realize that sampling functions as a tool of necessity and is similar to a resistant orality in this. Sampling began because rap musicians did not have access to studios, a full range of instruments, backup singers, and so forth. They took, therefore, from previously recorded releases and remixed parts of them into their own music out of necessity. The act of sampling thus is also a street-based response that, like the act of reading, uses other sources for its own ends. I think here of Le Roi Jones pointing out how the blues encourage individuals to respond to collective forms: "Blues was a music that arose from the needs of a group, although it was assumed that each man had his own blues and that he would sing them" (82). Similarly, Mullen explains why she wrote *Muse & Drudge* in the quatrain form: "Quatrains can be free standing and shuffled in and out of the work in the way that blues verses are shuffled in and out in any particular performance" ("Solo Mysterioso Blues" 654).

Talking differently, with its emphasis on resistance and communal acts of language such as slang, argot, homilies, and other cultural colloquialism, moves away from the moments when language defines what an individual is (the way the subject of the sentence and subjectivity slip into hierarchies of domination in language) and toward the way language can define a collective yet multivalent identity. I read Mullen's intent here as proposing alternative literacies, alternative reading practices. These ways of reading, with their emphasis on language's slippages, are not pursuing correctness or standards. Instead, they are aligned with the impudence and flexibility of talk, orality, and resistance.

Talk Back: Édouard Manet, Gertrude Stein, and Harryette Mullen

A PETTICOAT
A light white, a disgrace, an ink spot, a rosy charm.

—Gertrude Stein, *Tender Buttons*

A light white disgraceful sugar looks pink, wears an air, pale compared to shadow standing by. To plump recliner, naked truth lies. Behind her shadow wears her color, arms full of flowers. A rosy charm is pink. And she is ink. The mistress wears no petticoat or leaves. The other in shadow, a large pink dress.

—Mullen, *Trimmings*

When I speak of Mullen's "talking back," my interest is in how her work uses signifyin(g) as a tool of resistance, a tool that reads dominant culture and critiques it. It has not been unusual to notice, especially as concerns *Trimmings,* that Mullen's work is in dialogue with modernism in general and Stein in particular.[23] But the question again is one of the intent of this intertextuality. I read Mullen here as primarily talking back, as replying to modernism's at times problematic race, class, and gender politics. It is not that talking back is merely a tool of defiance or of anger. In *Trimmings,* Mullen uses modernist techniques of disruption, fragmentation, and making

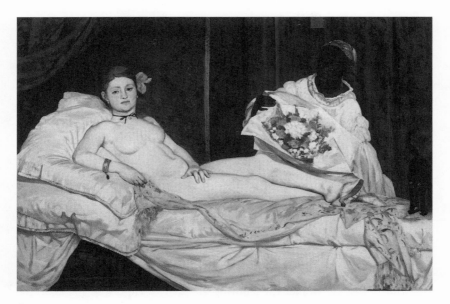

Édouard Manet, *Olympia* (1863, oil on canvas, Musee d'Orsay, Paris)

strange to expose the often limited political attention of Anglo-American modernism, and she also examines what these techniques have to add to discussions of race, class, and gender in the late twentieth century. It is necessary, since Mullen presents both a critique of modernism's content and an alliance with modernism's forms, to realize her intent as critiquing homage. Anglo-American modernism is clearly one source of influence for Mullen's work, but *Trimmings* approaches these influences with a measured ambivalence.

One of the most obvious and interesting moments of this dialogue with modernism occurs in *Trimmings* when Mullen takes Édouard Manet's *Olympia,* adds Stein's "A PETTICOAT" from *Tender Buttons,* and writes the two together to make something altogether different. As Stacy Hubbard points out, "the picture [that] suddenly looms into view, such that we may wonder at not having seen it in Stein's line all along, is Manet's *Olympia*" (4). In Mullen's words, the "light white" and "disgrace" of Stein's petticoat turns into the white woman's body of Manet's *Olympia* with "a light white disgraceful sugar looks pink" (15). Stein's ink spot turns into the black woman with "And she is ink" (15). And when Mullen writes "a rosy charm is pink" she refers multiply to the flowers, to the white woman's body, and to the black woman's pink dress.

Most see Manet's painting as one where viewers look and are made aware of their looking by the white woman's returned gaze. The painting appears to be all about equal exchange: the white woman and viewers exchange gazes. Plus they are as brazen, as indicted, as she is; their accusing gaze receives her accusing gaze; thus their gaze strips them and her gaze clothes her. When *Olympia* was shown at the 1865 Salon in Paris, spectators called it indecent, saw it as portraying "a kind of female gorilla," or otherwise mocked it.[24] While the painting comments on the classical and rereads, most obviously, the reclining nude of Titian's *Urbino Venus* into the modern (a project that would be similar to Mullen's rereadings of modernist works), it is the obvious flaunting exposure of the woman's body and her direct gaze at the spectator that made *Olympia* so controversial in its time.[25] This questioning of the traditional role of women in painting in turn disrupts the logic of the painter's (and spectators') gaze. Spectators are forced into confrontation with their own act of looking, and most of the critical attention on this painting concentrates on how one looks at the reclining white woman's body. Griselda Pollock points to a series of questions when she addresses this painting (and Manet's *A Bar at the Folies-Bergère*): "How can a woman relate to the viewing positions offered by either of these paintings? Can a woman be offered, in order to be denied, imaginary possession of *Olympia* or the barmaid?" (53). And part of the ambiguous power of this painting is that these questions go unanswered and are endlessly debatable.

By referencing Stein's *Tender Buttons*, Mullen adds another layer of examination to what gets perceived as conventional and acceptable and what does not. While Stein's *Tender Buttons* did not receive as much attention as Manet's *Olympia*, critics also reacted with disdain, and the book was notorious mainly as a work of nonsense. But as *Olympia* signaled the beginning of a new form of painterly perception, so Stein's *Tender Buttons* stands heralding literary modernism's attention to fragmentation. In *Tender Buttons*, Stein takes things domestic—objects, food, rooms—and rewrites them in a fractured, playful language. It is a work that is uniquely concerned with pushing issues of representation and language as far as they will go, and it encourages its readers to "act so that there is no use in a centre" (*Tender Buttons*

63). I read the work as being about, if one can say such a thing without being unnecessarily reductive, "what language can instruct any fellow" (41).[26] If Manet's painting raises questions about women's bodies, Stein's *Tender Buttons* raises questions about women's places and their relation to language. In "A PETTICOAT," Stein might describe ("a light white"), argue ("a disgrace"—the ink spot? or the exposure of the undergarment?), complicate ("an ink spot"), and defend ("a rosy charm") (22). But none of this is done through narrative. It is rather done through a description around an object. Or as she writes in *Lectures in America*, "I resolutely realized nouns and decided not to get around them but to meet them, to handle in short to refuse them by using them and in that way my real acquaintance with poetry was begun" (228).

Mullen talks back to these two works by using their techniques of looking elsewhere and fragmentation to question their claims to egalitarian politics. Instead of presenting a centered gaze as Manet does, or one that has no use in a center as Stein does, Mullen turns the gaze into a locus of relations. As Mullen is well aware, when one looks at the black servant woman in Manet's painting, one can only realize that any claims to an equality of gaze are fraudulent and privileged. Further, in Mullen's poem, it is not that the central subject of the painting is the white woman's returned gaze. The black servant woman in the shadow, off to the side, presents another gaze and another subject. In Manet's painting, the black woman is like the spectator, submissively looking. But when spectators look also at the black woman, they have to see at least a triangular relationship in which they gaze on a black woman serving a white woman. In this configuration, the center is no longer constitutive. Spectators' gazes are decentered and no longer equally exchanged. Spectators gaze also on race and class and—most importantly, because the painting requires its spectators to recognize themselves as spectators—their own role in these social structures. Mullen's talking back to the painting points to how that which is most obviously spectacular, most obviously central, is actually constituted by an equally constitutive marginality. Her move here is like Gayatri Chakravorty Spivak's "to point to the irreducibility of the margin in all explanations" (107). Spectators see a history of servitude for black women and realize the black woman's distance from the art history ideal of the white woman's body. So when Mullen writes that "the naked truth lies," she refers not only to how the woman's body lies across the bed but also to how it is deceptive and does not present a truth, an exposure, of a generic woman's body (15). One looks at the white woman's naked body and one looks also at how the black woman's body disappears into the background and how what is left is "a large pink dress" (15).

Talk Back: "Raise Your Hand If You're Sure You're Not"

Raise your hand if you're sure you're not

—Mullen, S*PeRM**K*T

There is no clear "I" in Mullen's later books. This is most literally exemplified by the title S*PeRM**K*T, which is the word "supermarket" with the letters "u are" missing. The missing "u are" is emblematic of the complicated way critique is manifested in Mullen's work. On the one hand, the "you" or the "I" that is clearly present in *Tree Tall Woman* is missing in the later works. But the asterisks in the title also point to a certain emphasis. What is crucial about Mullen's work is not that she erases the subject in the name of political critique (as many argue that language writing does), but that she rewrites it as a series of asterisks, or as present (in the sense that one reads "u are" as a statement of fact) but necessarily flexible, compounded, and fractured (because the asterisks are signs of non-dogmatic presence). Similarly, the pun that is present in the letters that remain suggest that "sperm" might come in a "kit," or that one can buy subjectivity at the grocery or arts and crafts store. So what Mullen's work presents is a more complex subject, one that breaks down the unnecessary dialectic between an essentialism that argues for a stable relationship to one's race or gender (and less commonly, one's class) and a constructivism that argues for an open performance of identity.

In Mullen's world, the subject that is most present and most accessible is most suspect. When the "you" does appear in S*PeRM**K*T, it is in a series of rewritten advertising jingles that Mullen talks back to: "Aren't you glad you use petroleum? Don't wait to be told you explode. You're not fully here until you're over there. Never let them see you eat. You might be taken for a zoo. Raise your hand if you're sure you're not" (n.p.). The phrases here are rewrites of advertisements for personal hygiene products such as "Aren't you glad you use Dial?" or "You're not fully clean until you are zestfully clean" or "Never let them see you sweat" or "Raise your hand if you're sure." Several of these are rewritten so that the discourse about purity and cleanliness which they invoke turns into statements that critique essentialist narratives of belonging: "You're not fully here until you're over there" and "Raise your hand if you're sure you're not." So one reading of the missing "u are" is that Mullen shows how subjectivity is made manifest by advertising and its language of purity in which cleanliness is privileged and placed on a continuum with goodness and whiteness. Also critiqued here are racial stereotypes of "others" as dirty and smelly. Throughout $S*PeRM**K*T$, Mullen points to the relation between the oppressive languages of race, gender, and class and the language of the supermarket, which she refuses to read as naive. Roach killer, Two Thousand Flushes, feminine hygiene napkins, milk, bread, and more, with their emphasis on clean whiteness, all speak in a language that walks hand in hand with the language of racism.

The revision of narratives of color also occurs in Mullen's continued engagements with Stein in *Trimmings*. While *Tender Buttons* often refers to what is "dirty,"[27] *Trimmings* rereads the dirty. As A. L. Nielsen notes, "Mullen finds ways to reread the influence of Gertrude Stein while deprivileging the racist markings so often found in Stein's works" ("Black Margins" 159). But differences between these two works are obvious. When Stein writes about "trimmings," she writes about them as red and white and plays with the associations among femininity, pinkness and whiteness, and sexuality: "A sight a whole sight and a little groan grinding makes a trimming such a sweet singing trimming and a red thing not a round thing but a white thing, a red thing and a white thing" (*Tender Buttons* 11). But instead of red and white, Mullen writes, "Her red and white, white and blue banner manner. Her red and white over black and blue. Hannah's bandanna flagging her down in the kitchen with Dinah, with Jemima. Someone in the kitchen I know" (*Trimmings* 11). Here colors resonate meaning: red and white femininity turns white and blue turns black and blue. As Mullen notes in the afterword to *Trimmings*, "The words pink and white kept appearing as I explored the ways that the English language conventionally represents femininity. As a black woman writing in this language, I suppose I already had an ironic relationship to this pink and white femininity" (69). This ironic relationship turns color into a troubled metaphor in Mullen's work. While the red and white of *Trimmings* is clearly not used as in the traditional sonnet, where the red of the woman's cheeks and lips is contrasted with the white of her skin, it is still hard to sort out if this red and white speaks ominously of the harsh red of blood which turns into the "black and blue" of a bruise; or if a "white and blue banner manner" is a kitchen servant's gingham or a reference to the purity implied in the term "blue bloods"; or if the red and white of Hannah's bandanna covers dark skin or bruised skin. Nielsen is right that Mullen deprivileges the racist markings in Stein's work, but she does it using the technique that Stein used in *Tender Buttons:* she refuses them by using them. Color in her work bears little "true" meaning, and the supposedly clear dividing line of the skin's color is constantly muddled. In the above passage, not only is it hard to recognize the ordering impulse of racial categories in which skin is read as representing a certain color, but also the emphasis on blood in this passage challenges the social and legal emphasis on blood as a site of quantifiable racial absoluteness. Blood, the sign of race, here spins out of control as red and white and black and blue cannot be separated into distinct identities. Mullen's concentration on blood's multiple colors emphasizes the fictitious biological foundation of laws which at one time established racial categories in the United States by using "a few drops of Negro blood" as judge.

Mullen's reply to absolute categories of subjectivity in *S*PeR M**K*T* is the asterisk as the sign of "u are." In *Trimmings* it is the practice of refusing by using. But in *Muse & Drudge,* this figure is the community. The identifications throughout this poem are connective ones, not individual ones. The connective here is presented as an arrangement of individuals, of collective utterances. As Mullen notes in an interview, "Any time 'I' is used in this poem, it's practically always quotation. . . . The 'I' in the poem is almost always someone other than myself, and often it's an anonymous 'I,' a generic 'I,' a traditional 'I,' the 'I' of the blues, that person who in reference to any individual experience also speaks for the tradition, speaks for the community, and the community recognizes the individuality of the speaker and also claims something in common" ("Solo Mysterioso Blues" 653). This community, I want to argue, is a community of readers, and it is what is crucial about Mullen's work and its engagements with reading. Her emphasis throughout her three later books figures reading as a reply to the authority of subjectivity, grammar, and overly reductive identity narratives. Mullen's emphasis is on reading as a communal act of resistance, a utopian, dissident space. And this emphasis is evident in Mullen's desire to integrate the room of the experimental and identity poetries with the more inclusive vision of *Muse & Drudge*.

Talk With: Sappho/Sapphire/Bessie Smith

Like a quince-apple
ripening on a top
branch in a tree top

not once noticed by
harvesters or if
not unnoticed, not reached

—Sappho (trans. Mary Barnard)

Sapphire's lyre styles
plucked eyebrows
bow lips and legs
whose lives are lonely too

my last nerve's lucid music
sure chewed up the juicy fruit
you must don't like my peaches
there's some left on the tree

you've had my thrills
a reefer a tub of gin
don't mess with me I'm evil
I'm in your sin

—Mullen, *Muse & Drudge*

Just as important as talking back's critique is talking with's revisionism. While talking back envisions readerly engagement as having elements of critique, talking with is more attentive to alliances. Throughout her work, Mullen emphasizes a continual tradition of resistance. While *Trimmings* and

S*PeR M**K*T do this work by resisting dominant culture, *Muse & Drudge* works to establish alliances with dominant cultures. Such emphasis is at its most obvious in *Muse & Drudge* where Mullen puts literary and extra-literary sources in dialogue. Her work willingly takes dictation from oral as well as written sources and insists on dialogic writing practices. This book is less critique and more homage. *Muse & Drudge* begins with Mullen talking with Sappho, Bessie Smith, and others.

It is Sappho, as is often noted, who begins the personal, lyric tradition. The fragment of the quince apple is found embedded as a quote in Syrianus's commentary on Hermogenes' *On Kinds of Style*.[28] It is often assumed to be a part of an epithalamium. It is typical of works by Sappho in that the complicated nature of the personal is brought to readers' consciousness through a seemingly innocent metaphor. The everyday of the apple suddenly becomes loaded with meaning, with the personal. And what appears to be an innocent statement about fruit ripening opens in many directions. The poem is built around fleeting states and formed so that ambiguities resonate off each other. It is a quince apple (or a sweet apple, depending on who is translating) that is the subject, not just any apple. This apple is ripening, not yet ripe. It has gone unnoticed, yet we notice it with the poem. It is above us, dangling, perfect. The poem itself is ambiguous as to why the fruit has escaped touch. It is either not noticed or not reached.

It is easy, and common, to read this poem as a metaphor for women and the difficult relationship between purity and sexuality. The fragment contains an easy moral for contemporary readers: one must work hard to get the sweet apple. If the poem is read as an epithalamium, it says that things do not come easily for those who want the best love. Even if one was to literalize and read the poem as just about an apple, then it still is about how, when looking differently, one sees the best fruit. Sappho's turn to the personal, lyric I in a world of heroic war poetry turns the apple from mythic fruit into the fragmented, domestic personal moment. Yet in this poem there is no "I" directly. The narrator is omniscient. The "I" is off holding the camera up at the unattainable, almost ripe whole. Readers are left dangling, as it were, in a suspended moment of betweens.

This metaphor—that of looking up at ripening fruit—comes down through the centuries, twisting around in different ways but growing in its relation to sexuality by the time one gets to *Muse & Drudge*. In fact, if there is a danger in these readings of the apple as women's sexuality, it is danger that is unavoidable after Adam and Eve's takeover of the apple (and there is but a short jump from the apple to the metaphor of all fruit being forbidden). In Mullen's poem, the sweet apple of Sappho turns into the peaches on the tree. The peaches reference can almost be endlessly unpacked. There are the peaches of the Steve Miller Band's "The Joker": "No don't worry mama. / Cause I'm right here at home. / You're the cutest thing / That I ever did see / Really love your peaches / Wanna shake your tree." Which is really the peaches of The Clovers' 1953 hit: "I really love your peaches wanna shake your tree / Lovey dovey, lovey dovey all the time." And there is a slightly different lineage of peaches that appears in the Beatles' "Matchbox," where "an old poor boy" laments and shifts the gender of the fruit here, "Well, if you don't want my peaches / honey please don't shake my tree." Which is really the peaches of Carl Perkins. Perkins's peaches come from the peaches of Blind Lemon Jefferson's "Matchbox Blues." And versions of this song are also sung by Larry Hensely (1934), Joe Shelton (1935), Roy Shaffer (1939), Roy Newman and His Boys (1939), the Shelton Brothers (1947), and Jerry Lee Lewis (1958).[29] But even before all this, Ma Rainey sang a song called "Lost Wandering Blues," which, while it does not reference the peaches and the tree, does contain the matchbox and is seen as the precedent for Blind Lemon Jefferson's "Matchbox Blues."

I doubt if I have unpacked the resonances of the peaches and the tree exhaustively. Does James Mtume's song "Juicy Fruit" resonate? Does Billy Holiday's "Strange Fruit" with its critique of racism resonate here?[30] Does Faulkner's *The Sound and the Fury*? Does St. Augustine's confession about stealing the pears from the tree? But I also doubt anyone could unpack it exhaustively. Part of the point is the impossible unpacking. Mullen's work in this book challenges the claims of hermetic competence that highly intertextual works and their readers often encourage or espouse. While this work allows readers to do the unpacking, as I just attempted, it is always a provisional unpacking because the markers are so loaded with culture that one cannot come up with an easily exhaustive answer. This work urges that readers abandon that feeling of cleverness, of being well trained, of successfully penetrating a work to an exhaustiveness, and instead recognize reading as connective. The most that can be said is that the peaches on the tree are bound with sexuality, the grand theme of poetry and blues.

When one arrives at Mullen in 1995, the metaphor of the ripe fruit in the tree that is unnoticed or at times unwanted has become part of a larger cultural detritus: something that might be the equivalent of a Sapphic fragment, a highly aesthetic reminder of something that cannot be recovered and all the more valuable for that reminder. *Muse & Drudge* begins referencing Sappho's lyre (*Sappho's Lyre* is the title of Diane J. Rayor's translations of archaic lyric and women poets of ancient Greece). Only here Sappho is marked as the African-American Sapphire. Resonating here is the "locus of confounded identities" that Hortense Spillers notes at the beginning of "Mama's Baby, Papa's Maybe: An American Grammar Book": "Let's face it. I am a marked woman, but not everybody knows my name. 'Peaches' and 'Brown Sugar,' 'Sapphire' and 'Earth Mother,' 'Aunty,' 'Granny,' God's 'Holy Fool,' a 'Miss Ebony First,' or 'Black Woman at the Podium': I describe a locus of confounded identities, a meeting ground of investments and privations in the national treasury of rhetorical wealth" (65). Also resonating here is Sappho's role as one of the first "outsider" poets.[31] And all that is in the quince apple fragment: the emphasis on in-between states, the personal told through the metaphoric, the desire to direct readers' attention to what is elsewhere, out of the easy gaze. Mullen quickly and easily joins Sappho to the blues tradition as Sappho's juicy fruit turns into the peaches left on the tree of the blues song. And then Fats Domino's "I found my thrill on Blueberry Hill" turns into "you've had my thrills" moves into Bessie Smith with "a reefer a tub of gin" and "I'm in your sin" sandwiched between something that might be Robert Johnson or Howlin' Wolf with "don't mess with me I'm evil" (1). Such referential pyrotechnics appear throughout *Muse & Drudge*. By moving through Sappho, the blues, and Juicy Fruit gum, Mullen exposes what concepts of tradition tend to overlook or leave out with their exclusionary lineages.

Avoiding Reading's Possible Imperialisms

We "know" that the Other is within us and affects how we evolve as well as the bulk of our conceptions and the development of our sensibility. Rimbaud's "I is an other" is literal in terms of history. In spite of ourselves, a sort of "consciousness of consciousness" opens us up and turns each of us into a disconcerted actor in the poetics of Relation.

—Édouard Glissant, *Poetics of Relation*

Black women's appropriation of materials from African-American oral traditions, as well as their interiorization of writing technologies productive of bourgeois subjectivity, are equally products of analysis and reflection upon their own and antecedent experiences passed from mothers to daughters. They were not the helpless victims of predatory literacy any more than they were passive and silent victims of their bodies' generative forces or of the abuse of masters and mistresses. On the contrary, they have frequently insisted upon a dialogic writing practice that operates against the tendency of the literate to view the illiterate and the oppressed as "voiceless."

—Mullen, "Runaway Tongue: Resistant Orality in *Uncle Tom's Cabin, Our Nig, Incidents in the Life of a Slave Girl*, and *Beloved*"

What has interested me about Mullen's work has been her attention to reading, an attention that is rooted in the intersection between language writing's pursuit of wild reading and autonomy- and identity-centered poetries' concerns with community building and alliance. Her work is just one example of an emerging tendency in contemporary writing to merge these two affiliations (which are often, rather unfortunately, seen as unaligned or unsympathetic to each other). This tendency can be found in any number of writers, but I would point in particular to related work by Myung Mi Kim, Edwin Torres, and Erica Hunt. These writers insist that culturally concerned writing has multiple roles, multiple forms. They point out that even writing which explores the concerns of uplift specific to racially defined communities should not sell the members of these communities short with limited or overly simplistic models of relation.

But also, Mullen's claim to be writing the future, for the offspring of an illiterate woman, suggests a rethinking of alliances in reading-orientated theory. Discussions of reading have tended to ignore the specificities that certain types of writing might demand of reading. There has been little work that addresses how works might alter the racial composition of a room, for example. Yet this literalization on a microcosmic level of reading communities by Mullen points to a profound rethinking of what reading literary works can do in and to community settings. It is not that Mullen makes grand utopian claims that all will begin to understand each other with this statement, but rather she suggests that the composition of work does shape larger community concerns.

An important exception to reading-orientated theory's avoidance of cultural specificities, however, is Doris Sommer's work on ethnically defined novels and testimonials.[32] The particular ways that her theories and the works they arise out of differ and intersect with works like Mullen's is also illustrative of the larger ramifications of community in these works of autonomy. Sommer is one of few critics to actually address the relation between ethnically defined works and reading. She usefully criticizes models of reading that lack self-reflection in their pursuit of mastery over a work. She examines works where the writers or narrators often refuse to divulge or claim to withhold crucial information necessary for understanding the racial or ethnic other. Such works, she argues, resist the attempts of both professional and nonprofessional readers to force an imperializing clarity, a clarity which assumes that readers can master the book, that the book is a territory that can be taken over, understood fully, consumed. These works, in order to avoid imperializing gestures where those who define themselves as outside racial or ethnic category claim to have understanding or the mastery of knowledge of the culture that the work is concerned with, deny identificatory fluidity. She writes: "They will refuse any conventional collusion between writer and reader, and flaunt an exclusive mastery meant to humble privileged outsiders" ("Who Can Tell?" 230).

Sommer's analysis is useful because it looks at moments of complication around issues of identity and does not propose a possible mastery. Her work represents a productive extension of reader-orientated theory by concentrating on moments of readerly difficulty as opposed to assumed communities of understanding. Her attention is to moments such as how "books resist the competent reader intentionally" and how this resistance differs from ambiguity, which "for some time [has been] a consecrated and flattering theme for professional readers" ("Textual Conquests" 147). These moments of resistance are moments that much reader-orientated theory avoids or does not consider an integral part of a work.

At the end of "Textual Conquests: On Readerly Competence and 'Minority' Literature," Sommer calls for a paradigm shift where we as readers recognize that "ambiguity cannot be conquered" (152). But at the same time, this shift requires that readers recognize "an inviolable border" (153). She writes: "From that border we can be 'ideal,' paradoxically, to the extent that we are excluded. We can be competent to the extent that we cannot conquer" (153). I appreciate (and want to align with) Sommer's desire to not further reading's possible imperialism. This chapter has been an attempt to look at works that suggest how reading can be non-imperial, non-universal. But while Sommer sees mainly two options—imperial reading or no reading—in the works she studies,[33] Mullen's work points to a theory of reading that acknowledges the dangers that Sommer points to yet at the same time points to reading as one way to explore more complex relations among ethnicity, reading, and politics. Instead of equating the ethnically defined work's refusal of an easy identificatory collusion with the actual preclusion of cross-identification, Mullen's work proposes other forms of identification and suggests that readers might approach these moments of withheld information using reading techniques that do not presume mastery.

I feel we ought to give a special weight to works that not only discuss the constructedness of race and ethnicity but also require readers to rethink this construction. Mullen's work, like the works Sommer studies, "neither assume[s] nor welcome[s] comprehension by the reader who would assimilate" it ("Who Can Tell?" 219). But the importance of Mullen's nonstandard language lies in how it manages to avoid the imperializing tendencies of reading not by denying information but by structuring her works so that this tendency is demonstrated to be inapplicable and suspect. The difficult moments in Mullen's work speak to a desire not to shut readers out but to invite them to abandon the standard ways of reading. Readers are invited to be constantly shifting locations, constantly struggling with a sampled and punned language, to talk back and to talk with. Her work is constructed around a challenge to readerly conventions and the necessity of readers' involvement. There is in her work a faith in readers' ability to be transformed by works and to move beyond silence and into knowledge. Rather than projecting racial or ethnic experience as something opaque, impermeable, or impossible to understand, her work establishes a productive space of rereading, a space in which cultural and textual authority are unceasingly undermined and re-inflected.

Viewing works as sites of complication rather than exclusion avoids the either/or of thought that so pervades systems of domination. Mullen's work demonstrates that reading is always a variable function beyond anyone's control, and that it is this which must be acknowledged (and encouraged) in order to adequately explore the complex relationships among race and ethnicity and reading. Her work proposes an alternative to the separatist intent that Sommer locates, yet it continues the anti-imperial attention to reading that Sommer rightly deems so important. The reading practice that Mullen's work pursues is one in which readers are forced to realize the variability of both reading and linguistic categories. It is this that her work cultivates to set up a space where productive, unsettled communication can begin between races and genders, as well as between readers and writers.

"Tertium Quid Neither One Thing Nor the Other"

Theresa Hak Kyung Cha's *DICTEE* and the Decolonization of Reading

Nothing could be more normative, more logical, and more au-
thoritarian than, for example, the (politically) revolutionary poetry
or prose that speaks of revolution in the form of commands or
in the well-behaved, steeped-in-convention language of "clarity."
. . . The language of Taoism and Zen, for example, which is per-
fectly accessible but rife with paradox does not qualify as "clear"
(paradox is "illogical" and "nonsensical" to many Westerners),
for its intent lies outside the realm of persuasion. The same holds
true for vernacular speech, which is not acquired through institutions—schools, churches, professions, etc.—and therefore not
repressed by either grammatical rules, technical terms, or key
words. Clarity as a purely rhetorical attribute serves the purpose
of a classical feature in language, namely, its instrumentality. To
write is to communicate, express, witness, impose, instruct, re-
deem, or save—at any rate to *mean* and to send out *an unambiguous message*. Writing thus reduced to a mere vehicle of
thought may be *used* to orient toward a goal or to sustain an
act, but it does not constitute an act in itself. This is how the
division between the writer/the intellectual and the activists/the
masses becomes possible. To use the language well, says the
voice of literacy, cherish its classical form. Do not choose the off-

beat at the cost of clarity. Obscurity is an imposition on the reader. True, but beware when you cross railroad tracks for one train may hide another train. Clarity is a means of subjection, a quality both of official, taught language and of correct writing, two old mates of power: together they flow, together they flower, vertically, to impose an order. Let us not forget that writers who advocate the instrumentality of language are often those who cannot or choose not to see the suchness of things—a language as language—and therefore, continue to preach conformity to the norms of well-behaved writing: principles of composition, style, genre, correction, and improvement.

—Trinh T. Minh-ha, *Woman, Native, Other: Writing Postcoloniality and Feminism*

loss, the absence, the ~~proper~~ object ~~presents~~ exposes the loss, the missing ~~thing is~~ left to the ~~one~~ imaginary.

—From Cha, *DICTEE*

"Correspondence. To Scatter the Words."

The section of Theresa Hak Kyung Cha's *DICTEE* entitled "CLIO HISTORY" opens with a photograph of Yu Guan Soon, the sixteen-year-old leader of the March 1, 1919, resistance movement against the Japanese occupation of Korea. Cha follows the photograph with basic biographical information about Yu and two full-page renderings in Chinese script of the words "woman" and "man." This in turn is followed by a six-page collage prose passage. The collage contains more biographical data, passages culled from F. A. McKenzie's *The Tragedy of Korea* (including a description of the Japanese hierarchy system, two articles from the *Korea Daily News,* and a petition from the "Koreans of Hawaii" to President Roosevelt protesting the Japanese colonization of Korea), and a discussion of the difficulties involved in trying to relate the Japanese colonization of Korea to the world. After the collage, Cha offers readers a brief description of the March 1 protest and of

Yu's death, a photograph of the execution of three Korean men by Japanese soldiers, and, finally, a page of her own handwritten notes for *DICTEE*.

"CLIO HISTORY" addresses two related issues. It examines the history of how "one nation has disregarded the humanity of another" (32) and, at the same time, raises the question of how to represent the reality of imperialism in a manner that adequately captures, or even enacts, its horror. In Trinh T. Minh-ha's terms, Cha is offering a form of writing that "constitutes an act in itself," rather than a description of acts external to it (16).

Cha claims that nations who have not experienced imperialist occupation cannot understand it: "To the other nations who are not witnesses, who are not subject to the same oppressions, they cannot know" (32). The problem, she maintains, is partially one of language: "Unfathomable the words, the terminology: enemy, atrocities, conquest, betrayal, invasion, destruction. They exist only in the larger perception of History's recording, that affirmed, admittedly and unmistakably, one enemy nation has disregarded the humanity of another. Not physical enough. Not to the very flesh and bone, to the core, to the mark, to the point where it is necessary to intervene, even if to invent anew, expressions, for *this* experience, for this *outcome,* that does not cease to continue" (32). By pointing to an apparent incommunicability of the experience of oppression, Cha starts from a position of cultural essentialism. However, she immediately moves into a critique of the standardized forms of thinking, writing, and reading that serve to make the experiences of being colonized incommunicable. She notes that the news articles she has collected from McKenzie are ineffective[1] because what she calls "uni-directional correspondance"[2] is incapable of approaching the truth:

> This document is transmitted through, by the same means, the same channel without distinction the content is delivered in the same style: the word. The image. To appeal to the masses to congeal the information to make bland, mundane, no longer able to transcend their own conspirator method, no matter how alluring their presentation. The response is precoded to perform predictably however passively possible. Neutralized to achieve the no-response, to make absorb, to submit to the uni-directional correspondance. (33)

It is the "uni-directional correspondance" of conventional reading that Cha tries to complicate as she writes *DICTEE*. She does this, in part, by writing in a variety of languages that are different from, and often opposed to, the balanced language of conventional reportage.

Conventional understandings of reading have tended to be caught between two paradigms, both uni-directional. In one, the model of New Criticism, literary works impose themselves on readers. In the other, the model of reader response, readers impose themselves on works. *DICTEE*—like its reproduced page of manuscript, liberal with crossings out, quotes, samplings, and revisions—offers a different model altogether. In place of simplistic, linear arrows of causality, Cha presents a model of relation in lines that are curved, meandering, and reciprocal. In her sense, reading involves not simply identifying and assigning meaning to certain works, but also entering into a creative and self-reflexive relation with them. Both readers and works matter. Thus, my interest in *DICTEE* is in how it decolonizes reading and challenges dominant patterns of thinking. My use of the term "decolonization" here is a mimicry of Cha's move from the Japanese colonization of Korea to her critique of reportage in "CLIO HISTORY." Yet I want to also point out that the decolonization of reading might play but a minor role in political decolonization movements. And so when I use this term I do not want to be guilty of suggesting that decolonizing reading would be "enough" or even a top priority of political response. Rather, I want to suggest that it might be a related project, that as Trinh suggests, "Clarity is a means of subjection, a quality both of official, taught language and of correct writing, two old mates of power: together they flow, together they flower, vertically, to impose an order" (16–17). Nor do I wish to establish Cha as a postcolonial writer. Her work is written from an immigrant's perspective and reflects those concerns. My intent here is not to degrade political decolonization by comparing it to reading, but to politicize reading so that it no longer resembles an imposing external power and is respectful of individual response, and so that it no longer represents an immigrant community's tendency to assimilation.

"What Transplant to Dispel Upon"

From A Far
What nationality
or what kindred and relation

what blood relation
what blood ties of blood
what ancestry
what race generation
what house clan tribe stock strain
what lineage extraction
what breed sect gender denomination caste
what stray ejection misplaced
Tertium Quid neither one thing nor the other
Tombe des nues de naturalized
what transplant to dispel upon

—Cha, *DICTEE*

—You have repeatedly defined the difference between making a political film and making a film politically.

—Yes, these two things are completely different. As Brecht already said, it's not important to know what are the real things but rather how things are real. The relation is in that reality.

An image is nothing. It's the relationship between the images that matter. Why are these relationships important? Marxism indicates what is the nature of the relationship between things. They are relations of production. A machine is not or a worker is not important by themselves, what matters is the relationship between that worker and the other works who from their own positions have relationships with the machine.

—Jean-Luc Godard, as qtd. by Cha in her preface to *Apparatus: Cinematographic Apparatus: Selected Writings*

DICTEE addresses domination in many forms: the Japanese colonization of Korea, the internal colonization of immigrants, the self-perpetuating privileging of dominant culture over minority cultures, the demands of teacher over student, of men over women. I must, therefore, apologize for my at times baroque language as I try to address a work that simultaneously addresses so many different power relationships. Also, as the collection of documents in "CLIO HISTORY" demonstrates, while *DICTEE* is a work written out of postcolonial and minority immigrant experience, it is unlike most of the literature that is categorized as representative of these experiences because of its relentless attention to reading and the reception of works. *DICTEE* was first published in 1982 by Tanam Press (a small alternative press that published mainly avant-garde works during the 1980s). That same year, Cha was murdered in New York City; the murder remains unsolved. The book was popular among the East and West Coast avant-garde scenes at the time, but always had a fairly limited general audience.[3] It was out of print in the 1990s. With the exception of Walter Lew's critical collage book, *Excerpts from Δikth /* 딕테/딕티 */ DIKTE for DICTEE (1982), DICTEE* received little attention after its original publication until 1995 when Third Woman Press in Berkeley reissued *DICTEE* and published *Writing Self Writing Nation: Essays on Theresa Hak Kyung Cha's "DICTEE."* Of the writers I discuss in this book, Cha is perhaps least like the others in terms of influence and social association. Andrews, Hejinian, and Mullen all know each other. All are in direct dialogue with Stein. Cha was in California and New York at the time language writing was emerging, but was more closely associated with the performance art and video scene.

DICTEE was written out of minority immigrant experience, but it is unlike most of the literature that is categorized as representative of these experiences. It is built around discomfort. It has little reading ease. It often teases and encourages readers to question what they take as proper, correct, or true. It gives false information, both obvious and not so obvious, along with verifiable facts. A quote from Sappho ("May I write words more naked than flesh, stronger than bone, more resilient than sinew, sensitive than nerve" [n.p.]) that begins the book is not part of the works that are generally assumed to be authored by Sappho. Cha names "Elitere" as the muse of lyric poetry instead of Euterpe. Sam Choy, the Honolulu chef, appears in a list of elements representing "Heaven, Earth, and Humans" (173).

The complicated construction of *DICTEE,* the way it is willing to be elliptical, even "wrong," to be difficult or deceptive, often provokes critics. And it is not unusual for critics, even those sympathetic to the book's complicated relationship to colonialism and nationalism in the Korean context, to admit this. Elaine Kim writes: "The first time I glanced at *Dictée,* I was put off by the book. I thought that Theresa Cha was talking not to me but rather to someone so remote from myself that I could not recognize 'him'"

("Poised on the In-Between" 3). Li Hyun Yi Kang writes: "My subjective positioning in relation to the text was most evident during the very first encounter when I found myself literally yelling at the book. . . . It angered me that the text was not always accessible, that it seemed to speak to a highly literate, theoretically sophisticated audience that I did not identify with. Most of all, Cha herself remained elusive" (75–76). Shu-Mei Shih notes: "Immensely difficult to decipher, the text often seems to drown in its own fragmentation, refusing to make any straightforward, easily consumable signification" (149).[4] Granted, these essays manage to move beyond this initial resistance and provide detailed and sophisticated readings.[5] However, rather than glossing over in an attempt to move beyond the provocative tensions Cha creates, I read them, and the resistance they inspire, as the place to dwell. It is not without intention that *DICTEE* appears remote, appears written by an "other" (Kim's "him"), appears elusive. As one reads *DICTEE,* therefore, one must ask: what is Cha's intent in creating a work that is richly diverse and difficult to contain under conventional paradigms of reading? In this context, it seems foolish to insist on self-expression as *the* answer. And just as foolish to say that Cha wants to value the dialogism, polysemy, syncretism, or any of those words of cultural pluralism as positive values in themselves.

My argument in this chapter is that Cha pursues and presents not simply a critique of colonization on the level of content, but that she also writes her work so as to decolonize reading. Her work challenges the forms of reading that subtly remove literature from cultural concerns, from the world that produces and surrounds it. "You read," Cha writes, "you mouth the transformed object across from you in its new state, other than what it had been" (131). Cha wants readers who, as they read, as they mouth the words, transform. My use of the term "decolonization" here has come after much thought. In terms of content, *DICTEE* is about both colonization (the Japanese occupation of Korea) and immigration (the narrator's move from Korea to the United States). And the narrator's subjectivity in this work is more immigrant than (post)colonial. (I do not consider *DICTEE* to be an example of postcolonial literature; the narrator, like Cha, escapes colonialism through immigration, and to call this work, with its attention to immigrant difficulties, "postcolonial" would be to risk overwriting the specificities of colonial and postcolonial concerns with those of minority immigrants.) But as political decolonization's intent is to dislodge dominant and externally imposed ideas and ideologies, so Cha wants to dislodge dominant and externally imposed methods of reading. Cha wants political reading, and to make reading political she writes a work that decolonizes as it collages together different cultural products, as it is polylingual, as it uses second-language, nonstandard English and French. I use "decolonization" here because Cha uses the attention of various decolonization movements to language politics to resist a tradition of assimilationist immigrant literature.

DICTEE also complicates the assumption that works which address colonialism and/or minority immigrant experience should propose clear selves, group solidarities, easy nationalisms, traditional values, or the preservation of absolute cultures and identities. Like many of the works that Doris Sommer examines, *DICTEE* holds readers off at moments, reminds them that their knowledge may be incomplete. But it also engulfs readers in an uneasy embrace of particularism. *DICTEE* challenges everything that makes things clear and concise. It questions readers' right to read for mastery or development or identification or conclusion, for mysteries that can be solved with well-practiced research skills, and yet at the same time it questions their desire to back away from it, to remain uninvolved.

Language politics are endlessly difficult, endlessly variable. Ngũgĩ wa Thiong'o calls colonial English a cultural bomb that "annihilate[s] a people's belief in their names, in their languages, in their environment, in their heritage of struggle, in their unity, in their capacities and ultimately in themselves. It makes them see their past as one wasteland of nonachievement and it makes them want to distance themselves from that wasteland. It makes them want to identify with that which is furthest removed from themselves; for instance, with other people's languages rather than their own" (3). This relation between colonialism and language is very clear in Korean history, as the Japanese, during the 1910–1945 occupation, outlawed the Korean language.[6] But Salman Rushdie replies to Thiong'o: "I don't think it is always necessary to take up the anti-colonial—or is it post-colonial?—cudgels against English. What seems to me to be happening is that those peoples who were once colonized by the language are now rapidly remaking it, domesticating it, becoming more and more relaxed about how they use it—assisted by the English language's enormous flexibility and size, they are carving out large territories for themselves within its frontier" (64). While Ngũgĩ points to how English has been used repeatedly in colonial situations to police and regulate, to govern and restrict, Rushdie points to how the colonized have turned the English language against dominant culture. In many ways, Cha's work provides a way out of these opposed positions, both by documenting and exposing the intrusive policing that accompanies colonialism's desire to impose a language and by demonstrating ways to disrupt this policing limitation through collage, non-native language practices, translation, and multilingualism. I see her work as saying "yes, but . . . " to both Ngũgĩ and Rushdie. Yes, there is continual remaking, but that remaking is merely an apolitical word game if one does not continually take up cudgels. The larger concern of this chapter, which I discuss in greater detail below, is to suggest that these decolonizing techniques are crucial to considerations of works that address postcolonial and minority immigrant and exile experience. It is interesting and telling that this way out, this different positionality, comes from a writer who has negotiated between both a colonial and an immigrant subjectivity, a writer who refuses to give up on one or the other too easily. While my chapter on Mullen looked at more specific examples of reading communities, this chapter concludes by looking at the limitations and possibilities of a global or cosmopolitan work. If we are truly looking for a work that reconfigures and challenges the conventions of colonial thinking, then we need to examine works that challenge how we read to categorize, conquer, penetrate, and settle. We need to question the poststructuralist assumption that works are constructed by readers, for this may be just another form of imperialism, the obverse of an orientalism that presents Western writers actively writing about passive subjects. These issues seem especially pertinent when examining works written out of or in response to dominant cultures.

"Cracked Tongue. Broken Tongue. Pidgeon. Semblance of Speech."

Cracked Tongue. Broken Tongue. Pidgeon. Semblance of Speech.

—Cha, *DICTEE*

Dictée, or dictation, is a technique often used in the teaching of foreign languages. Its premise is that repetition is the first step toward mastery. But dictation has many mutant forms, such as parody, quotation, collage, or sampling, and thus can become a space for cultural comment. In these forms, receivers manipulate the received object as they resist the role of passive consumer and retransmit the old information in a new form. The model here is of receivers (readers) who are also conduits: two-pronged figures who take in information and pass it on. Dictation turns here from a passive act that mimics brainwashing into an active one with its own, often political, agenda. In this section I examine Cha's formal revision of dictation through collage, nonstandard English and French, translation, and multilingualism.

1. *On Collage*

Collage brings to the work (here the ethnographic text) elements that continually proclaim their foreignness to the context of presentation. These elements—like a newspaper clipping or a feather—are marked as real, as collected rather than invented by the artist-writer. The procedures of (a) cutting out and (b) assemblage are of course basic to any semiotic message; here they are the message. The cuts and sutures of the research process are left visible; there is no smoothing over or blending of the work's raw data into a homogeneous representation. To write ethnographies on the model of collage would be to avoid the portrayal of cultures as organic wholes or as unified, realistic worlds subject to a continuous explanatory discourse. . . . The ethnography as collage would leave manifest the constructivist procedures of ethnographic knowledge; it would be an assemblage containing voices other than the ethnographer's, as well as examples of "found" evidence, data not fully integrated within the work's governing interpretation. Finally, it would not explain away those elements in the foreign culture that render the investigator's own culture newly incomprehensible.

—James Clifford, *The Predicament of Culture: Twentieth-Century Ethnography, Literature, and Art*

Most obviously, *DICTEE* is a work of mutant recitation as it is mixed-genre collage. It joins literature, photographs, news reports, and historical documents. It is written in a series of sections, or chapters, each titled with the name of a muse and her domain. What always surprises me when teaching this work is that in addition to the many forms of domination addressed, there are many themes: the difficulty of language acquisition, cultural impermanence and interconnection, colonialism's betrayals, troubled identities. The materials are gathered so that one theme does not dominate another. Although one might want to privilege for political reasons what Elaine Kim calls the attention to "Korean and Korean American nationalism," to apply that one narrative seems as arbitrary as any other does ("Preface" x). One could also point to language acquisition or immigrant histories or religion or relations between men and women. And these concerns bleed together throughout the book. When I teach *DICTEE* to undergraduates I work toward getting a sense of the large cosmology of the work by having them map the book out. I assign groups of students different sections, and I have them list the documents and approaches included in that section. Then together we list these sections on the board. Each class produces a different chart, but taken together they are a testament to the sheer variety of data in this book.

The fragments that comprise *DICTEE* tend to be about how things are "neither one thing nor the other" (20). With its emphasis on collage as cross-cultural mixing, *DICTEE* is a prime textual example of what Mary Louise Pratt calls a "contact zone": "social spaces where disparate cultures meet, clash, and grapple with each other, often in highly asymmetrical relations of domination and subordination" (4). Much of the narrative within *DICTEE* also takes place in or concentrates on actual, geographic contact zones: a long passage describes the highly charged DMZ-esque space of customs, and the "CALLIOPE EPIC POETRY" section tells the story of Hyung Soon Huo living in a Korean community in Manchuria. Also, the formal construction of the book is itself a contact zone. As Kang notes, Cha "moves amongst multiple positions of enunciation and representation; she is a storyteller, a scribe, a transmitter, a revisioning historian, a translator, a camera lens, a Catholic penitent, a poet writing in French, a student reciter" (78). It also moves between photographs, quotations, translations, confession, and language lessons. It is part autobiography, part biography, part personal diary, part ethnography, part autoethnography, part translation.

The structure of *DICTEE* shapes its resistance to conventions of reading. While developmental narratives, such as novels or life writing, tend to keep to defined points of view, collage abandons this pretense as it abandons conventional perspective by placing what would be considered often unrelated information on the same plane to avoid a unified gaze and to discourage a penetrative reading practice. Collage leaves out the connections and the transitions as it leaves in the marks of disparate cuts, of assemblage. The fractures of collage point to how we only have partial views into complex events and situations. The form, rather than reaffirming a need for all data, presents knowledge as a system that is limitless, guided by input, storage, and retrieval, that is resistant to overarching developing narratives. As James Clifford notes in his examination of ethnographic collage, the form brings to the work "elements that continually proclaim their foreignness" (146). Clifford's analysis of collage usefully points to its dual nature: its claim to the real and its denial of organic wholes or unified experiences. Cha uses this proclamation of foreignness to its fullest as she explores the themes of language acquisition and immigration as moments necessarily shaped by this foreignness.

2. On Nonstandard English and French

Personally, I believe there is no such animal as a "native speaker."
The more I study it, the more it seems a myth propagated by linguists.

—Thomas M. Paikeday, *The Native Speaker Is Dead*

Within a generation or two of Columbus, it seems, language instruction materials had become part of imperialism's educational apparatus.

—John Willinsky, *Learning to Divide the World: Education at Empire's End*

One of the most dramatic and insufficiently questioned aspects of language politics is the privileging of Anglo-European speakers of English as native and other speakers as non-native. The nonstandard language practices of second-language speakers tend to get defined as mistake instead of as deviance.[7] At times, even those who learn their English from birth in India or parts of the Pacific or the Caribbean or even in the United States can still be excluded from linguistic definitions of "standard English" or native-language practitioner. But work by Braj B. Kachru, Thomas M. Paikeday, and Larry Smith, among others, questions the whole idea of a native speaker because all languages are process and construction.[8] I see Cha's use of a second-language English and French as similarly questioning this linguistic convention that only "native" speakers have the right to create new vocabulary, to expand the language, to contribute to the evolutionary history of English and French, while "non-native" speakers only misuse these languages. The book claims affiliation not with the overtaker's correctness (and it seems important to note here that English and French are the two major languages of colonial expansion), but rather with the provisionality of the second languages of those overtaken. While Cha, who immigrated to the United States in 1962, was a second-language speaker of these languages, her use of these "mistakes" is strategic rather than unintentional. By writing in the stutters and misspellings of a second-language speaker, she resists the cultural hegemony of language acquisition that smooths over the stutter, the atypical pronunciation. She misspells and puns words like "correspondance," "mimicks," and "pidgeon" (33, 3, 75). She exposes the constructed nature of language by using forms of grammatical hesitation, such as spaces or periods between phrases ("She call she believe she calling to" or "The delivery. She takes it. Slow. The invoking. All the time now. All the time there is. Always. And all times. The pause. Uttering. Hers now. Hers bare. The utter." [15, 5]) and fractured words ("uni formed" and "American Pass port" [57, 56]). And, importantly, the dialog-esque passages in this book are not separated out with quotation marks. Nor is their strangeness emphasized by italics, as often happens in dialogic works from the nineteenth-century regional novel to Langston Hughes's *Weary Blues* to more contemporary works like Haunani-Kay Trask's *Light in the Crevice Never Seen*. For Cha, the dialogic moment is not a diversion from the standardized correctness of English, but rather that which forms the stuff of language.

Further, in the opening section, Cha mimes and remakes the language instruction materials that Willinsky points out as part of the "imperial educational apparatus" (191).[9] While these passages critique colonial educational practices, they do so without resorting to postcolonial and immigrant literature's much used trope of the white, repressive, culturally insensitive, and usually female schoolteacher.[10] Cha's critique in this section is of the educational apparatus, not the individual. Instead, the only personalized school-teacher in *DICTEE* is Hyung Soon Huo, who teaches in Japanese to Korean schoolchildren in occupied Manchuria. And the introductory section of *DICTEE* directly addresses the politics of language acquisition in a manner that is abstract without becoming impersonal. It is composed of sections that instruct "Ecrivez en francais," "Traduire en francais," and "Complétez les phrases suivantes." But the phrases in these sections tend to be ominous and have as an underlying theme the colonizing practices of language acquisition. One "Ecrivez en francais" exercise is "The people of this country are less happy than the people of yours" (8). The "Traduire en francais" section is concerned with the interpersonal politics of speaking:

1. I want you to speak.
2. I wanted him to speak.
3. I shall want you to speak.
4. Are you afraid he will speak?
5. Were you afraid they would speak?
6. It will be better for him to speak to us.
7. Was it necessary for you to write?
8. Wait till I write.
9. Why didn't you wait so that I could write you? (8–9)

These exercises work doubly. They are both language textbook and a parodic form of cultural mediation. This is even more explicit in the "Translate into French" section, which turns fragmentary and questions the ability to ever translate anything into standardized language. Exercise number three, for example, reads in its entirety "Near Occasion" (14). Number five stutters,

She call she believe she calling to she has calling because there no response she believe she calling and the other end must hear. The other end must see the other end feel
she accept pages sent care of never to be seen never to be read never to be known if name if name be known if name only seen heard spoken read cannot be never she hide all essential words words link subject verb she writes hidden the essential words must be pretended invented she try on different images essential invisible (15)

Through these mock exercises, *DICTEE* exposes the myth of a transparent, standardized language practice divorced from socioeconomic or cultural forces. It demonstrates how linguistic change in the modern era is defined by frisson as different language systems meet each other both geographically and within the arena of large political economic systems such as colonization and transnational labor migration. She directly connects new words with mapping when she writes, "She begins the search the words of equivalence to that of her feeling. Or the absence of it. Synonym, simile, metaphor, by-word, byname, ghostword, phantomnation. In documenting the map of her journey" (140). This documentation of the process of becoming a speaker and writer represents the cultural mixing that defines many readers' encounters with a work.

3. *On Translation*

The post-colonial desire to *re-translate* is linked to the desire to *re-write history*. Re-writing is based on an act of reading, for translation in the post-colonial context involves what Benjamin would call "citation" and not an "absolute forgetting." Hence there is no simple rupture with the past but a radical rewriting of it. To read existing translations against the grain is also to read colonial historiography from a post-colonial perspective, and a critic alert to the ruses of colonial discourse can help uncover what Walter Benjamin calls "the second tradition," the history of resistance. . . . Translation, from being a "containing" force, is transformed into a disruptive, disseminating one.

—Tejaswini Niranjana, *Siting Translation: History, Post-Structuralism, and the Colonial Context*

Although *DICTEE* mimics and mocks language instruction materials, Cha is not opposed to language acquisition or translation or other forms of communication. Rather, *DICTEE* is aware of the possibilities and limitations that accompany any attempt to speak across cultures and languages. It proposes a more formally complex model of dialogue, one that complicates the easily overlooked power relationships among participants in a dialogue. Like much of Stein's work, it acknowledges that just because people are talking with each other does not mean that they are understanding each other or even listening. The book, for example, begins with a bilingual/translated passage where punctuation is turned from symbol to word:

> Aller à la ligne C'était le premier jour point Elle venait de loin point ce soir au dîner virgule les familles demanderaient virgule ouvre les guillemets Ça c'est bien passé le premier jour point d'interrogation ferme les guillemets au moins virgule dire le moins possible virgule la réponse serait virgule ouvre les guillemets Il n'y a q'une chose point ferme les guillemets ouvre les guillemets Il y a quelqu'une point loin point ferme les guillemets

> Open paragraph It was the first day period She had come from a far period tonight at dinner comma the families would ask comma open quotation marks How was the first day interrogation mark close quotation marks at least to say the least of it possible   comma the answer would be open quotation marks there is but one thing period There is someone period From a far period close quotation marks $(1)^{11}$

These techniques cultivate resistant reading by interrupting reading's absorptive nature. When punctuation symbol turns to word, as the act of vocal proofreading makes clear, it no longer functions as a silent director of reading that monitors the flow of the sentence. When reading a passage such as this, readers become, like the narrator, unable to read smoothly and easily. Instead they are set adrift, forced to doubt and question the normalizing practices of reading.

This frustrating and yet necessary aspect of dialogue is literally represented in the layout of the pages in the "URANIA ASTRONOMY" section. Here, Cha places French text on the left pages and English text on the right pages. The pages are set up as quasi-mirror images of each other (what is said in French on the left loosely resembles what is said in English on the right), so they gesturally represent the close relationship between dialogue and translation. While the layout is mirrored, the relationship between the two texts is, of course, never one to one. At one point the left side reads,

> Là. Des année après
> Impossible de distinguer la Pluie.

Cygnes. Paroles souvenus. Déjà dit.
Vient de dire. Va dire.
Souvenu mal entendu. Pas certain. (66)

And the right side reads:

There. Years after
no more possible to distinguish the rain.
No more. Which was heard.
Swans. Speech. Memory. Already said.
Will just say. Having just said.
Remembered not quite heard. Not certain.
Heard, not at all. (67)

This whole section of "URANIA ASTRONOMY" plays with translation and
with what it means to speak. Speaking is figured in this section as difficult,
painful:

Mordre la langue. Avaler. Profondément,
Plus profondément. Avaler. Plus encore.
J'usqu'a ce qu'il n'y aurait plus d'orange. (70)

and:

Bite the tongue. Between the teeth. Swallow
deep. Deeper. Swallow. Again, even more.
Until there would be no more organ. (71)

The text as mirror image points both to how difference is transferable and
translatable and also to how the translation is always imperfect. (This section
also serves as an interesting counterpoint to the "ERATO LOVE POETRY"
section; here text and white space have an inverse relationship: where there
is text on the left side there is no text on the right, and vice versa.)

Translation is, like dialogue, another cross-cultural encounter loaded
with hope and yet always in danger of going wrong. While translation, post–
Walter Benjamin, is no longer presumed to contain or clarify another lan-

guage (or its accompanying culture), it still represents the need for one culture to speak and learn about another. In his study of translation and Christian conversion in Tagalog society, Vicente L. Rafael points out that translation, especially in religious contexts, is not just the transfer of information: "The fact that translation lends itself to either affirmation or evasion of social order is what gives it its political dimension. It draws boundaries between what can and cannot be admitted into social discourse even as it misdirects the construction of its conventions. Translation in whatever mode, leads to the emergence of hierarchy, however conceived. This tendency raises another possibility that haunts every communicative act: that at some point translation may fail and the social order may then crumble" (211).[12] Yet as Rafael also notes, translation has "tended to cast intentions adrift" (21). Or, as much as it instills order it points to a separation between the original meaning and the received meaning that allows room for various subversions. It is this "casting adrift" that gets emphasized in *DICTEE*. Cha's use of translation here points to transferable difference; her work suggests that what one can say in English one can say in French. And yet, at the same time, what gets said in one language is not always the same as what gets said in the other. In *DICTEE*, because the terms of the translations remain visible and verifiable, they expose translation as an apparatus that is always failing. It is not that Cha wants to deny the possibility for meaning to cross cultures; rather, her work insists on exposing the limitations as much as the possibilities of language exchange.

4. *On Multilingualism*

If art is the form of perception
    a way of seeing and hearing,
perhaps consciousness,
        to join and to cut,
    the double movement of the weaver

is the art,
        el con de la continuidad,
the togetherness of union, *allqa.*

—Cecilia Vicuña, *Quipoem: The Precarious*

Poethical poets, whether or not they have themselves used the "h," enact the complex dynamics that criss-cross through these boundaries. The model is no longer one of city or nation states of knowledge each with separate allegiances and consequences, testy about property rights and ownership, but instead the more global patterns of ecology, environmentalism, bio-realism, the complex modelings of the non-linear sciences, chaos theory. You can see this now with more and more poets using multiple languages in their work—not as quotation, but as lively intersection, conversation. . . . What better thing for poets to do right now than to begin in one language and end up in others.

—Joan Retallack, "The Poethical Wager"

ha'-l(i)-s-du-tlv'-ga Bend yourself on something.

i-da-nv'-ni-da Let's be sitting around.

That's what it is to make an easement. To share a place where *talking* can happen. For the purpose of *refielding.* For understanding. For making the adjustments which survival adjusts.

—Diane Glancy, "A Fieldbook of Textual Migrations"

Within the United States, language politics are most publicly present in movements like "English First" and in media controversies over bilingual schools.[13] But such movements always seem strangely out of sync, for while the nation has always been multilingual and always will be so,[14] there are not many places where languages other than English are institutionally visible. Most government documents, even in the constitutionally bilingual state of Hawai'i, are in English. The educational system teaches few multilingual works. And what gets categorized and taught as American literature is written almost exclusively in English, despite the fact that the United States has a rich tradition of works written in more than one language or entirely in languages other than English. These literatures tend to be absent from anthologies and studies of American literature. Marc Shell notes: "Even as the American university claims to foster a tolerant heterogeneity of cultures, then, it perseveres in the traditional American homogenization of the world as English. . . . [F]ew American literary critics work on the vast multilingual literature of the United States. Most simply raise up English-language works written by Philomelan members of American's various 'ethnic' and 'racial' groups—often in the name of multicultural diversity—even as they erase, or put down, American literary works written in languages other than English" ("Babel in America" 120, 121). Multilingual works themselves are often seen as suspect, as Babel. Foreign words, for instance, are often viewed either as impure (the current "English First" movement provides ample evidence of this) or as connoting intellectual pretension (Ezra Pound's and T. S. Eliot's multilingualism is often read this way).[15]

While Joan Retallack points out that multilingual works suggest "lively intersection, conversation," it is not necessarily true that every multilingual work performs such emancipatory functions (295).[16] It is crucial to avoid conflating quantitative issues with qualitative ones by simply listing the number of languages presented in any given work. A quantitative consideration would merely propose a simplistic, arithmetical alternative to the standardized work written in a single language. And such a straightforward accumulation of language/capital does not really question the difficult politics of grammar that Stein's work makes so clear. Rather, it leaves intact, or even reproduces, the existing social inequalities that walk hand in hand with concepts of standardized language. Édouard Glissant points to a more progressive definition of multilingualism, one that I feel also defines *DICTEE*: "What is multilingualism? It is not only the ability to speak several languages, which is often not the case in our region where we sometimes cannot even speak our oppressed mother tongue. Multilingualism is the passionate desire to accept and understand our neighbor's language and to confront the massive leveling force of language continuously imposed by the West—yesterday with French, today with American English—with a multiplicity of languages and their mutual comprehension" (*Caribbean Discourse* 249). *DICTEE*, as it enacts this "passionate desire," avoids multiplying oppressive structures by focusing on the divergent syntaxes and semantics of second-language practices.

At the same time, however, *DICTEE* has a shifting and variable degree of "accessibility." The ease of one's passage through the work depends on one's mastery of English, French, Korean, Chinese, ancient Greek, and Latin, as well as one's ability to recognize the book's uncaptioned pictures. What happens when readers are not fluent in all the languages that comprise such a work? What sort of effect can the work claim over its less-than-fluent readers?

While it could be argued that such a work alienates those readers who might not possess the requisite language skills (or alienates those who have not had immigrant experiences), I want to argue the reverse. *DICTEE*, whether encountered by readers with a multilinguality that matches its own or by readers without such skills, speaks to a dialogic linguistic relation rather than an isolating one. *DICTEE*, for example, with its beginning emphasis on the pronunciation of foreign languages, is not an alienating work but rather a provocative, empathic one. It engages readers in discussions of the difficulties of negotiating different linguistic systems as its narrator attempts to negotiate "Cracked tongue. Broken tongue. Pidgeon. Semblance of speech" (75). An understanding of Cha's text is undeniably enhanced and complicated by multilingual readers, but readers of just one or several of the languages in this book are not excluded from understanding and identifying with the work as a whole. It is important in this context to keep in mind that while this book is in many ways difficult, it is not finally impenetrable. The information in *DICTEE* that requires an unconventional fluency is cultural (languages can be learned by anyone who wishes to do so), not personal (such as elliptical childhood references).

The issue of readers' potential alienation has to be located in those readers' own ingenuity. Readers who lack mastery of all six language systems in *DICTEE* have a number of options: they can just ignore the sections that are not readily interpretable to them; they can translate the work themselves with the assistance of a dictionary or someone who knows the language; or they can go out and learn the language and return to the work at a later date (I am ignoring here options that reject the reading process altogether, like throwing the book down in disgust, because these options are available when reading any book). The latter two possibilities have the value of cultural crossing. The multilingual work that provokes readers to consult an outside work in pursuit of knowledge can claim a priority in stimulating thinking at the same time that it points to the necessary intercultural, weblike nature of all knowledge systems. This flaunting awareness of the dynamics of our current cultural situation, one whose prime characteristic is diversity, can serve as a weapon against, or a cure for, singular reading practices.

But, even for readers who adopt the most passive of these responses and simply skip over the sections they cannot read, reading the multilingual work points to their implication in a colonialist system and its limitations. Instead of questioning how to master the text, passive, skipping readers must confront, at each place they encounter an undecipherable language, a number of questions: Who speaks to whom? What does my lack of fluency in this language mean? What does it mean to read without understanding, without total mastery? These readers are forced to confront how they cannot own or control the work, cannot assume reading's colonizing powers. They also cannot—as it could be argued of readers who translate—naturalize or domesticate the divergent multiplicity of the work. The untranslated work serves as a clear reminder to readers that they have access to only one language pattern in the midst of a larger world of multiple communication systems that are not easily appropriated and owned as sovereign territory.

Plural Text: Making Active, Making Visible

I hope that this book in its totality will serve as an object not merely enveloping its contents, but as a "plural text" making active the participating viewer/reader, making visible his/her position in the apparatus.

—Cha, "Preface," *Apparatus: Cinematographic Apparatus: Selected Writings*

And I should say to myself:
"And most of all beware, even in thought, of assuming the sterile attitude of the spectator, for life is not a spectacle, a sea of griefs is not a proscenium, a man who wails is not a dancing bear. . . . "

—Aimé Césaire, *Return to My Native Land*

Western thought has led us to believe that a work must always put itself constantly *at our disposal,* and I know a number of our folktales, the power of whose impact on their audience has nothing to do with the clarity of their meaning. It can happen that a work is not written *for someone,* but to dismantle the complex mechanisms of frustration and the infinite forms of oppression.

Demanding that in such a situation they should be immediately understandable is the same as making the mistake of so many visitors who, after spending two days in Martinique, claim they can explain to Martinicans the problems in their country and the solutions that need to be implemented.

—Glissant, *Caribbean Discourse*

Critics from Roland Barthes on have examined the twists and turns of the reading act. From Mikhail Bakhtin on they have lauded dialogism. But less often has the relation of literary form to larger issues, such as its political effect on readers, received much attention. Or, when pushed, it has not been unusual to man the barricades and argue that traditional Western forms are in some sense "natural."[17] So while the politicization of literary studies has done much to correct the sexism, racism, and classism of the canon, this new canon tends to avoid exploring how the values of dominant culture define assumptions about genre.[18] Plus, there is an increasing omission of poetry from critical studies because it is assumed to not be a politically, theoretically, and culturally astute art (an attitude that has unfortunately been perpetuated by M.F.A. programs and their continuous reproduction of works of milk-fed confessionalism).[19] Too often, genre divisions, which assume that prose is for serious objective and political work and that poetry or mixed-genre forms are for personal or subjective explorations, are not evaluated. And while the writers I examine in this book clearly challenge this, they are often perceived as being outside mainstream discussions. In the final section of this chapter I want to examine what prioritizing a work like *DICTEE* might add to discussions about cosmopolitanism. While in some ways it might be important to avoid adding any more works written in the United States to this discussion, in other ways *DICTEE*'s attention to contact zones between the United States, Europe, and Asia has much to add. Further, such an investigation seems justified because a pervasive disinterest in nontraditional forms of literature is present in the utopian rhetoric that surrounds the discourse of cosmopolitanism. Bruce Robbins, for instance, writes:

> When we speak today of world literature or global culture, we are not naming an optional extension of the canon. We are speaking of a new framing of the whole that revalues both unfamiliar and long-accepted genres, that produces

new concepts and criteria of judgment, and that affects even those critics who never "do" world literature or colonial discourse at all—that affects all critics, that is, by shifting criticism's whole sense of intellectual enterprise. In an unprecedented and somewhat mysterious way, what it means to be an intellectual or a critic seems to have become worldly or transnational or—to use a whilefully provocative word—cosmopolitan. ("Comparative Cosmopolitanisms" 246)

Regardless of what one thinks of the term "cosmopolitan,"[20] it is obvious that Robbins's rhetoric sees it as an expansion of critical activity. He offers new frames, new concepts, new criteria, and new intellectual enterprises while pointedly avoiding new theories of reading and new genres. The critic's territory expands to new vistas without a concomitant broadening of the work's formal possibilities.

Tim Brennan, who tempers the utopian rhetoric of cosmopolitanism with his argument that it is just another form of Westernization, points out that while cosmopolitanism values writers from elsewhere, it values only "those whose sympathies finally belong here" (*At Home in the World* 39). He also argues that cosmopolitanism flattens or ignores influences, emphasizes "unity and complementarity," is impatient with or distrustful of decolonization movements, and lauds a literature of "complexity, subtlety, irony, and understatement" (39, 40). Brennan challenges the formal conventions of the literature that cosmopolitanism canonizes:

> It is very difficult and thankless to challenge both the content of a social illusion and a profession's argumentative codes at the same time. But consider a question commonly raised by documentary filmmakers: Can a politically challenging content produce a new consciousness when a film relies on the "talking heads" format of mainstream television? Without a frontal assault on form as well as ideas, there are built-in limits to transformations in thought. The values under attack are only reinscribed, now from a more moral or more widely informed vantage point. (79)

Brennan's reminder here of the interconnection between forms and ideas is useful to keep in mind when reading a work like *DICTEE*. Similarly, it is important to remember that there might be political (and cultural) reasons behind unfamiliar forms.

As I discussed in the chapter on Mullen's work, it is not unusual for nontraditional forms to be called "complex" because they are different or unusual, and then, in contrast, for traditional forms to be read as mimetic of thought patterns and thus easily understood. Both the literary critical establishment and the major media establishment have been complicit in labeling anything that does not resemble what has come before as too complex or too hard. Both establishments have done this without actually looking at how works engage readers and have also made assumptions about the limitations of these readers.

I am not arguing that Robbins would dismiss *DICTEE* out of hand. His work suggests otherwise. At the same time, however, his lack of attention both to reading and to the effects that works' forms have on reading seems dangerously close to a sort of intellectual mercantilism where one collects works from different geographies and cultural positions solely for their representative value. It is not enough to merely laud the world literature of a global culture solely for its more inclusive politics. To only consider literature as representative of certain identity positions not only devalues the work itself, but also reduces it to a one-dimensional representation rather than an engaged and ongoing political act. As much as we look at what works mean and what they say, we must also look at how they mean and what sorts of readers they enable or construct. Are readers mere spectators, or can they be active participants? Are they to identify with the sentimental and individual, or with the cultural and collective? Are they isolated from the work, or part of its community? These sorts of questions alter ideas of literature and culture, allowing for an approach to world literature that is more than an exotic travelogue or a static appraisal of individual, authorial representation. Looking at *DICTEE*'s alliances with nonstandard speakers of languages, for instance, unsettles many assumptions about artistic mastery at the same time that it points to the importance of forms of reading that are not mastery-dependent. Thus the concern for a political literature extends beyond more inclusive syllabi and into the works themselves, into what sorts of authorities works give to the localism of readers.

Yet before the fairly recent move to reclaim the idea of cosmopolitanism, Fredric Jameson addressed many of these issues and argued that global postmodernism isolated readers. His arguments both parallel and diverge from my own in a manner that is particularly illuminating. In *Postmodernism: Or,*

The Cultural Logic of Late Capitalism, Jameson is centrally concerned with the effects that artistic forms have on readers. And while this book is almost ten years old, his arguments still well represent the concerns of a number of academic critics who are resistant to more formally innovative work for political reasons. In Jameson's somewhat bleak view, the art of late capitalism is an assembly-line product. He complains that postmodern works cause reading to become "colonized and miniaturized, specialized, reorganized like some enormous modern automated factory somewhere, [while] other kinds of mental activities fade out and lead a somewhat different, unorganized or marginal, existence within the reading process" (143).[21] For Jameson, "perhaps the supreme formal feature of all the postmodernisms" is "the emergence of a new kind of flatness or depthlessness, a new kind of superficiality in the most literal sense" (9). The postmodern cultural product brings together different systems of knowledge into an increasingly global space. But, because of the cultural product's alienating formal composition, this global space is itself alienated, "demoralizing and depressing," ultimately separating readers from the possibility of political action or response (49).

Jameson's work is an important critical exception to the tendency of literary criticism to avoid questioning the relationship between readerly activity and textual form. For this reason, his work has frequently informed my own. We diverge, however, in our definition of what constitutes an "alienating" or "colonizing" literary form.

In his study of Claude Simon, Jameson argues that "reading undergoes a remarkable specialization and, very much like older handicraft activity at the onset of the industrial revolution, is dissociated into a variety of distinct processes according to the general law of the division of labor" (*Postmodernism* 140). While Cha's *DICTEE* is a world apart from the nouveau roman of Simon, it prominently uses the very techniques that Jameson holds responsible for the "colonizing specialization" of readerly labor: "the possibilities that [the words] may be themselves a quotation, and that we are reading someone else's reading," and "the inserted foreign languages or the reproduction of letters printed in other typefaces" (141).[22]

In Jameson's formulation of the relationship between reader and work, a one-to-one equation is proposed: the fractured forms of postmodernism create a fractured reading practice. A result of this fractured reading process is an unengaged and distant reader. Jameson's formulation of reading assumes it is a passive act. When readers enter into relations with fragmented works, they are susceptible to a fragmented consciousness. Thus his definition of postmodernism pays attention mainly to the surface ramifications of this relationship. He does not examine the possibility of readerly agency arising out of moments of dissonance. But, even more troubling, reading is assumed to be an act with a mimetic relationship to the mind: what one reads, one's mind mimics. He leaves little room for agency within the work and does not seriously address or reply to the political claims of works that deliberately trouble mimesis as part of their philosophical investigation. While it is not clear how his mimetic model of reading allows for it, Jameson suggests that the active, politically capable reader must learn to control and use the work rather than be used by it. He further implies that this is most possible when reading coherent, nonfractured, developmental narratives. Again, while confident about the "why" of this transaction, he is unclear about how the one-to-one correspondence of such lockstep readerly activity fosters critical thinking. For Jameson, readerly agency seems to be simply a matter of digesting the right combination of simply understood ideas. His position involves a strange mixture of traditional Western ideas of textual mastery and a sort of vanguardist notion of literature as a form of straightforward propaganda. In either case, works that question what gets left out of univocal, developmental narratives, works that use turbulent, multilingual forms to challenge readerly passivity and that pursue alternative lexical patterning in order to undermine standardized reading habits, are elided. In fact, for Jameson, these works are lumped together under the category of colonizing postmodern literature to become not challenging but complicit.

Jameson's portrayal of multilingual works as a form of colonizing specialization is especially troubling in the context of a large tradition of postmodern works that use this technique to examine and critique the impact of colonialism and economic migration. Dismissing the fragmented work as too "difficult" or too alienating borders on an ethnocentric dismissal of the "difficulty" of postcolonial or immigrant experience. But I would also argue that assuming mimetic theories of identification between readers and works is often inapplicable with works written by immigrants or other members of socially marginalized groups.[23] As Glissant notes, "Western nations were established on the basis of linguistic intransigence, and the exile readily admits that he suffers most from the impossibility of communicating in his language" (*Poetics of Relation* 15). These works often explore the ramifications of cultural dissimilarity rather than similarity and question the usefulness of generic forms for expressing such dissimilarity. They often put readerly identification to their own strategic use. Toni Morrison, for example, constructs *Beloved* so that white, middle-class readers might identify with Sethe rather than the schoolteacher, and Cha writes *DICTEE* so that readers must read as someone new to English and French. Although Jameson never addresses this tradition of postcolonial, immigrant, and/or minority postmodern works in *Postmodernism*,[24] his approach borders on a sort of linguistic intransigence. Works like *DICTEE* suggest a model of interaction between readers and works that is less about readers identifying with that which is similar, whether linguistic or subject-oriented, and more about works that grant possibilities to their readers.

"Reader Analogue Final Abandonment"

[k]

Whether it hardens more and binds the opening veins

Claw and correspondence

Receive the shape of the flexile elm

The habits of the place what it refuses what it produces

Reader analogue final abandonment

Distrust the planes of things.

—Myung Mi Kim, "Primer," *The Bounty*

Dead words. Dead tongue. From disuse. Buried in
Time's memory. Unemployed. Unspoken. History.

Past. Let the one who is diseuse, one who is mother
who waits nine days and nine nights be found.
Restore memory. Let the one who is diseuse, one
who is daughter restore spring with her each ap-
pearance from beneath the earth.
The ink spills thickest before it runs dry before it
stops writing at all.

—Cha, *DICTEE*

At their best, the theoretical discussions around cosmopolitanism have negotiated the difficult terrain between the desire for a more inclusive canon and
the fear that a global literature might be complicit with Western capitalism's
expansive, colonial opposition to the specific nationalisms of sovereignty
movements. Often universalism and sovereignty have been presented as antithetical or irreconcilable. And often in response there has been a tendency
to look for a global literature that engages neither of these categories. In
"The World and the Home," Homi K. Bhabha writes:

> Where the transmission of "national" traditions was once the major theme of
> a world literature, perhaps we can now suggest that transnational histories
> of migrants, the colonized, or political refugees—these border and frontier
> conditions—may be the terrains of world literature. The center of such a study
> would neither be the "sovereignty" of national cultures nor the "universalism"
> of human culture but a focus on those "freak displacements:—such as Morri-
> son and Gordimer display—that have been caused within cultural lives of post-
> colonial societies. (449)

I admire Bhabha's emphasis on such "freak displacements," just as I admire
his interest in and revision of Freud's "unhomely": the place where "the border between home and world become confused; and, uncannily, the private
and the public become part of each other" (445). Still, I am not convinced
that this sensitivity to the contingency and permeability of borders necessarily
demands an abandoning of the particularism of sovereignty, the universalism
of global culture, or the productive tension between the two. Such abandonment makes little sense in the light of works like Cha's *DICTEE* that attempt

to encourage cross-cultural communication without drowning out the culturally specific voices that demand sovereignty and separatism as forms of survival.[25]

DICTEE suggests there is no standoff between universalism and particularism. As a multilingual work, it both addresses the global dominance of colonial languages and gives voice to colonized, non-native speakers. At the same time, DICTEE's formal innovations insist that, in order to be relevant in today's globalized culture, a political art form must engage the political dynamics of reading itself if it is to enable and authorize the localism of its readers. By destabilizing the reading practices of mastery, DICTEE calls attention to—rather than elides—all that is least assimilable about readers' particular connections to works, making this an integral part of what must be read. Yet Cha does not stop there. Rather than simplistically valorizing localism, the disruptive moments of untranslated or nonstandardized second-language usage in her work serve as subtle shocks that jolt the reader out of particularism without reestablishing the absorptive reading practices of universalism. This maintenance of the fruitful contradictions between universalism and particularism is apparent throughout DICTEE.

For example, Cha draws numerous connections between Yu Guan Soon and Joan of Arc.[26] She writes: "The identity of such a path is exchangeable with any other heroine in history, their names, dates, actions, which require not definition in their devotion to generosity and self-sacrifice" (30). Individual self-sacrifice here is further sacrificed to Cha's sense of the generalized interchangeability of historical heroines. Yet it is only Yu's story that Cha tells fully. Joan of Arc receives mention only through the filter of others: as a reference in Yu's story, in a photograph of St. Thérèse de Lisieux portraying her in a convent play, in a still of Maria Falconetti portraying her in Carl Dryer's *The Passion of Joan of Arc*.

Similarly, Cha tells the full story of Hyung Soon Huo: a woman in a Korean village in Manchuria, a child of the Korean diaspora that followed the Japanese occupation of Korea, a teacher who uses the enforced Japanese language to teach uprooted Koreans in a Japanese-occupied province of China. Hyung's section of the book ends with someone—it may be Hyung or her daughter—returning home and passing through customs:

> You see the color the hue the same you see the shape the form the same you
> see the unchangeable and the unchanged the same you smell filtered edited

through progress and westernization the same you see the numerals and innu-
merables bonding overlaid the same, speech, the same. You see the will, you
see the breath, you see the out of breath and out of will but you still see the
will. Will and will only espouse this land this sky this time this people. You
are one same particle. You leave you come back to the shell left empty all this
time. To claim to reclaim, the space. Into the mouth the wound the entry is
reverse and back each organ artery glad pace element, implanted, housed skin
upon skin, membrane, vessel, waters, dams, ducts, canals, bridges. (57)

In this passage, Westernization is the filter, but it can never totally filter out
the will, the breath, the unchanged same: the numerable and innumerable
particularities of self and nation. Using the infrastructural language of the
body and of the land, Cha asserts the colonized's need to claim and reclaim,
despite the fact that what is reclaimed is a liminal collection of fluids and
borders (membranes, water, ducts, and bridges).

In a related move of unsettled reclamation, Cha opens *DICTEE*, before
even its title page, with a photograph of graffiti:

These words translate as: "Mother, I miss you, I'm hungry, I want to go
home."[27] While English and French texts appear throughout *DICTEE*, Cha's
first language, Korean, is represented only by this scrawled call for help. But

even this single, originary photograph (which looks badly photocopied and several generations from the original) teases, plays with our sense of origins. Its blotchiness and obvious distance from the original suggests an impure product, an image that is several removes even from Cha. There is also some controversy about the origin of the graffiti itself.[28] It is generally assumed to have been written by a Korean laborer in Japan during the period of occupation. Some claim that the words are inscribed on the wall of a mine, others that the wall is part of a tunnel attached to a castle that was being constructed during World War II to provide a safe haven for its Japanese owners. However, some linguists have argued that the script follows the grammatical rules of Han-gul that were adopted after Korea's liberation from Japan—which might mean that the inscription is fake, written perhaps by later Korean nationalists in Japan.

Cha chooses to begin *DICTEE* with a document that complicates the discourse around the universal and the particular. The graffiti author's context has decayed and faded away, but Cha brings the text back, rescues it, as it were, without glossing the context. The photograph, appearing without any clarifying narrative of connection, speaks in varying registers to Korea's formidable history of repeated colonization, to its resistance and nationalist movements, and to the difficult role of immigrant culture in Japan or places like the United States. Yet it remains fraught with questions of truth and origin. And it is haunted by the possibility of a nationalist rewriting of history. It affirms the need for, and power of, cultural resistance while at the same time emphasizing the questionable particularism of national authority.

Sixty pages later, Cha begins the "URANIA ASTRONOMY" section of *DICTEE* with the description of someone having a blood sample taken. The passage begins in the first person: "She takes my left arm, tells me to make a fist, then open" (64). But, beyond this opening sentence, first-person pronouns disappear and the rest of the passage uses a technical, descriptive language that dissolves the individual specificity of voice:

> She takes the elastic band and ties it tightly around the left arm. She taps on the flesh presses against it her thumb. She removes the elastic to the right arm. Open and close the right hand, fist and palm. She takes the cotton and rubs alcohol lengthwise on the arm several times. The coolness disappears as the liquid begins to evaporate. She takes the needle with its empty body to the skin. (64)

As the needle approaches and then crosses the boundary of skin to enter the body, Cha employs technical terminology like "Sample extract" and "Specimen type" (64). Once the needle is in, however, language becomes less specific: "One empty body waiting to contain. Conceived for a single purpose and for the purpose only. To contain. Made filled" (64). As the "specimen" is taken, the possibility of "specimen type" disappears. Instead, Cha shifts to a broader, metaphorical prose with more generalized implications and references: "Contents housed in membranes. Stain from within dispel in drops in spills. Contents of other recesses seep outward" (64). While it takes only seconds for the blood to be drawn and contained by the needle, blood continues to spill from the hole the needle has made in the arm. Cha writes:

> *Stain begins to absorb the material spilled on.*
> She pushes hard the cotton square against the mark.
> *Stain begins to absorb the material spilled on.*
> Something of the ink that resembles the stain from the interior emptied onto
> emptied into emptied upon this boundary this surface. More. Others. When
> possible ever possible to puncture to scratch to imprint. Expel. Ne te cache pas.
> Révèle toi. Sang. Encre. Of its body's extention of its containment. (65)

The cotton square, the clotting mechanism used to halt the blurring of boundaries, cannot maintain the separation of internal and external. Instead, it is itself absorbed by the stain as the interior is "emptied onto emptied into emptied upon this boundary this surface" (65).

Cha further enacts the lack of clear boundaries in this passage by moving between French and English and by blurring the distinction between blood (*sang*) and ink (*encre*).[29] Thus, while one has the blood or language of a certain nation or race in one's veins or on one's tongue, *DICTEE* constructs a notion of cultural exchange that is defined by leakage and reciprocal absorption, even as it is shaped by and through individual resistance. The absolutes of blood and ink, of nation and language, become metaphors both for the continual transcendence of universalism and for the specificity of one's particular, however destabilized, origins. While *DICTEE* is centrally concerned with the relations among nation and race and language and personal identity, it does not grant or restore determinacy to any of them. Nor does it valorize pluralism for pluralism's sake. Instead, it negotiates between cultural determinacy and cultural transcendence, employing a sort of fluid particularism that validates the personal linguistic practices of second-language speakers and the pluralism of their multilingualism. Testimony of how Cha's work encourages readers to re-create are the numerous works written in dialogue with *DICTEE:* Catalina Cariaga's *Cultural Evidence,* Carla Harryman's *In the Mode of,* Myung Mi Kim's *Under Flag* and *The Bounty,* Walter Lew's *Excerpts from* Δ*ikth /* 딕테 / 딕티 / *DIKTE for DICTEE (1982),* and Trinh Minh-ha's "Grandma's Story" in *Woman, Native, Other.*

For Cha, no place is, or has ever been, monocultural or monolingual. She neither imagines a "true" home nor proposes to construct one. This does not mean, as some might argue, that *DICTEE* is an obscurely relativistic work divorced from postcolonial or immigrant minority experience. Rather, it is written from within the vicissitudes of that experience and works to complicate, and in many ways dissolve, exceptionalist and isolationist narratives of "national character" or "ethnicity," without forfeiting the specific forms of resistance that have historically invoked them.

Conclusion

An Unquiet House, An Uncalm World

The house was quiet and the world was calm.
The reader became the book; and summer night

Was like the conscious being of the book.
The house was quiet and the world was calm.

The words were spoken as if there was no book,
Except that the reader leaned above the page,

Wanted to lean, wanted much most to be
The scholar to whom the book is true, to whom

The summer night is like a perfection of thought.
The house was quiet because it had to be.

The quiet was part of the meaning, part of the mind:
The access of perfection to the page.

And the world was calm. The truth in a calm world,
In which there is no other meaning, itself

Is calm, itself is summer and night, itself
Is the reader leaning late and reading there.

—Wallace Stevens, "The House Was Quiet and the World Was Calm"

As I finish this manuscript, Rob Wilson sends me an email concerned about my use of the word "autonomy" in the title. He writes, "I cannot help thinking that even Althusser, perhaps the most overbearing Marxist theorist of the postwar era, could only allow for the 'semi-autonomy' of the spheres, meaning culture and the arts and politics as moments of self-determination." He suggests jokingly that I call the book *Everybody's Semi-Autonomy* because the word "autonomy" by itself risks "playing into the biggest liberal mythos of the American poetry and art market, namely the autonomy of the self to shape the codes and myths to make them user-friendly for expansionism of private liberation and one's own sublime." I have left the title as it is less out of a stubborn conviction and more out of a desire for simplicity. I think Wilson's worries about the word "autonomy" are justified; and I want to conclude by stressing that I do not wish to suggest by "autonomy" a literature of private liberation or self-autonomy. In contrast to Wallace Stevens's poem, this book has asked, But what if one is not reading alone in the night, if the house is not quiet, if the world is not calm? I want to stress that a semi-autonomy rooted in the community is the most I can suggest in answer.

One of the goals I have had in this book is to investigate the sorts of autonomies the turn to community, to coalition, might suggest. I realize that making it everybody's does not escape the Althusserian critique. In some ways it just multiplies it, and it is a dangerous multiplication because liberalism has often been found to be inadequately attentive to the varieties, the specificities, and the separations that define many communities. Even as I feel sympathetic to the utopianism of liberalism (or pluralism or universalism or cosmopolitanism or any of those other words that come around every so often to reinstate liberal humanism), I have to agree with those who point out how the discourse that surrounds conventional liberalism often avoids the political by not acknowledging how the conversation can be angry or how models of community can be separatist as a result.

Although Wilson sees the word "autonomy" as a code word for liberal humanism, the model of autonomy that I have had in mind draws from anarchism's negotiation between individuality, community, and coalition. Whereas an anarchic autonomy is also implicated in liberal humanism, I have also found it suggestive for its pursuit of flexible and plural connections that are self-governed. In terms of literature, the individual matters (the author; the reader) and yet so do his or her alliances (the community; the coalition).

By using anarchism as a model for reading literature, I am attempting to suggest a nonintrusive model for acknowledging the cultural connections, the semi-autonomy, that occurs in literature. I want this model to be one that recognizes asymmetries of power and their resulting inequalities and respects separatism even as it values dialogue. And I want to join dialogue with politicized readings of forms in order to increase the complexity of models of the relations between readers and works without totalizing. Anarchic reading as I have envisioned it here values elasticity of responses. It suggests aesthetic coalitions instead of dominant models of culture or literature. It allows a turn to localities, to communities, to the specific engagements that writers make with their own languages and identities at the same time that it is attentive to how literature reaches out to readers who might not share those languages.

Although this book has been limited to few works, in conclusion I want to spin it out and off into the world. Analogies and connections can be troubling moves: one person's relation can be another person's appropriation. Looking at formal (or aesthetic) similarities runs the risk of depoliticizing, of totalizing, or of eliding asymmetries of power. But one must also be careful not to reject the possibility of a shared forms assembled, used, or reinterpreted among groups across their varying and uneven degrees of marginalization and/or dominance. Thus I want to point cautiously to a cluster of literary works that begin to use nonstandard and atypical and polylingual grammars for the purposes of cultural critique and communally rooted and reformatory reading. This cluster more or less begins in the early 1900s with Stein and Joyce, continues in works by late modernists Charles Reznikoff and Louis Zukofsky, and then dominates from the 1970s on. This literature turns away from stories of nation states and toward the possibilities in site-specific discourse, to identities rooted in communities. In the United States, this occurs most pervasively in the 1960s and 1970s with the rise of both a literature that intensifies modernism's turn to engage the audience or reader directly (often called avant garde) and a literature of identity that is often rooted in dialect or other nonstandard Englishes. Although these two communities often did not explore alliances, both of them are in dialogue with grassroots protests against imperialism, racism, and sexism.

This work carries on into the twenty-first century in multiple ways. The contemporary tendency is evident in polylingual works such as Gloria

Anzaldúa's *Borderlands: La Frontera: The New Mestiza;* Alfred Arteaga's *Cantos;* M. Nourbese Philip's "Universal Grammar," "Discourse on the Logic of Language," and "The Question of Language Is the Answer to Power" in *She Tries Her Tongue: Her Silence Softly Breaks;* Mercedes Roffé's "Love Poem in Twelve Tongues"; Anne Tardos's *Uxudo;* and Xu Bing's "Introduction to New English Calligraphy" and "A Book from the Sky."

The tendency is evident in the contemporary usages of indigenous forms in works such as Darryl Keola Cabacungan's "He Song of Parting Ma Mākaha"; María Sabina's *The Midnight Velada;* Ray Young Bear's "Mesquakie Love Songs"; and Kuʻualoha Meyer Hoʻomanawanui's "Electric Lava," "Lei Waiʻaleʻale," and "Wailuanuiahoʻāno ('The-Great-Twin-Waters-of-[the-Chief] Hoʻāno')." It is also evident in works in which what Kamau Brathwaite calls "nation languages" rub up against dominant languages, such as Kathy Dee Kaleokealoha Kaloloahilani Banggo's *4-Evas, Anna* or Brathwaite's own *Trench Town Rock.*

Other works pursue the spaces of in-between, such as Diane Glancy's "The Woman Who Was a Deer Dressed for the Deer Dance"; Edwin Torres's "Seeds Sown Long Ago: Are You the Layer?" "Taxi-Toxic-Tiction," and "Portorico N Prague"; and Cecilia Vicuña's *Quipoem: The Precarious.*

Although the current trend is to insist that these literatures of identity have nothing to do with radically experimental poetries—such as the fake language poetries of David Melnick's *Men in Aida* or Javant Biarujia's "Purges"; or the chance-influenced work of John Cage's *Themes and Variations,* Jackson Mac Low's *Virginia Woolf Poems,* and Joan Retallack's *How to Do Things with Words* and *Mongrelisme*—I want to suggest similar forms and a similar attention to critique among these works even while there is not a socially united front or a coalition of alliance or an agreement on what most needs to be critiqued among the authors.

My list here is deliberately ahistorical, and it is by no means all-inclusive. It merely brings together a swirling mass of different language practices coming out of different political situations, different class and gender and race positions. As a whole, it is resolutely not site specific. Yet it is made up almost entirely of site-specific and community based poetries that disrupt the conventions of standard English. The common complaints about these works—that they are fragmented and unusual, that they lack a coherent position or theory or subjectivity, that they speak too specifically, and that they are written in a "bad English"—reveal their strengths. As Bernstein notes, "[n]ew forms provide new methods of critique" ("Poetics of the Americas" 20). These works all pursue similarities while resisting unifying totalities. They suggest a late-twentieth-century interest in the possibilities of nonstandard language practices. They constitute a literature that acknowledges the peculiarities of local contexts and that uses these contexts to respond to the neat facade of single-language, single-meaning internationalism.

Anne Tardos's *Uxudo*, for example, is a work that engages the local in interesting ways. At first glance, *Uxudo* appears to be all about plurals, about cosmopolitanism. *Uxudo* is one of the more extreme examples of multilingual writing that I have read; it is written in English, French, German, Hungarian, and neologisms. Yet *Uxudo* is an interesting example of the complex negotiation that occurs between cosmopolitanism and specificity in many contemporary works.

The poems are spread across two pages: The pages on the right contain words and images (the images are of Tardos's family and friends). The pages on the left contain something that resembles translation. Tardos's work is cosmopolitan in several obvious ways. It uses many languages and many of these languages are European ones, yet its subject matter is more specific and personal than cultural. One dominant concern of the book is connection. The diverse languages in *Uxudo*, for instance, are carefully connected; so the right side of the first piece states in part:

Panic in the
Strassen kein
viszivilág.
Watery armory
hip-hop Gefäss (19)

Then a parallel translation of sorts is on the left side:

viszivilág = [*vee-see-vee-lag*] = viszi = carries off / nimmt mit sich / emporte
(világ = world / Welt / monde) (18)

Languages are mixed on the right side. The left side, which presents footnotes of a sort to the content on the right, connects through translation. This connective intent in *Uxudo* points to how there is something familiar, something intimate about languages. One way to read these poems is as a peculiar sort of realism for Tardos's life of polylingual fluency. Tardos is so fluent because her parents were in the French resistance and thus were constantly moving to avoid the rise of anti-Semitism that accompanied World War II. To just say such work represents a sort of realism for Tardos, however, seems to be underestimating *Uxudo*. Nevertheless, *Uxudo*, written out of languages learned in avoidance of anti-Semitism, does not, cannot, have the utopianism of cosmopolitanism. It is too aware of the various political upheavals that have forced people to negotiate a range of languages. Instead of unified pluralism, instead of melting pots, Tardos presents a right page of joined languages (perhaps of cosmopolitanism) but then a left page that respectfully sorts it out with specificities, the multilingual translations pointedly joined with equal signs. *Uxudo* is, thus, as sensitive to the presence and specificity of borders as it is to their permeability, It presents borders as contingent and responds to them with a connective work that encourages the cross-cultural communication desired in cosmopolitanism; yet it does so without drowning out specific, culturally rooted language practices.

I have been limiting my examination here to form. Yet I want also to acknowledge that language carries specific cultural information and this specificity can be used to resist a too easily politicized formalism. Many people who write a poetry concerned with identity write from and for very specific communities. Many people write a poetry that is directly aligned with political struggle in a way that Tardos's work is not. I still have much to learn from Hawai'i where the discourse of the local is so insistent. And I do not want to over write the insistence, the specificities, that some works might carry with them in this brief conclusion. Some works written in pidgin (or Hawaiian Creole English) or in a multilingual English and Hawaiian, such as Joe Balaz's *Ola* and Haunani-Kay Trasks's *Light in the Crevice Never Seen*, present an insistent specificity rather than a cross-cultural one. In these works there is little desire for negotiation. Some works written in Hawaiian pidgin exemplify a literature of "nation language" more than Brathwaite's own work, which is quick to turn to T. S. Eliot as influence. Such work is valuable and has contributed to my thinking as I wrote this book because it points to how one can write a poetry out of the local that is for the local, that is directly tied to political struggles to regain land. Moreover, it has helped me rethink literature that appears at first glance to be mainly cosmopolitan. Basically, poetry that is in some ways in opposition to cosmopolitanism has given me a way to think about the insistent localism of polyvocal work.

In this context of specificity, my interest in reading is not without motivation; for when I consider the question of what we need from the written word, my answer tends to utopian ideals of conversation, shifts in conventions of thought, exchanges of ideas. Reading has a complex social role. It is one of the most important ways human beings take in knowledge, learn, and go about the business of what Stein could call, with her fondness for gerunds, being human. Without a reading that pursues ideals, all this is at risk. Without pursuing reading's renewal, we hazard no longer thinking of ourselves as doers or undoers, as shifters of patterns of thought. The issue here might be a larger one of convention or pedagogy than of obtuseness. Many are taught to see themselves as speakers of standard English, as mono- or dominantly lingual. This is a mundane example that risks trivializing, but I remember being told over and over by my mother not to speak like I was from southern Ohio. It more or less worked, and I identify as a dominant, standard English speaker and not to do so would be to claim a marginality that I do not possess. I bring this up because I have often thought that it was the southern Ohio part of me that could read Stein as an ally, not the college part of me (which learned to catalogue Pound's allusions). It might be time, in other words, for us to question our pedagogies, the complicity between normative reading and passivity of thought, rather than to keep insisting that these works are too difficult for some imagined general public. Similarly, the tendency of much criticism concerned with the political ramifications of works is to assume that some undefined concept of the people requires a simple literature.

Part of reading, as these works make clear, is a cutting away of convention, an abandoning of the Dick and Jane story that taught us to read, and an embracing of reading as something that transforms the everyday. I have found when teaching many of these works that they open up the classroom in dramatic ways. These works shift language's conventions and thus shift readers' understanding of the world. This shift has within it the possibility of seeing existing structures of linguistic power while allowing one to imagine a response from somewhere else, from somewhere specific. It is this response from somewhere specific that we most need to hear in this era of monocultural and monolingual expansionism brought on by globalism.

Notes

Introduction

1. It has been argued that the emphasis placed on Douglass's literacy by critics such as Henry Louis Gates, Jr., and Robert B. Stepto has ignored what Valerie Smith calls "indirect, surreptitious assertions of power" in women's narratives ("Gender and Afro-Americanist Literary Theory and Criticism" 488). Smith argues further that "by demonstrating that a slave can be a man in terms of all the qualities valued by his northern middle-class reader—physical power, perseverance, literacy—[Douglass] lends credence to the patriarchal structure largely responsible for his oppression" (*Self-Discovery and Authority in Afro-American Narrative* 27). This is a valid critique of readings of Douglass that have emphasized the writerly product of his literacy over the reading act. But at the same time, it might not be necessary to see Douglass as the bad guy. Douglass's narrative is wonderfully dual in its insistence on both the communal and the individual. Even in a narrative like Douglass's that carries questions of complicity, one realizes that reading is more communal than individual—more resistant than complicit—than one finds in most reader response theory. Douglass's idea of reading's literacy is broad, as he uses both literary (*The Columbia Orator,* Whittier's poetry) and extraliterary (abandoned copies of *Webster's Spelling Book,* bread, the shipyard, the newspaper, conversations) resources to obtain the pathway to freedom. He figures reading as collective production and emphasizes it as an act that is dependent on the interrelation of forms of knowledge. Reading, in this narrative, is thus a force that can be channeled for utopian resistance against predatory assimilation. But it is obvious at the same time—and Douglass's narrative points this out—that reading is not necessarily emancipatory.

2. While rewriting this introduction I read Samuel R. Delany's *Time Square Red Times Square Blue.* While Delany's subject matter is very different from mine (his is Times Square jerk off theaters), his theories of connection in this work guided rewrites. He writes, for instance, "Given the mode of capitalism under which we live, life is at its most rewarding, productive, and pleasant when large numbers of people understand, appreciate, and seek out interclass contact and communication conducted in a mode of good will" (121).

3. See Martha C. Nussbaum's *Love's Knowledge: Essays on Philosophy and Literature*.

4. All the writers I examine here are well schooled in theoretical concerns. Stein wrote several essayistic studies of literature (*Narration* and *Lectures in America*). Andrews is a noted essayist and political theorist. Hejinian has taught in the Poetics Program at the New College in San Francisco. Mullen is a critic and also teaches at UCLA. Cha edited an important early collection of essays on film (*Apparatus: Cinematographic Apparatus*). It might be fruitful at some point to examine the relationship between contemporary writing and literary theory not as indictment (it seems as if, since the rise of M.F.A. programs and their agenda of confessionalism, the theoretical interests of writers are suspect rather than indicative of engaged thinking about larger issues), but as evidence of the growing popular influence of literary theory.

5. Charles Bernstein notes similarly, "The university environment is not just non-poetic, which would be unexceptional, but antipoetic. And this situation has remained constant as we move from literary studies to the more sociologically and psychoanalytically deterministic approaches to cultural studies" ("What's Art Got to Do with It?" 29).

6. For more on poetic cultures see Christopher Beach's *Poetic Culture: Contemporary American Poetry between Community and Institution;* James Clifford's *The Predicament of Culture: Twentieth-Century Ethnography, Literature, and Art* (especially the introduction); Maria Damon's "When the NuYoricans Came to Town: (Ex)Changing Poetics" and "Avant-Garde or Borderguard: (Latino) Identity in Poetry"; Édouard Glissant's *Poetics of Relation;* Greg Sarris's *Keeping Slug Woman Alive: A Holistic Approach to Native American Texts;* Jerome Rothenberg's *Technicians of the Sacred;* José Saldívar's *Border Matters: Remapping American Cultural Studies;* and Susan Stewart's "The State of Cultural Theory and the Future of Literary Form." See also issues of *Alcheringa* and *XCP: Cross Cultural Poetics*.

7. See, for instance, Roland Barthes's *The Pleasure of the Text;* Stanley Fish's *Is There a Text in This Class? The Authority of Interpretive Communities;* Janice Radway's *Reading the Romance: Women, Patriarchy, and Popular Literature;* and John Fiske's *Understanding Popular Culture.* Jameson's *Postmodernism* is an important exception to this argument. I discuss this more later.

8. An interesting contrast to reading primers is Gertrude Stein's *First Reader and Three Plays.* Stein's "first reader," as I briefly discuss later, concentrates on words that mean doubly.

9. De Certeau argues, "There remains the literary domain, its modalities and its typology (from Barthes to Riffaterre to Jauss), once again privileged by writing but highly specialized: 'writers' shift the 'joy of reading' in a direction where it is articulated on an art of writing and on a pleasure of re-reading. In that domain, however, whether before or after Barthes, deviations and creativities are narrated that play with the expectations, tricks, and normativities of the 'work read'; there theoretical models

that can account for it are already elaborated. In spite of all this, the story of man's travels through his own texts remains in large measure unknown" (170). See also Jane Tompkins's collection *Reader Response Criticism: From Formalism to Post Structuralism* and Robert C. Holub's *Reception Theory: A Critical Introduction.*

10. I mention this because I feel that at times the relation that gets made between experimental poetry and more indigenous and/or communal, cultural poetry risks being oversimplistic in its desire to suggest alliance. Various sorts of ethnopoetics, for instance, have had a tendency to point to similar sorts of formal dissonance between these two types of poetry and yet to not give much attention to how these works come out of dramatically different contexts, political desires, and cultural resonances. Further, this alliance has tended to be a one-way street (the "dialogue" here seems to happen more within experimental poetry communities, rather than across the poetries themselves). An important exception here is the recent editing work done by Mark Nowak in his journal *XCP.*

Chapter 1

1. See Howard Zinn, *A People's History of the United States* 261.
2. See Jürgen Eichhoff, "The German Language in America."
3. Eliot writes in "The Waste Land":

I sat upon the shore

Fishing, with the arid plain behind me
Shall I at least set my lands in order?
London Bridge is falling down falling down falling down
Poi s'ascose nel foco che gli affina
Quando fiam uti chelidon—O swallow swallow
Le Prince d'Aquitaine à la tour abolie
These fragments I have shored against my ruins
Why then Ile fit you. Hieronymo's mad againe.
Datta. Dayadhvam. Damyata.
Shantih shantih shantih" (*Complete Poems and Plays* 50)

4. See especially the "Revolution of the Word" section in issue 16–17 (June 1929). For more on Jolas and politics, see Marjorie Perloff's "'Logocinēma of the Frontiersman': Eugene Jolas's Multilingual Poetics and Its Legacies."

5. See, for instance, "Black Rhythms" by Reuben T. Taylor in *Transition* 21 (1932).

6. North's reading of "Melanctha" as a form of masking or racial masquerade

is insightful and does much to puzzle through this endlessly complicated work. His work—and those which are built off of it, such as Carla Peterson's argument that the rhythms of "Melanctha" mimic African-American musical traditions and Corinne E. Blackmur's examination of masking in "Melanctha"—point to how Stein's language is full of the culture of the time. But it troubles me that North, Peterson, and Blackmur tend only to mention in passing that "Melanctha" is but one part of *Three Lives*. The other chapters, "The Good Anna" and "The Gentle Lena," which reflect the linguistic anxiety of the time in related ways but suggest a more complicated nexus of influences and alliances, get more or less overlooked. But even more troubling is how the crucial works of Stein's that come later almost never enter into discussions of race and Stein. These works are remarkably different from *Three Lives* in construction and intent. Most obviously, Stein abandons the grammatical approximation of black dialect that makes "Melanctha" both stunning enough that Richard Wright called it "the speech of my grandmother, who spoke a deep, pure Negro dialect" and troubling enough that numerous critics have flatly declared it racist (M15). Wright tells this story: "Believing in direct action, I contrived a method to gauge the degree to which Miss Stein's prose was tainted with the spirit of counter-revolution. I gathered a group of semi-literate Negro stockyard workers—'basic proletarians with the instinct for revolution' (am I quoting right?)—into a Black Belt basement and read *Melanctha* aloud to them. They understood every word. Enthralled, they slapped their thighs, howled, laughed, stomped and interrupted me constantly to comment upon the characters" (M15). For more on Wright and Stein see M. Lynn Weiss's *Gertrude Stein and Richard Wright: The Poetics and Politics of Modernism*. Catharine R. Stimpson notes: "The facts that Stein disliked raw racial injustice and that a black author, Richard Wright, praised 'Melanctha' itself must be balanced against the fact that racial stereotypes help to print out the narrative. Not only does white blood breed finely-boned blacks, but the primitive darker race, especially in the South, embodies sensuality" ("The Mind, the Body, and Gertrude Stein" 140). A. L. Nielsen writes: "When we hear the libidinous blues of *Melanctha* in response, we are hearing the stirrings of white desire passed through a fictive veil of blackness, a passage which has been integral in the most despicable of racist cant" (*Reading Race* 28). North, Peterson, and Blackmur are all more interested in the difficulty of the work and reluctant to make absolute statements. North writes: "By making her dialect both direct and indirect, distinct and very slippery, Stein also undermines the associated differences of race and gender. The masks worn by her characters, which transform Stein herself into Dr. Jeff, correspond to these verbal masks. Like the dislocations of Picasso's finished canvas, which preserve in altered form the secret history of race and sex change, Stein's verbal dislocations represent in the final text the indeterminacy that made her hover between male and female, white and black" (75). Peterson notes: "In short, if we need to question Stein's total adherence to Flaubert's and Cézanne's 'realism of composition' and modernist criticism's exclusive focus on the experimental quality of her writings, we also need to avoid the caricaturing of Stein as a 'white supremacist' guilty of offensive racial stereotyping" (145). Blackmur notes: "Stein, unlike other white authors of her day, broke from the minstrel tradition of rendering black vernacular speech through orthographic distortions, such as mutilated spelling and elision, designed to reinforce the sense of linguistic caricature and parody by making the language comically or pathetically aberrant and broken. Rather, Stein deploys the African mask to disassemble the system of verbal correctness that creates the distinction between 'normal' and 'deviant' language" (250). One of the only studies to address racialized language in Stein's experimental works is Lorna J. Smedman's "'Cousin to Cooning': Relation, Difference, and Racialized Language in Stein's Nonrepresentational Texts," which argues that Stein was drawn to racialized language and that she attempted in various ways to "defuse this language, to disempower it" (585). Although finally, Smedman concludes, "That she failed to do so shows how deeply rooted these linguistic formulations are in American speech and writing" (585).

7. I tend to use the term "experimental" as shorthand for Stein's nondevelopmental and linguistically nonstandard works. By experimental work I refer to Stein's work after *Three Lives* and before *The Autobiography of Alice B. Toklas* (1914–1933). I apologize for the baroque language. By using it, I do not mean to suggest that there is no experiment in the more narrative-based words or that there is no narrative in what I am calling the experimental ones. The term is for convenience only.

8. For more on the German language in the United States see Peter Conolly-Smith's "'Ersatz-Drama' and Ethnic (Self-)Parody: Adolf Philipp and the Decline of New York's German-Language Stage, 1893–1918"; Marc Shell's "Hyphens: Between Deitsch and American"; and Edward Sagarin and Robert J. Kelly's "Polylingualism in the United States of America: A Multitude of Tongues amid a Monolingual Majority." Paul Bowles discusses Stein's dislike of Roosevelt as elitism in an interview by Florian Vetsch: "And she disapproved very much of Roosevelt. Of course, the people who read that magazine [*Saturday Evening Post*] also disapproved of Roosevelt. Generally they don't like him. He was in favor of democracy and they didn't like that idea" (643). But it might make as much sense to think of it as anger against Roosevelt's treatment of German-speaking immigrants at this time.

9. Laura Riding (Jackson) noted this in 1928's "T. E. Hulme, the New Barbarism, and Gertrude Stein" when she concludes by noting that Gertrude Stein is "many different authors in one. She might seem more intelligible if it were possible to read her as many authors" (199). See also Charles Bernstein's essay "Professing Stein/Stein Professing" in *A Poetics* (142–149) and his and Bruce Andrews's edited collection of different statement readings in *The L=A=N=G=U=A=G=E Book* (195–207); Harriet

Scott Chessman's emphasis on the dialogic possibilities and enactments in Stein's works; both Ulla Dydo's textual scholarship on the manuscripts and her attention to Stein's often forgotten works (see especially her *A Stein Reader* and "Landscape Is Not Grammar: Gertrude Stein in 1928"); Peter Quartermain's intricate close readings in *Disjunctive Poetics: From Gertrude Stein and Louis Zukofsky to Susan Howe;* and Neil Schmitz's wandering, associative readings in *Of Huck and Alice: Humorous Writing in American Literature.*

10. Damon argues: "Stein's text gives permission to hold multiple possibilities in question and to move in multiple directions, and this is also what the metaphor of Yiddish does; it speaks of a language that constantly generates new meanings and can neither be pinned down nor killed off" (*Dark End of the Street* 217). Yet her argument is one of similarity of intent, not of actual influence (she even puts the word "Yiddish" in quotation marks in the title of her chapter: "Gertrude Stein's Doggerel 'Yiddish': Women, Dogs, and Jews").

11. Marjorie Perloff said this about Stein's work during a talk at the Kelly Writer's House on October 20, 1999. Talk is available at http://www.english.upenn.edu/~wh/webcasts/.

12. Quartermain's chapter on Stein is excellent, but he strangely avoids giving too much attention to this observation in his close readings of her work. It is, in his reading, as if Stein's work sprang out of but then away from her early language history.

13. That one can read Stein's work as patriotic is well represented in the collection *Gertrude Stein's America.* See also Herbert Stein's "The Cubist Republican: What Gertrude Stein and I Share—Beyond a Last Name" in *Salon.*

14. Charles Bernstein writes, for instance, "I think this is the meaning of Stein's great discovery—call it invention—of 'wordness' in the last section of *The Making of Americans* and in *Tender Buttons:* satisfaction in language made present, contemporary; the pleasure/plenitude in the immersion in language, where language is not understood as a code for something else or a representation of somewhere else—a kind of eating or drinking or tasting, endowing an object status to language, if objects are realized not to be nouns; a revelation of the ordinary as sufficient unto itself, a revelation about the everyday things of life that make up a life, the activity of living, of speaking, and the fullness of every word, *of*s and *in*s and *as*s, in the communal partaking—call it meal—of language arts" (*A Poetics* 143).

15. In her study of immigration, Priscilla Wald points to how "[i]mmigrant narrators who depict themselves as Americans, who spell out their changes of being—or conversions—into Americans, assure an anxious native-born population that they intend not to disrupt but to assume an American identity" (243). In contrast, as Wald notes of *The Making of Americans,* Stein "calls attention to those contradictions and

disruptions to analyze the anxiety experienced and generated by immigrants at the turn of the century and thereby tell the story of the making of Americans" (243). This story refuses both the standard tropes of immigrant narratives and the tradition of ethnic burlesque with its emphasis on exaggerated and mutilated pronunciation.

16. As linguists make a distinction between "deficiency" (a mistake) and "difference" (a systematic deviation from the standard), Stein's nonstandard usages are differences. See Braj B. Kachru's "World Englishes 2000: Resources for Research and Teaching" and also "Models for Non-Native Englishes" for more on this distinction. In the latter, Kachru explains that a mistake is a nonstandard usage that "cannot be justified with reference to the sociocultural context of a non-native variety; and it is not the result of the productive processes used in an institutionalized non-native variety of English" (45). On the other hand, a "deviation" is "systematic within variety" (45).

17. For Stein's take on the differences between English and American literature see her essay "What Is English Literature" in *Lectures in America;* for discussion of this lecture see Jennifer Ashton's "Gertrude Stein for Anyone."

18. Kachru summarizes: "[T]he prolonged colonial period substantially changed that situation in the linguistic fabric of the English language, and extended its use as a medium for ethnic and regional literatures in the non-Western world (e.g. Indian English, West African English; see Kachru, 1980). The extreme results of this extension can be observed in the 'Sanskritization' and 'Kannadaization' of Raja Rao's English, and in the 'Yorubaization' and 'Igboization' of Amos Tutuola and Chinua Achebe. The labels indicate that these authors have exploited two or more linguistic—and cultural—resources which do not fit into the paradigms of what Kaplan (1966) terms 'the Platonic-Aristotelian sequence' and the dominant Anglo-Saxon thought patterns of the native speakers of English. Recognition of this mixing of Western and non-Western resources has implications for our use of terms such as *cohesion* or *coherence,* and even *communicative competence*" ("The Bilingual's Creativity" 126).

19. Stein's role in choosing the photographs for *Everybody's Autobiography* was advisory only. When Bennett Cerf first suggested photographs for the edition, she asked Van Vechten (who was playing the role of Stein's agent in the United States) for a list of photographs by various people. Van Vechten wrote back that he wanted to use his photographs exclusively. Stein agreed. From there on out the placement and the inclusion of photographs were Van Vechten's decisions. Stein did, however, suggest this photograph of herself surrounded by a crowd of students. See pages 552–566 of *The Letters of Gertrude Stein and Carl Van Vechten* for more information.

20. See Leo Stein's *Journey into the Self* and B. L. Reid's *Art by Subtraction.*

21. Perelman strangely does not address the large, and often positive, influence Stein's work has had on writers who do not identify primarily as academics. He avoids, for instance, talking about how the language writing scene uses her work.

22. Perelman writes: "I don't think the beginning of the *Geographical History*, 'In the month of February were born Washington Lincoln and I,' is meant as an outrageous joke" (*Trouble with Genius* 153). For more on Stein and ego see Sandra Gilbert and Susan Gubar's *No Man's Land*, Susan Schultz's "Gertrude Stein's Self-Advertisement," and Catharine Stimpson's "Gertrude Stein and the Lesbian Lie."

23. See also Stimpson, "Gertrude Stein and the Lesbian Lie," where Stein's autobiography is read as reflective of a specific genre, the lesbian lie.

24. As Stein notes in "And Now," "In the first place Picasso and I are no longer friends. All the writers about whom I wrote wrote to me that they liked what I wrote but none of the painters. The painters did not like what I wrote about them, they none of them did" (*How Writing Is Written* 64). The lie of the book has often been the very basis of accusation against it. After its publication, friends and enemies of Stein had enough ire to fill an entire supplement to the magazine *Transition* (supplement to *Transition* no. 23) debating minutiae of truth. But undeniably the foregrounding of the lie in this autobiography is what made it into the hugely popular book that it was. For Stein's amused reaction to the *Transition* pamphlet see *The Letters of Gertrude Stein and Carl Van Vechten* 404.

25. During her U.S. lecture tour Stein insisted to Harcourt that "this extraordinary welcome that I am having does not come from the books of mine that they do understand like the Autobiography but from the books of mine that they did not understand" (*Everybody's Autobiography* 8). Later in the autobiography she writes: "I was upsetting everything, I definitely did not intend to do any of the things that Bradley wanted me to do. I would not sign a contract for the autobiography the idea of which at that time I did not find interesting and anyway I was certain that I would not sign a contract to do anything, and I had not quarreled with my editor Harcourt because I had never written to him or met him actually when I did although he only wanted autobiographies to print and I wanted everything I did not quarrel with him" (129). See Bryce Conrad's "Gertrude Stein in the American Marketplace."

26. Stein's refusal of identity categories of sameness seems important, considering that Stein was a Jew who did not write much about Judaism (even though she lived through the Nazi occupation of France), a lesbian who wrote what are often considered to be coded and nonspecific works, and a woman who was partial to what are often considered antifeminist statements (such as Adele's declaration of "I always did thank God I wasn't born a woman" in *Q.E.D.* [58] and her claim that, while she does not mind the cause of women, "it does not happen to be her business" [*The Autobiography of Alice B. Toklas* 102]).

27. Maria Damon, in "Gertrude Stein's Doggerel 'Yiddish': Women, Dogs, and Jews" (in *The Dark End of the Street*) also draws an analogy between Deleuze and Guattari's concept of a minor literature and Stein's ditties on relations between identity and dogs.

Chapter 2

1. Stein has been central to the language movement's canon. See, for instance, the section "Reading Stein" in *The L=A=N=G=U=A=G=E Book* (Andrews and Bernstein 195–206). Andrews and Hejinian both present themselves as under the influence of Stein. Andrews often quotes from her. Hejinian mentions Stein directly in *My Life,* and she has also written two essays on Stein, "Language and Realism" and "Grammar and Landscape" (collected in *Two Stein Talks*). See also Steve Evans's "1978: Reading Stein." He writes: "In bringing to bear on the work of this crucial predecessor in the anglophone avant-garde tradition the commentary of ten contemporaries, *L=A=N=G=U=A=G=E* No. 6 simultaneously reproduces, renews, and in important ways appropriates, the linguistic problematic personified by Gertrude Stein. The process of transforming Stein into an icon of American avant-garde literary production began much earlier, perhaps most notably (leaving aside Stein's own formidable strategies of auto-canonization) in John Ashbery's 1956 interpretation of Stein's *Stanzas in Meditation.* The process reached a kind of provisional conclusion recently when Douglas Messerli—whose Sun & Moon Press, taking over the role New Directions played at mid-century, positions itself as the most visible of the independent presses— supplemented his practice of reprinting Stein's work in single volumes by instituting an 'award' bearing Stein's name to be distributed annually to a (rather large) number of experimental writers. The forum in *L=A=N=G=U=A=G=E* marks a crucial intermediate phase in this process of valorization and interpretation" (247).

2. See Jeffrey T. Nealon's *Double Reading: Postmodernism after Deconstruction* for a good discussion of the relation between postmodernism and deconstruction.

3. Norman Finkelstein, for instance, argues that the optimism of language writing has been appropriated. See pp. 103–104 in Finkelstein's *The Utopian Moment in Contemporary American Poetry* and my discussion of this argument later in this chapter.

4. It is also important to note that several writers associated with language writing have questioned the possibility of utopian reading. Erica Hunt writes, for instance: "One troubling aspect of privileging language as the primary site to torque new meaning and possibility is that it is severed from the political questions of for whom new meaning is produced. The ideal reader is an endangered species, the committed reader has an ideological agenda both open and closed, flawed and acute, that we do not

address directly" (204). Bob Perelman agrees that language writing's "primary tendency is to do away with the reading as a separable category" (*Marginalization of Poetry* 31). Yet he offers a more nuanced critique. Perelman gives serious attention to what he calls Watten's "disidentification with . . . physical and political surroundings" and believes readers capable of handling Silliman's new sentences, which break up "attempts at the natural reading of universal, authentic statements" and imply "continuity and discontinuity simultaneously" (122, 65, 67). But in contrast, he argues about Bernstein's attempts at a radically democratic poetry that "the utopian politics of liberated textualities are also cloudy" (90). In his reading of Bernstein's "A Defence of Poetry" (this is a poem in which Bernstein plays with nonstandard language by writing a poem that discusses meaning and nonsense in a sort of approximation of English where most words are misspelled), Perelman argues that the poem's project fails because it gets reinscribed as intellectual. Similarly, he dismisses Andrews's work for leaving only a "narrow margin for readers" (108). Watten also complains that there has been a "lower-case formalism" that has "led, beyond a defunct politics satisfied to claim that the reader is 'empowered' to make meaning from material texts, to a poetics of 'possibility'—that to say what writing wants to accomplish as politics is the same as to do it; that to describe literary possibility is to represent a form of agency, in a circular fashion, as a critique of representation" (3–4). Unfortunately, he does not specify whom he finds guilty of such formalism.

5. Although Alan Golding's "'Provisionally Complicit Resistance': Language Writing and the Institution(s) of Poetry" in *From Outlaw to Classic: Canons in American Poetry* comes closest, a survey that examines in detail the reception of language writing (especially one that gives special consideration to who is affiliated with this group of writers as an insider and who is not) has yet to be done. But just looking at the MLA program in the last five years seems to reveal that academic critics have been much less resistant to language writing than a number of contemporary poets (although often poets mention this reception by academics with scorn). Rasula writes: "The resentment within some poetry circles that Language Writing has caused in recent years is a sign of rudimentary alarm at the specter of a group, particularly one so efficiently organized. It's a singular phenomenon that poets should come together as active *readers* and conceptually adroit *critics* of one another's work rather than, as is the custom, mutual celebrants of poetry as initiatory cult. The term 'Language Writing' should be taken strictly as a historical marker for the willingness of a few dozen American poets to go public, in the 1970s, in a mutually supportive way. But there was no manifesto of party doctrine in the manner of Surrealism. If anything, the heterogeneity of the group was its most significant bonding agent. Debates within the group have periodically resulted in withering assessments of a kind rarely associ-

ated with supposed 'members' of a doctrinal league" ("The Politics of, the Politics in" 319).

6. *Apex of the M* was edited by Lew Daly, Alan Gilbert, Kristin Prevallet, and Pam Rehm. The editorial has no primary authorship attributed to it.

7. I discuss Jameson's arguments in *Postmodernism* in more depth in the chapter on Cha's work. For more on Jameson and language writing see George Hartley's chapter "Jameson's Perelman: Reification and the Material Signifier" in *Textual Politics and the Language Poets* and Perelman's reply to Jameson in "Parataxis and Narrative: The New Sentence in Theory and Practice."

8. This collection crucially refigures and responds to what was the dominant American poetry at the time, a poetry that Robert von Hallberg calls a "poetics of accommodation," a poetics of the suburbs (228). Many of the poets who define the poetry of protest in this period (and also today) are included: Allen Ginsberg, Le Roi Jones (Amiri Baraka), Jerome Rothenberg, Ed Sanders, and Gary Snyder. This anthology claims diversity in its organization, although in this case it tends to be geography (not race and gender) that guides. The poets are divided into geographic categories: Black Mountain, San Francisco Renaissance, New York Poets, Beat Generation, and a fifth group without geographical definition. For more on the importance of this anthology see *The American Poetry Wax Museum: Reality Effects, 1940–1990* by Jed Rasula and "Whose New American Poetry? Anthologizing in the Nineties" by Marjorie Perloff. My argument here is especially informed by Perloff's article that traces the impact of *The New American Poetry* in some detail. For an even narrower, and consequently irrelevant, collection of political poetry see Todd Gitlin's *Campfires of Resistance: Poetry from the Movement*.

9. This poem, written in 1966, was not included in *The New American Poetry*. Andrew Ross writes: "Above all, in most of the work of the Beats and the Black Mountaineers, modernity—urban, technological, and massively commodified—is either passed over entirely for some preindustrial cause or else pilloried for its dark Satanic birthright in Capital (if Vietnam was a *crise de conscience* for many of these writers, it was more often than not cast in the same technological-voodoo drama—Ginsberg's *Wichita Vortex Sutra* is the best example and is quite symptomatic); only the New York school stood by its acceptance of modern life, even if that acceptance often took the form of an undiscriminating optimism (a Foster-like faith in personal friendship), the other side of the utopian coin" (364).

10. In this article, at times it is hard to tell whether Altieri is critiquing McGann or language writing in general. In "Contemporary Poetry, Alternate Routes," McGann quickly summarizes and supports a number of claims about the political possibility of language writing. Then Altieri replies with an attack that he directs

toward McGann by name but is often concerned with language writing in the larger sense ("Without Consequences Is No Politics"). It is difficult to figure out where one ends or begins. See also McGann's "Response to Charles Altieri" and Rasula's "The Politics of, the Politics in."

11. Much academic writing on language writing, Perloff's work in particular, has avoided this.

12. Marianna Torgovnick usefully worries about the "we." She writes: "I do not object to the 'we' voice in and of itself. What I object to is the easy slide from 'I' to 'we' that takes place almost unconsciously for many users of the first-person plural or its equivalents—and is often the hidden essence of cultural criticism. This slide can make the 'we' function not as a device to link writer or reader, or as a particularized group voice, or even the voice of 'the culture,' but rather as a covert, and sometimes coercive, universal" (48–49). I argue in this chapter, however, that the "we" of these works is one that links writers and readers. Rather than a slide from an "I" to a "we," the "I" is refigured as necessarily a "we." This is not in any sense unconscious or an assumed universal.

13. Against genius, see Bob Perelman's *The Trouble with Genius: Reading Pound, Joyce, Stein, and Zukofsky*.

14. Michael Greer notes that the political claims of various writers associated with the movement "rest not so much on the expression of a 'position' or an agenda as they do on an effort to change the way we attend to texts, 'poetic' and otherwise" (335). Watten uses the metaphor of the development of the assembly line in his essay. He writes: "The move from the revealed moment of the 'word in the head' to the durational forms of Language Writing (as from the spark of the internal combustion engine to the start-up of the entire assembly line, as it were) took place, arguably, over the first half dozen issues of *This*, which witnessed a reflexive recognition on the part of numerous writers of new possibilities. This recognition was not 'author-centered' but 'socially reflexive,' if by social we mean the development of communities of writers in San Francisco and then New York" (24).

15. Perelman writes: "Kit Robinson, Steve Benson and I began a writing project almost as soon as we met in San Francisco in 1976. One of us would read from whatever books were handy and two of us would type. These roles would rotate; occasionally there would be two readers reading simultaneously to one typist. The reader would switch books whenever he felt like it, and jump around within whatever book was open at the time. Truman Capote's slam at Kerouac's work—that this was typing, not writing—would have been even truer here, though none of us could type as fast as Kerouac, who apparently was terrific as a typist, an ability which undoubtedly helped give his writing its enviable fluidity" (*Marginalization of Poetry* 32).

16. They write: "While we are flagrantly writing this article as a group, the per-

ceptive reader will already have noticed that until this point neither the 'Language School' nor 'Language Poetry' have been named. This is no accident; the politics of group identity are a problem (and challenge) particularly for those alternately identified within and without it. We would all, in short, admit to being primarily interested in our own work—but does that release us, or it, from social context?" (272–273). Silliman almost always uses terms like "so called language writing" in his writing. Basically, language writing gets called language writing, or L=A=N=G=U=A=G=E writing, after the journal *L=A=N=G=U=A=G=E* edited by Bruce Andrews and Charles Bernstein from 1978 to 1982. Watten critiques the emphasis on *L=A=N=G=U=A=G=E* and proposes instead *This,* the journal he edited with Rob Grenier, as the pivotal foundational moment for language writing in recent talks and also in his essay "The Bride of the Assembly Line: From Material Text to Cultural Poetics" (although I suppose that Clark Coolidge and Michael Palmer could present *Joglars* or Silliman *Tottel's* as similar pivotal moments). The term "language writing" has been much contested and defined, and I do not wish to retread this territory. The criticism on language writing often spends so much time on such definitions of the movement that it at times becomes its central preoccupation. See, for instance, Michael Greer's "Ideology and Theory in Recent Experimental Writing, or the Naming of 'Language Poetry.'"

17. They edit journals (*This, Hills, Roof, L=A=N=G=U=A=G=E, Tottel's, Qu, Poetics Journal*), create publishing houses (The Figures, Tuumba, Roof, Segue, Sun & Moon), edit anthologies (*In the American Tree,* ed. Ron Silliman, *"Language" Poetries,* ed. Douglas Messerli, *From the Other Side of the Century,* ed. Douglas Messerli), create distribution agencies (Segue), establish cooperative housing (Segue), establish prizes and contests with fancy names (The Gertrude Stein Awards in Innovative American Poetry, the Ferns, The New American Poetry Award), infiltrate academic presses (Southern Illinois University Press in the beginning, but now Northwestern University Press and University of Alabama Press), organize long-running and established reading series and talks, and set up academic centers of research (the Poetics Program at SUNY at Buffalo).

18. Bernstein writes: "Let me be specific as to what I mean by 'official verse culture'—I am referring to the poetry publishing and reviewing practices of *The New York Times, The Nation, American Poetry Review, The New York Review of Books, The New Yorker, Poetry* (Chicago), *Antaeus, Parnassus,* Atheneum Press, all the major trade publishers, the poetry series of almost all of the major university presses (the University of California Press being a significant exception at present). Add to this the ideologically motivated selection of the vast majority of poets teaching in university writing and literature programs and of poets taught in such programs as well as the interlocking accreditation of these selections through prizes and awards judged by

these same individuals. Finally, there are the self-appointed keepers of the gate who actively put forward biased, narrowly focussed and frequently shrill and contentious accounts of American poetry, while claiming, like all disinformation propaganda, to be giving historical or nonpartisan views. In this category, the American Academy of Poetry and such books as *The Harvard Guide to Contemporary American Poetry Writing* stand out. . . . Official verse culture is not mainstream, nor is it monolithic, nor uniformly bad or good. Rather, like all literary culture, it is constituted by particular values that are as heterodox, within the broad context of multicultural American writing, as any other type of writing. What makes official verse culture official is that it denies the ideological nature of its practice while maintaining hegemony in terms of major media exposure and academic legitimation and funding" (*Content's Dream* 247–249).

19. Things do seem to be slowly changing. Witness, for instance, the half-hearted inclusive gesture by the Academy of American Poets to add Lucille Clifton, Robert Creeley, Louise Gluck, Yusef Komunyakaa, Heather McHugh, Michael Palmer, Adrienne Rich, Rosanna Warren, and Charles Wright after being critiqued for exclusive race and gender politics in 1999. Publishing sales figures are hard to get. But when actual marketplace figures slip out, the differences between an official and an unofficial verse culture are not so clear. According to an e-mail by Bill Luoma, Alfred Corn's *Autobiographies,* for instance, had sold only 1,024 copies and William Logan's *Vain Empires* had sold only 2,182 as of August 1999 (both these poets tend to be well represented by the prize- and grant-giving circuit), while Hejinian's *My Life,* according to Douglas Messerli, has sold around 8,000 copies so far (private e-mail). In the world of prizes and grants, as Rasula's book documents, there seems to be a clearer indication of who is an official and who an unofficial verse poet.

20. Alan Golding replies: "There are a number of reasons, then, why we need not swallow whole the argument that the assimilation of poetic and cultural critique into the academy negates or compromises entirely the force of that critique, especially when the last few years' culture wars suggest how many Americans see an academically based cultural criticism as threatening and potentially effective. First, a distinction should be made between the address, reception, and use of Language writing on the one hand and the institutional status of individuals on the other. To be specific: relatively few Language writers make a full-time living in English departments, and even fewer are employed *as poets,* to teach creative writing. Second, 'assimilation' is a matter of degrees. . . . Paul Hoover's *Postmodern American Poetry: A Norton Anthology* is the first anthology from a major trade press to contain a substantial number of Language poets. Third, at least some Language writers can be read as 'assimilating' the academy as much as it is assimilating them" (148). Maria Damon also points out that poets

begin to enter the academy at the same moment that arts funding gets dramatically cut ("Poetic Canons: Generative Oxymoron or Stalled-Out Dialectic?").

21. See, for instance, Howe's critical work *My Emily Dickinson*. But also recent "poems," such as "Melville's Marginalia" and those in the collection *Pierce Arrow*, work between genres. See Perelman's critical poem "The Marginalization of Poetry" and "A False Account of Talking with Frank O'Hara and Roland Barthes in Philadelphia" in *The Marginalization of Poetry*.

22. Instead, it is not unusual to hear language writers claim to be marginalized and use this claim to avoid investigating their own complicity with systems of power.

23. I have used one of Jackson Mac Low's *Virginia Woolf Poems*, Howe's "Bride's Day," and a selection from Mullen's *Muse & Drudge* to great success. All these poems are fairly disjunctive and yet also open easily to new readers. I have written a more detailed explanation of this assignment in the script for the Institute for Writing and Thinking's "Poetry: Reading, Writing, and Teaching" workshop. Joan Retallack, who also uses this exercise, has used poems from Melanie Nielson's *Civil Noir*. All these works are distinctively disjunctive and lack a story-like narrative. When discussing this exercise with Retallack before the *Poetry and Pedagogy* conference, she recommended not using a narrative-based poem, pointing out that a narrative poem often does not lead to the speculative thinking that is the purpose of this exercise. My classroom experience backs this up. I have had very bad results doing this exercise with Lois-Ann Yamanaka's "Yarn Wig" in *Saturday Night at the Pahala Theatre* (most of the students chose the "turn" as their phrase and did not provide much new interpretative information to the poem beyond personal anecdote). See also Lisa Samuels and Jerome McGann's "Deformance and Interpretation" for more on pedagogy and other sorts of reading.

24. When I talk to secondary school teachers about the difficulties of teaching poetry, they often state that they do not know how to teach poetry because students often claim an interpretative right and say that anything they say is a legitimate reading of the poem. I have often suggested that this sort of exercise can be an antidote. It avoids setting up any one reading of the poem and encourages various interpretations. But because students must interact closely with the poem itself, it guides them into justifying their engagements with the work and the larger public of the classroom.

25. Detractors often vilify Andrews's work more than that of other language poets because it relentlessly refuses at any moment to resort to poetry's seductive charms, to what conventionally gets called "poetic" or "lyrical." Lazer writes: "Tokenizing provides one example for a lack of critical attention to Andrews's work; the particular difficulties of Andrews's writing provides another" (*Opposing Poetries* 77). Wat-

ten's work similarly avoids the poetical and the lyrical and is similarly often vilified; other language writers, such as Bernstein, Harryman, Hejinian, and Howe, often have a more complex engagement with the lyrical in their work. For more on lyric and language writing see Lazer's "The Lyric Valuables: Soundings, Questions, and Examples," Mark Wallace's "On the Lyric as Experimental Possibility," Susan Schultz's "'Called Null or Called Vocative': A Fate of the Contemporary Lyric," and the introductions to the first three issues of *Apex of the M*. In 1999, Women Poets at Barnard held a conference called "Where Lyric Tradition Meets Language Poetry: Innovation in Contemporary American Poetry by Women."

26. For a much less utopian view of the avant-garde see works like Peter Bürger's *Theory of the Avant-Garde*.

27. And the project continues. See Hejinian's "My Life in the Early Nineties." Messerli of Sun & Moon reports that *My Life* is one of his better-selling books. This poem has received a lot of critical attention in recent years. Christopher Beach, however, argues that *My Life* is still a marginal and underappreciated work in "Poetic Positionings: Stephen Dobyns and Lyn Hejinian in Cultural Context" in *Poetic Culture* (this essay was originally published in 1997). Interestingly, sales suggest both poets to be doing equally well. Luoma notes that Dobyns's *Velocities: New and Selected Poems* sold 9,421 copies as of August 1999 (a single title such as Dobyns's *Body Traffic* sold 3,066); Hejinian's *My Life* has sold around 8,000 copies as of September 1999. In 1997 Samuels published an article where she critiques the critical (she calls canonical) attention given to *My Life*. I discuss Samuels's article in greater depth later and in note 31 below.

28. I have used the later Sun & Moon edition for all citations of *My Life*.

29. Adams writes: "Of all this that was being done to complicate his education, he knew only the color of yellow. He first found himself sitting on a yellow kitchen floor in strong sunlight. He was three years old when he took this earliest step in education; a lesson of color" (5). Thanks to Stacy Hubbard who pointed this out to me originally.

30. See Hilary Clark for more on mnemonics. She writes: "Replacing chronology is an overall numerical structure and an ongoing development by mnemonic techniques of association and repetition of ideas, images and phrases. *My Life* challenges the view that the events of a life form an ordered sequence culminating in an always-foreseen fullness of being—the writer's present life and vocation" (316).

31. Samuels's argument basically is that *My Life* is being canonized because it is a clear, understandable, accessible, and happy work. Her argument on canonization is sketchily based on three articles published on *My Life* in the last four years (which is even more sketchy when she implies that Hejinian has received a disproportionate

amount of the attention compared to Howe, Silliman, or Andrews; the MLA Index in September 1999 has eight articles on Hejinian but twenty-eight on Howe, seven on Silliman, and two on Andrews). Her argument at moments assumes that autobiography means representative of the author (she writes: "It has been pointed out that Hejinian represents an all-American girlhood; but most of the book's events are more those of the *expected surface* of a privileged American childhood in the prosperous 1950s. So far so good, born in 1941, and educated at Harvard, as Hejinian was" [106]) and grants little strategy to Hejinian's engagement with how childhood gets represented as generic. The quote that Samuels uses to support her assertion that *My Life* is the story of Americans who make good emotionally does not really provide convincing evidence for such a claim. Samuels quotes only the parts that I have marked in italics in this string of phrases: "I confess candidly that I was adequately happy until I was asked if I was . . . we are filled with scruples about individualism and . . . a disturbance on the lapping—*happiness is worthless, my grandfather assured me when he was very old, he had never sought it for himself or for my father, it had nothing to do with whether or not a life is good*" (115). In its full context, this quote investigates the relation between privilege and happiness (if there even is one) in a much more complicated manner. Hejinian herself sees the book as refining its critique through its two editions. In an interview with Larry McCaffery and Brian McHale, McCaffery asks her to describe the difference between the two editions. Hejinian states, "It's [the second edition] a fuller account intellectually. Those seven years coincided with the beginning of the Reagan era, and I continually experienced an enormous increase of skepticism and critical abilities. Everything was again open to examination but not as it had been in the sixties, which is where I built my social consciousness and my aesthetics" (142). Nonetheless, Samuel's accusation of the bourgeois tendencies of this book deserves serious consideration.

32. This from an interview by McCaffery and McHale:

"BM: How come your autobiography is so unlike those autobiographical poems, the expressive lyric, which are really the stable of American poetry? As far as I'm concerned, once you've read one of these, you've read them all.

"LH: My overriding concern as a writer is *epistemology*. My work is nearly always concerned with the question, How do you know anything? Whereas the conventional beginning point is, I know something and want to express something about this. Well, in *My Life* I wanted to write a work in which 'I' is tremendously mediated by knowing prior to being 'I.' I tried to do this with all the snippets of language that are in quotes which are a kind of ambient constructing of the I or contextualizing of the I: social, parental, and familial contextualizing, even things that go through my head, like chronic ideas, all those things that modify and mediate the I that's knowing. I wanted this sort of tumbling effect in which context and I roll along, an effect that would be to some extent cumulative, to some extent fragmenting, dispersing" (136).

33. Paul Naylor points to a similar sense of strategy throughout this chapter on *My Life* in *Poetic Investigations: Singing the Holes in History:* "Hejinian, then, uses language in order to point out language's own limits in order to articulate the self as an entity in the process of creating a life in the world as well as in the text, in, to be specific, an open text such as *My Life*" (123).

34. See Silliman's *The New Sentence* for closely related ideas.

35. It is not unusual for those associated with language writing to deny any sort of lineage with their love of incendiary rhetoric. While Silliman, for instance, acknowledges Vietnam as a moment that defines language writing, he is also partial to creation myths. He locates the beginnings of language writing in Robert Grenier's 1971 "I HATE SPEECH" statement in *This* (86). Silliman's pivotal anthology *In the American Tree* begins with this statement: "'I HATE SPEECH.' Thus capitalized, these words in an essay entitled 'On Speech,' the second of five short critical pieces by Robert Grenier in the first issue of *This,* the magazine he cofounded with Barrett Watten in winter, 1971, announced a breach—a new moment in American writing" (xv). Similarly, Perelman notes that the phrase, "in hindsight, was an important literary gesture . . . important in its positing of literary space" (*Marginalization of Poetry* 40, 41). Watten complicates this rhetoric by arguing that "By analogy, the work of *This* stands at the beginning of the Language School because it is the first continuous self-conscious and self-reflexive literary venue of what 'will have been' the Language School once it developed as it did, even if its formal characteristics could be assembled from other sources. Organization, here, is central; given this fact, it is not at all accurate for Perelman and Silliman to cite Grenier's breach with the literary past as an inaugural event" (17). Yet in his essay Watten wants to have it both ways. He argues both for a social network and for the uniqueness of language writing. In other words, he envisions language writing as having horizontal influences, but few vertical ones. I understand the impulse here. Grenier's statement is persuasive as a break because it is so beautifully succinct in how it separates language writing from the speech-based writings of the New American poets and the dominant lyrical modes of the poetries of accommodation. Yet it also rings false because language writing is interestingly involved with many of the same concerns of the New American poets.

36. See Steve Evans's "1978: Reading Stein," especially the tables, and also Lazer's "Language Writing; or, Literary History and the Strange Case of the Two Dr. Williamses" in *Opposing Poetries* for more on language writing and their canon. A useful recent anthology for its range of attention to earlier and overlooked works is McCaffery and Rasula's *Imagining Language: An Anthology.*

37. See Howe's "Some Notes on Visual Intentionality in Emily Dickinson," "Women and Their Effect in the Distance," and "These Flames and Generosities of the Heart: Emily Dickinson and the Illogic of Sumptuary Values."

38. For more on the 1960s see Todd Gitlin's *The Sixties: Years of Hope, Days of Rage;* Sohnya Sayers, Anders Stephenson, Stanley Aronowitz, and Fredric Jameson's *The Sixties without Apology;* and Julie Stephens's *Anti-Disciplinary Protest: Sixties Radicalism and Postmodernism.*

39. To return to "Wichita Vortex Sutra," it, like much New American poetry, locates its politics in an inclusive pluralism: "I am the Universe tonite" (397); "not only my lonesomeness / it's Ours, all over America" (405); "I search for the language / that is also yours—" (406).

40. This is partially adapted from "A Partial Chronology" by Jameson, Stephenson, and Cornel West.

41. George Hartley's *Textual Politics and the Language Poets* does an excellent job of placing language writing in the context of 1970s and 1980s literary theory. See also Nealon's *Double Reading: Postmodernism after Deconstruction.*

42. Zinn notes in his *A People's History of the United States,* "Bruce Andrews, a Harvard student of public opinion, found that the people most opposed to the war were people over fifty, blacks, and women. He also noted that a study in the spring of 1964, when Vietnam was a minor issue in the newspapers, showed that 53 percent of college-educated people were willing to send troops to Vietnam, but only 33 percent of grade school–educated people were so willing" (483).

43. While autobiography is a complicated genre and an ideal place for investigating how to represent the subject without resorting to individualism, whenever this happens in a work it tends to no longer be considered autobiography. A collection as provocative as the Personal Narrative Group's *Interpreting Women's Lives: Feminist Theory and Personal Narratives* privileges the well-made "life narrative" that "forces the author to move from accounts of discrete experiences to an account of why and how the life took the shape it did" (4). And Nancy Miller writes: "[T]he postmodernist decision that the Author is Dead and the subject along with him does not . . . necessarily hold for women, and prematurely forecloses the question of agency for them" (*Subject to Change* 106). Nonstandardized forms of life writing are often seen as unskilled, not alternative. Elizabeth Hampsten and Lynn Z. Bloom, for example, both propose rewriting the nonstandardized language practices of certain forms of life writing. Hampsten's desire is to make these stories, "in spite of their gaps and improbabilities," become "more truly what they are" (135). Hampsten, in an article tantalizingly called "Considering More Than a Single Reader," describes the characteristics of private life writing by women outside the scholarly community in a language that could interestingly be speaking directly about *My Life.* Such work, she

writes, often "appears—possibly with a title such as 'My Life'—that might speak to
a wider audience, but one nevertheless with limited patience" (130). What tries
Hampsten's patience, as she demonstrates in her discussion of Mary Anna Burckhard's
"My Story," are narratives often written "in small increments barely connected to one
another" that focus "on details, one by one, in a nearly encyclopedic manner" that
"take place sequentially in time, but not in relation to each other" (131). Bloom urges
a form of "modern midwifery" where the scholar rewrites the "sparse, workaday prose
of the original documents" into "a narrative of literary distinction" and "when the
scholar is herself a good writer, the subject can be reborn with even greater vitality
than she had during her days on earth" (12). The point in these articles is unfortunately not to investigate how these stories challenge narrative's conventions as learned,
not innate. Instead, they both urge a form of enforced collaboration between scholar
and author that would smooth over the nonstandardized moments of the narrative.
Hampsten's and Bloom's desire to bring marginalized voices forward is, I believe, a
valid one full of conviction and concern. Their fault lies in wanting to make these life
stories "more truly what they are" through collaboration with scholars more successful
in wielding narrative's normative conventions.

Undeniably, there are important exceptions to this argument. The collections
De/Colonizing the Subject: The Politics of Gender in Women's Autobiography (see especially in this collection Anne Goldman's "'I Yam What I Yam': Cooking, Culture,
and Colonialism" and Greg Sarris's "'What I'm Talking about when I'm Talking about
My Baskets': Conversation with Mabel McKay") and *Getting a Life: Everyday Uses of
Autobiography* by Sidonie Smith and Julia Watson have done much to expand the
genre. Yet their collection *Women/Autobiography/Theory*, which is intended to be a
survey of thinking in this area, reestablishes the dominant genre conventions. (See
Cynthia Franklin's review in *Biography*.) What I am pointing to here is a conservative
and self-policing aspect of life writing studies that allows other forms of life writing
into the definition as long as they are marginal to it.

44. See her article "*Stanzas in Meditation*: The Other Autobiography."

45. For more on Anzaldúa, see Diane P. Freedman, "Writing in the Border-
lands: The Poetic Prose of Gloria Anzaldúa and Susan Griffin"; Lourdes Torres, "The
Construction of the Self in U.S. Latina Autobiographies"; and Sidonie Smith, "The
Autobiographical Manifesto: Identities, Temporalities, Politics," in *Autobiography and
Questions of Gender*. See also Keating's interview with Anzaldúa. Although this argu-
ment of multiple subjectivity is one that Anzaldúa openly embraces, Kingston's work,
I think, in many ways resists such a reading. Nonetheless, see Lisa Lowe, "Heteroge-
neity, Hybridity, Multiplicity: Marking Asian American Differences"; Malini Schueller,
"Questioning Race and Gender Definitions: Dialogic Subversions in *The Woman*

Warrior" and "Theorizing Ethnicity and Subjectivity: Maxine Hong Kingston's *Trip-master Monkey* and Amy Tan's *The Joy Luck Club*."

46. See Nealon's *Alterity Politics: Ethics and Performative Subjectivity* for a discussion of the limitations of defining subjectivity as a negative or an emptiness.

47. For Samuels this "I-centeredness" and "this focus on the human" makes *My Life* not a language work (113). She notes: "If word focus and phrasal repetition make *My Life* a Language text, its I-centeredness does not" (113).

48. Another possible useful context for comparison is the academic memoir, a genre that became very popular with star academics in the mid-1980s. See Franklin's "Turning Japanese/Returning to America: Race and Nation in Memoirs by Cathy Davidson and David Mura" and "Recollecting *This Bridge* in an Anti–Affirmative Action Era: Literary Anthologies, Academic Memoir, and Institutional Autobiography" for more on the bourgeois memoir.

49. Reading *My Life* is just the first step in examining non-normative linguistic forms and their relation to constructs of identity. The autobiographical work of connection raises useful questions: How might the very linear structure of narrative, which in autobiography centers around the subject, further perpetuate essentialist notions of the subject? How might the grammatical structures of our language, in which being is continually bestowed on the subject by its primacy in the hierarchy of the sentence, do the same? What might these very moments that are erased in scholarly rewritings of life narratives tell us about the narrator's relationship with language and society? And more specifically, beyond *My Life*, what might autobiographical works—such as Hannah Weiner's *Clairvoyant Journal*, which reflects its author's psychic premonitions and voices and accompanying confusions of subjectivity through typographically merged levels of discourse, or Johanna Drucker's *History of the/My World*, which is an autobiography of the lie as Drucker writes herself into world history—tell us about reading? How might these works provide access to other works written by subjects with outsider relationships to standardized discourse?

50. Hejinian, through her classes at the New College, brought together and, in Renee Gladman's words, "gave a sense of confidence and cohesion" to an interesting loosely affiliated group of writers in San Francisco (e-mail to author). Gladman writes about Hejinian's influence among herself and other younger writers (writers who come after language, born in the mid-1960s and later): "Anyway, my point is that Lyn's *My Life* represented for me (and I think others who were at the beginning of figuring out how experimental writing would impact their approach to language) a dialogue between Language poetry and my own interest in the difficulties of narrative and memory. I was drawn to that book because it gave experimental writing an integrity that I had yet to find. I saw, in *My Life*, how experience could complicate linearity,

how one might have to expand their use of language and ways of interpreting and conveying life in order to derive meaning, in order to think while doing. That's pretty deep when I think about it because it's still the principle on which I write. So I guess she influenced me a lot. I think Scalapino influenced me more because her early work seems more explorative of the how/why and absurdity of experience, which is really where I see myself. It seems to me that her early work (e.g., *Considering How Exaggerated Music Is*) is a study or a series of studies into the person and perspectives of inference" (e-mail to author).

51. At the same time, I do not wish to discredit the influence language writing has had on a more diverse group of younger writers now in their twenties to late thirties. One could also point to more cross-cultural journals like Paul Naylor's *River City* and Mark Nowak's *XCP* as exceptions (although I imagine that Nowak would not attribute his attention to cultural issues in *XCP* to language writing; rather, *XCP* reads as an important revision of the concerns of ethnopoetics). Bernstein's more recent essays are also an important exception here. See, for instance, his "Poetics of the Americas" essay. For a reply to Bernstein, a reply that seems to me indicative of how language writing wants at times to make identity politics into a racially blind complicated morass, see Watten's "The Bride of the Assembly Line." For more on Bernstein and Brathwaite see Perelman's "Write the Power" in *The Marginalization of Poetry*.

52. Morrison writes: "Let me propose some topics that need critical investigation. First, the Africanist character as surrogate and enabler. In what ways does the imaginative encounter with Africanism enable white writers to think about themselves? What are the dynamics of Africanism's self-reflexive properties? . . . A second topic in need of critical attention is the way an Africanist idiom is used to establish difference or, in a later period to signal modernity. . . . Third, we need studies of the technical ways in which an Africanist character is used to limn out and enforce the invention and implication of whiteness. . . . Fourth, we need to analyze the manipulation of the Africanist narrative (that is, the story of a black person, the experience of being bound and/or rejected) as a means of meditation—both safe and risky—on one's own humanity" (*Playing in the Dark* 51–53).

53. Shelley Fisher Fishkin's "Interrogating 'Whiteness,' Complicating 'Blackness': Remapping American Culture" has a good survey of the criticism in this area. See also "The White Issue" of *Minnesota Review* 47 (1997).

54. Shelley Fisher Fishkin, for example, in *Was Huck Black? Mark Twain and African-American Voices,* argues that Huck Finn's speech is rooted in black vernacular. And much recent work on modernism, such as Ann Douglas's *Terrible Honesty: Mongrel Manhattan in the 1920s* and Michael North's *The Dialect of Modernism: Race, Language, and Twentieth-Century Literature,* point to exchanges between black and

white artists and writers. These studies importantly point to how there is no racially pure writing and at the same time suggest the appropriative possibilities of an uninvestigated pluralism.

55. This is Cynthia Franklin's argument in "Recollecting *This Bridge* in an Anti–Affirmative Action Era: Literary Anthologies, Academic Memoir, and Institutional Autobiography": "[I]f the recent MLA call for conference papers or its special issue on 'ethnicity' are indicative of the current state of affairs in literature departments, explorations of 'whiteness' too often seem to accompany a diminishing amount of attention to the decreasing numbers of people of color in universities, not to mention the worsening conditions for racial minorities in an era characterized by anti-affirmative action, anti-immigration legislation, and an exponential growth in what Angela Davis calls the prison industrial complex, which criminalizes the poor and people of color" (14). As example she points to the controversial January 1998 *PMLA* special issue on "ethnicity" where three of the six articles are on Jewish ethnicity. See also AnnLouise Keating for a related critique of white studies. She writes that "theorists who attempt to deconstruct 'race' often inadvertently reconstruct it by reinforcing the belief in permanent, separate racial categories. Although they emphasize the artificial, politically and economically motivated nature of all racial classifications, their continual analysis of racialized identities undercuts their belief that 'race' is a constantly changing sociohistorical concept, not a biological fact" ("Interrogating 'Whiteness,' (De)Constructing 'Race'" 902).

56. Andrews's attacks on identity have gotten more intense in *I Don't Have Any Paper So Shut Up (Or, Social Romanticism)*. A more detailed study than I provide here would require placing this work in the context of evolving changes in identity politics in the 1980s.

57. Ngai's essay is one of the more provocative ones on contemporary poetics in recent years. She locates a poetics of disgust in Andrews, in a number of language-influenced Canadian writers such as Kevin Davies, Jeff Derksen, Dorothy Trujillo Lusk, and in several harder-to-define U.S. writers such as Lori Lubeski and Judith Goldman. She argues that this writing is against desire and instead exemplifies disgust. This disgust, she argues, "*thwarts seductive reasoning*," "*thwarts close reading*," and, finally, "*thwarts its own use as a critical paradigm*" (102, italics in original). I agree with much in Ngai's essay. I am especially interested in her argument that this writing is not friendly to close reading. Yet what worries me about "disgust" as the frame for reading this work is that it mainly rejects and thus avoids connection. It is disgust's "negative potentiality" that interests Ngai—its exclusions (102). Because Andrews has given so much attention in his theoretical writings to how readers connect with works, it seems crucial to address the role of connection in any reading of his work. But further, and this is purely personal, I worry about the value of a poetics that

leaves one merely with disgust. The rejection of pluralism that Ngai notes is crucial, but without some sort of social connection, a poetics of disgust just leaves readers with a recognition of indignation. Yet critique (of capitalism or of white dominance) has to have some sort of connection in order to function as critique.

Chapter 3

1. Most of the criticism on Mullen's work reads it as a form of signifyin(g). Elizabeth Frost, who places Mullen's work more in the tradition of Stein than anything else, mentions signifyin(g): "In choosing Stein as an intertextual companion, Mullen uses what Henry Louis Gates identifies as a strategy frequently employed in African-American writing: the elaboration of repetition and difference. . . . Strikingly matching Gates's theory of signifying, Mullen's version of Steinian writing involves an assertion of difference" (14, 15). Kate Pearcy notes: "Both these representational modes, however, intersect with, and are animated by, other roles and poetics practices, frequently grouped under the larger practictional term Signifyin(g), which exhibit a 'double voicedness,' a more ambiguous relation to the voice" (3).

2. Mullen writes: "my most immediate and influential model of a black poet engaged in formal innovation was Lorenzo Thomas, a poet born in Panama, reared in New York, and transplanted to Houston, Texas" ("Poetry and Identity" 88).

3. Mullen interestingly discusses this categorical tension in biographical terms in "Poetry and Identity," in an interview with Barbara Henning, and in another interview with Farah Griffin, Michael Magee, and Kristen Gallagher. In the latter, she points to it in linguistic terms: "The population of Chicanos is much larger in Fort Worth, or at least it was when I was a child. So I had the feeling we were growing up between the Anglos and, as we called them then, the Mexicans, you know. I was aware of Spanish being spoken; and in our community, a black Southern vernacular was spoken, which my family didn't exactly speak. When it came to class, our income and the neighborhoods we lived in, at first, were working-class, while our values and aspirations were middle-class, so in terms of class, we were also borderline. I also knew the prejudice of Northerners against the languid Southern drawl and the nasal Texas twang. I sound more Southern now than I did when I was a kid. And, you know, partly I sound more Southern, I guess, because I had to get with the program and blend in with my peers. My mother, my grandmother, the people who raised me, were from Pennsylvania. They were from Harrisburg. So my whole relationship to black English, like that of a lot of middle-class black people, is, you learn it to keep your butt from getting beat in the streets. You know, what we spoke at home was basically what I would call black standard English. You'd learn the vernacular on the streets

and playgrounds in order to have some friends out there. The essentializing of black English as the natural way that black people are supposed to speak is problematic for me. Of course, I enjoy using different linguistic registers and I enjoy throwing Spanish words into my poems, you know, and I think that the variety of languages and dialects makes life more interesting" (n.p.).

4. She states in the interview with Griffin, Magee, and Gallagher: " . . . the idea of problematizing the subject. You know, there was a joke that circulated among minority (and some women) graduate students: 'It's that white male subjectivity that needs to be put on hold. . . . We can just put a moratorium on that, and the rest of us need to step up to the plate, you know (laughter). We need our subjectivity.' And then I began to think, well, in what ways would I want to problematize my black female subjectivity, and going to California from Texas was one of the experiences that gave me some ideas about that. For instance, where I grew up, in Fort Worth, Texas—and I was born in Alabama, you know I'm a Southerner, basically—you see a black person . . . you speak to black folks whether you know them or not. We'd assume a connection to other black folk, I mean, even if it is in some cases very superficial. In California it's different. I'd walk up to people and they don't even make eye-contact, or maybe their whole idea of who they are is so utterly different from who I think they might be just because they're black. So, I thought about my first book, *Tree Tall Woman*, which is very much in the tradition of the 'authentic voice.' Most of those poems have a persona who speaks from the black family, from the black community, with a certain idea of who was a black person. Without even consciously thinking about it, I suppose I more or less assumed a black person was someone with Southern roots and someone who ate collard greens and someone who was probably a Protestant. Once I left the South, I had to rethink all of that. Those were ways that I began to relate what I did in my work to what they were doing. I had to reimagine what they were doing in other terms. Maybe that's answering your question or beginning to answer your question" (n.p.).

5. "Joy to the World" is a traditional Christmas carol. The lyrics go: "Joy to the world / The Lord is come / Let earth receive her King / Let every heart prepare Him room / And heaven and nature sing / And heaven and nature sing / And heaven and heaven and nature sing."

6. "My Favorite Things" (by Rodgers and Hammerstein) is sung by Julie Andrews in *The Sound of Music*, a musical about the rise of the Nazis in Germany.

7. "Swing Low, Sweet Chariot" is a popular spiritual or gospel song. The lyrics go: "Swing low, sweet chariot / Comin' for to carry me home; / Swing low, sweet chariot / Comin' for to carry me home."

8. Booker T. Washington wrote an autobiography titled *Up from Slavery;* W. E. B.

Du Bois wrote *The Souls of Black Folk*. Their arguments on self-determination for African Americans are often considered together for what are perceived as the concise opposition of their positions.

9. One of the many subplots of *Uncle Tom's Cabin* involves a character named Topsy.

10. Lady Godiva was an Englishwoman who supposedly protested the tax hike that her husband imposed upon the people of Coventry by riding naked on horseback through the town.

11. See Freud's *Dora: An Analysis of a Case of Hysteria*.

12. Baker started on the American stage but came to represent "le jazz hot" for the French. In 1925 she starred in Paris in *La Revue Negre* as a dancer clad only in a string of bananas.

13. Ivory soap's trademark is "99 and 44/100% Pure: It Floats."

14. See Michael Awkward's discussion in *Negotiating Difference: Race, Gender, and the Politics of Positionality* 28–32.

15. Gates's study has had a huge resonance in American studies. But it seems only fair to note that writers such as Amiri Baraka, writing before Gates, argued similarly. In 1972 Baraka takes pains to rehistoricize Pound by stating, "Make it New attributed to Ezra Pound is Eastern. It is the African (and Sufi) explanation of why life, even though contained by an endless circle, or not contained, *is* an endless cycle can be, is worthwhile" ("Notes" 46).

16. But despite all this theorizing, there remains a tendency that limits much minority writing with a policing rhetoric of accessibility or clarity. Or as Mullen herself has noted, *Tree Tall Woman* presents her as a "digestible black poet," and if her work is to be included in an anthology of African-American poets it is work from this collection that is usually chosen. But the more linguistically unconventional books that follow *Tree Tall Woman* garner her a series of subcategories: "innovative women poets of minority background" ("Poetry and Identity" 87).

17. Nielsen's *Black Chant: Languages of African-American Postmodernism* does important recovery work of experimental writers in the Black Arts movement.

18. Mullen discusses this in greater detail in "Poetry and Identity." Lubiano notes: "African-American literary critics of the first two eras of African-American criticism, the integrationist poetics critics and the black aesthetic critics, also privilege realism as the key mode for narration without reflecting on their hegemonic compliance. Both eras of critics internalized to some degree the demands of Euro-American culture: the integrationist critics in their assumption that the forms of English and American literature had universal application, and the black aesthetic critics, black cultural nationalists, in their insistence upon the imposition of another 'truth,' another realism—

a monolithic, absolutist, and essentialist 'black truth' or 'black reality' to counteract the white 'lies' about black culture and history" (215).

19. I have taken the term "talk back" from Mullen's critical writing. See her article "Runaway Tongue: Resistant Orality in *Uncle Tom's Cabin, Our Nig, Incidents in the Life of a Slave Girl*, and *Beloved*."

20. Amiri Baraka writes: "We talk about the oral tradition of African people, sometimes positively, many times defensively (if we are not wised up), and it's always as a substitute for the written. What this is is foolfood, because we were the first writers, as well . . . Thot is the God of writing, its inventor, an African" ("Introduction" 4). Nathaniel Mackey quotes this passage from Baraka and notes that "We hear from him too that whatever taint may be attached to literacy has more to do with the alien 'weight of dominant ideologies' to which Glissant alludes than with anything intrinsic to writing" (261). As A. L. Nielsen notes, "One problem with continued privileging of orality is that such privileging too often leads to a critique that inadequately listens to the relationship between script and performance" (*Black Chant* 21).

21. In the interview with Griffin, Magee, and Gallagher, Mullen says, "I want to claim the oral as much as the written tradition. That vernacular tradition is important, of course, but it's important not to lose sight of our tradition of writing and literature. Yes, Dunbar, Hughes and James Weldon Johnson were working with a vernacular tradition in their poetry, but it was written, and we had access to it through books. In my family, books were important, just as public speaking, and the ability to communicate face to face were important. I think the playful aspect of my work is certainly connected to that vernacular tradition, and some of that tradition I know only from books or media—just like you usually won't hear traditional black spirituals in black churches today. As a child, I knew the spirituals only because of records, movies, and the occasional recital by one of the black opera singers. We might have sung 'Swing Low, Sweet Chariot' in the chorus at school, and we'd have to learn it with sheet music. It was part of the oral tradition at one time, but now it exists only because someone cared enough to write it down. And writing something down changes it. Turning something into a poem changes it. Langston Hughes didn't write blues poems that were exactly like the traditional blues. He did something else to them. He was, in a way, digesting the blues tradition and synthesizing it with other traditions in order to create this poetry. And Dunbar didn't write down exactly the way people spoke dialect, in fact Dunbar was a standard English speaker. Growing up in Ohio and being the one black student in his class, the class poet, you know he spoke standard English. We tend to overlook all those poems he wrote in standard English and traditional verse. So, there's the balance between the two and, you know, a speakerly text may also be a very writerly text. When I look at *Invisible Man,* it's both" (n.p.).

22. For more on sampling see Tricia Rose's "Soul Sonic Forces: Technology, Orality, and Black Cultural Practice in Rap Music" in *Black Noise: Rap Music and Black Culture in Contemporary America* 62–96; Tim Brennan, "Off the Gangsta Tip: A Rap Appreciation, or Forgetting about Los Angeles"; and Dick Hebdige, *Cut N Mix: Culture, Identity, and Caribbean Music.*

23. See Frost, Hubbard, and Pearcy.

24. See Georges Bataille's *Manet* 61–63. The painting, as is often noted, heralded a new aesthetic, one that would soon replace all that was conventional at the time. As John Berger points out, "Manet represented a turning point. If one compares his *Olympia* with Titian's original, one sees a woman, cast in the traditional role, beginning to question that role, somewhat defiantly" (63).

25. Griselda Pollock notes: "Surely one part of the shock, of the transgression effected by the painting *Olympia* for its first viewers at the Paris Salon was the presence of that 'brazen' but cool look from the white woman, on a bed attended by a black maid in a space in which women, or to be historically precise bourgeois ladies, would be presumed to be present" (54 n).

26. Readings of *Tender Buttons* have been extreme and various. See for instance, William Gass's "Gertrude Stein and the Geography of the Sentence," Lisa Ruddick's *Reading Gertrude Stein: Body, Text, Gnosis,* and Marianne DeKoven's *A Different Language: Gertrude Stein's Experimental Writing* for three very different readings. Gass does an extreme psychosexual reading. Ruddick reads the book as about gnosticism. DeKoven argues that it is presymbolic language.

27. Consider, for instance, these references in the first few pages of *Tender Buttons* alone: "It shows that dirt is clean when there is a volume"; "Dirty is yellow"; "The resemblance to yellow is dirtier and distincter"; "Dirt and not copper makes a color darker"; "If lilies are lily white if they exhaust noise and distance and even dust, if they dusty will dirt a surface that has no extreme grace" (10, 12, 13, 14). See also Richard Bridgman, *Gertrude Stein in Pieces,* 126.

28. Campbell, *Greek Lyric,* 131

29. Nick Tosches, *Country: The Twisted Roots of Rock 'n' Roll* 63.

30. "Southern trees bear a strange fruit / Blood on the leaves, blood at the root / Black bodies swinging in the Southern breeze" (as quoted by Angela Davis 181). Song is written by Lewis Allen. See Davis 181–197 for more detailed discussion.

31. See Page Du Bois 1–30 for more on Sappho's possible complicated positionality. While it is generally assumed that she came from an established family, she did live on an island and was somewhat isolated from the mainland center of culture. There is also an early description (late second or early third century A.D.) of Sappho as "quite ugly, being dark in complexion and of very small stature" (which, like all

descriptions of Sappho, or information about her, may or may not be true). See Campbell, *Greek Lyric* 3.

32. There has also been a series of studies that examine the race of the reader/critic, such as Elizabeth Abel's "Black Writing, White Reading: Race and the Politics of Feminist Interpretation," Michael Awkward's "Introduction: Reading across the Lines" and "Race, Gender, and the Politics of Reading" in *Negotiating Difference: Race, Gender and the Politics of Positionality*, and Margaret Homans's "'Women of Color' Writers and Feminist Theory."

33. One possible reason for this division is that Sommer's attention is, as most writing about reading, focused on the rigorously developmental narrative work. Her canon of works includes Cirilio Villaverde's *Cecilia Valdes: O, la loma del Angel; Novela de costumbres Cubanas*, Rigoberta Menchú's *I, Rigoberta Menchú: An Indian Woman in Guatemala*, Richard Rodriquez's *Hunger of Memory: The Education of Richard Rodriquez*, and Toni Morrison's *Beloved*. And, in rigorously narrative works, the only way to open up a space is to leave a blank.

Chapter 4

1. As Elaine Kim points out about the ineffectiveness of this petition, "the U.S. signed a secret pact with Japan, the Taft-Katsura Pact, that year. This agreement allowed Japan free rein in Korea in exchange for her promise to allow the U.S. to dominate the Philippines, which had already been acquired in the Spanish-American War" ("Poised on the In-Between" 10).

2. Because I read Cha's nonstandard spelling as full of intent, I have reproduced it without the use of the intrusive [*sic*]. I have also capitalized the title of the book when I refer to it, but when quoting someone else on *DICTEE* I follow his or her usage. Brian Kim Stefans notes: "There has been a debate about how the title of the book should appear in print. Lew and others claim that a significant pun is created by the use of upper-case letter in the word's appearance on the cover, making it mean both 'dictation, the act of dictating' and 'one to whom something is being dictated,' while others feel that the accent aigu has been suppressed simply, because, in French, it is optional when a word appears in upper-case" (16 n. 3).

3. Cha was also a filmmaker and a performance artist, and in 1980 she had published a collection of essays, *Apparatus: Cinematographic Apparatus: Selected Writings*.

4. Stefans notes: "*Dictee* has been dismissed for almost a decade by the Asian American critical establishment, and was labeled as 'white' and not concerned with community or feminist issues" (5). Shelley Sunn Wong notes: "Asian American critics' silence regarding *Dictée* cannot be explained in simple terms of a critical orthodoxy

resisting challenges to its authority, or of tradition-bound (and largely realist) forms resisting avant-garde experimentation. Instead, that silence needs to be understood in the context of changing frameworks of reception within the Asian American community, changes that are the result not of transitory literary fashions but, rather, the conjunction of several historical developments in the 1970s and 1980s: major demographic changes within the Asian American community from 1965–85; the growing strength and influence of the women's movement; the postmodernist concern with fragmentation and multiple positionalities; and the emergence of new social movements that necessitated the rethinking of oppositional strategies" (103–104). See also Shu-Mei Shih's discussion of this in "Nationalism and Korean American Women's Writing."

5. I am not arguing with these essays; I rely on them extensively in this chapter. I've found especially illuminating Kang's observation that "Cha has constructed her book as *a process* of mutually active collaboration. If language would always already be implicated, predetermined and expectant for both reader and writer, Cha's strategy is to explicitly posit an active relationship between writer and reader as central to the challenging of the authorizing and alienating structure of language and literary transmission" (78).

6. See Patricia E. Tsurumi's "Colonial Education in Korean and Taiwan" for more information on the importance of not only language education but more general cultural education to Japan's colonial project.

7. See Braj B. Kachru's "Models for Non-Native Englishes."

8. See Kachru's *The Alchemy of English: The Spread, Functions and Models of Non-Native Englishes,* Paikeday's *The Native Sparker Is Dead!,* and Larry Smith's two edited collections, *Discourse across Cultures: Strategies in World Englishes* and (with Michael L. Forman) *World Englishes 2000.*

9. For more on the history of the spread of the English language, see David Crystal's *English as a Global Language.*

10. In recent reading I have encountered this figure in Sia Figiel's *Where We Once Belonged* and Lois Ann Yamanaka's *Blu's Hanging.* There are complicated revisions of this trope in Toni Morrison's *Beloved* and Cheikh Hamidou Kane's *Ambiguous Adventure.*

11. In *Writing Self Writing Nation,* Wong astutely points out that "two punctuation commands in French—'ferme les guillemets' and 'ouvre les guillemets'—have been omitted from the English translation. While the omission of the punctuation commands reveals the student's failure to accurately reproduce the original, it also calls attention to the fact that, contrary to established conventions, the commands have been written out rather than simply and unobtrusively inserted as punctuation marks" (119).

12. Talal Asad warns: "Take modern Arabic as an example. Since the early nineteenth century there has been a growing volume of material translated from European languages—especially French and English—into Arabic. This includes scientific texts as well as 'social science,' 'history,' 'philosophy,' and 'literature.' And from the nineteenth century, Arabic as a language has begun as a result to undergo a transformation (lexical, grammatical, semantic) that is far more radical than anything to be identified in European languages—a transformation that has pushed it to approximate the latter more closely than in the past. Such transformations signal inequalities in the power (i.e., in the *capacities*) of the respective languages in relation to the *dominant* forms of discourse that have been and are still being translated. . . . A recognition of this well-known fact reminds us that industrial capitalism transforms not only modes of production but also kinds of knowledge and styles of life in the Third World. And with them, forms of language" (158).

13. See James Crawford's *Hold Your Tongue: Bilingualism and the Politics of "English Only."*

14. Marc Shell notes: "The actual linguistic makeup of people inside and outside the often changing borders of the American colonies between 1750 and 1850 is relevant here. For if ever there were a polyglot place on the globe—other than Babel's spire—this was it. Here three continents—North America, Africa, and Europe—met one another" ("Babel in America" 105).

15. See, for instance, Alfred Arteaga's "An Other Tongue."

16. But even while it is obvious that multilingualism counters the emphasis on purity or on the cultural centrality of monolingualism by replacing a single voice with a necessary dialogue, this cannot necessarily be utopian. Tzvetan Todorov writes a bit melodramatically but nonetheless with pertinence, "I believe I saw silence and insanity looming on the horizon of boundless polyphony, and I found them oppressive, which is doubtless why I prefer the bounds of dialogue" (214). And while invocations of Babel seem unnecessary, the politics that have accompanied bilingualism in places like Quebec have not necessarily been without problems. Also, Eliot's and Pound's work, and that of other high modernists, demonstrates the conservative possibility within multilingual works.

17. This sort of argument characterizes much of the rhetoric of New Formalism. Brad Leithauser, for instance, writes: "Given the demands and restrictions of the human body, it may well turn out that free verse is inherently barred from the very grandest heights of poetry" (12). Frederick Turner writes: "Metered poetry is a cultural universal, and its salient feature, the three-second LINE, is tuned to the three-second present moment of the auditory information-processing system" (102–103). See Thomas B. Byers's "The Closing of the American Line: Expansive Poetry and Ideology" for a cogent critique of these arguments.

18. The most mundane example of this is the difference between the Norton anthology and the Heath anthology. As Bernstein notes, "Despite the fact that the Heath anthology does a better job of 'representing' the touchstones of American culture than Norton, I see no radical conceptual difference between the two. Both have the primary effect of taking a very heterogeneous field and domesticating it. Both represent literature in measured doses, uniform typography, and leveling head- and footnotes—making poetry the subject of its frame rather than presenting poetry itself as a context—a conflict—of frames" ("What's Art Got to Do with It?" 25).

19. Bernstein discusses this in greater detail in his essay "What's Art Got to Do with It?": "The university environment is not just nonpoetic, which would be unexceptional, but antipoetic. And this situation has remained constant as we have moved from literary studies to the more sociologically and psychoanalytically deterministic approaches to cultural studies" (29).

20. A great deal of critical energy has been put into semantic distinctions between terms such as "globalism," "cosmopolitanism," "transnationalism," and "internationalism." I've found Amanda Anderson's "Cosmopolitanism, Universalism, and the Divided Legacies of Modernism" a useful summary of these issues. See also Cheah and Robbins's *Cosmopolitics: Thinking and Feeling beyond the Nation*, Wilson and Dissanayake's *Global/Local: Cultural Production and the Transnational Imaginary*, Robbins's *Secular Vocations: Intellectuals, Professionalism, Culture*, and Brennan's chapter "Cosmopolitanism and Method" in *At Home in the World: Cosmopolitanism Now*.

21. While I have, on the advice of Maria Damon, avoided the word "postmodern" throughout this book as much as possible, I think most people would probably consider *DICTEE* a postmodern work. It was written post–*Gravity's Rainbow*, and it does not follow realist conventions.

22. Tzvetan Todorov is similarly skeptical of multilingual works: "'Unbounded polyphony,' therefore, according to the account just given, leads to schizophrenia, taken in its commonly understood sense of split personality, mental incoherence, and attendant distress. Doublethink is also a kind of madness, since it implies a decision to accept incoherence or even contradictions. It is like a vaccine the Party wants to use to inoculate everyone" (206).

23. The possibility of a reader who identifies on the basis of difference or who enters into identification with a work for reasons other than self-affirmation rarely gets explored. Even when critics discuss the possibility of identifying across gender, race, or class lines—a position of undeniable prominence in studies of more popular genres such as science fiction or fantasy literature—these assumptions tend to be based on the reader's becoming (however momentarily) like the character. As Carol Clover points out in her study of slasher films, there has been a tendency to underestimate readers/viewers and to see them as identifying only with what is similar to them.

Clover concludes her introductory discussion of the movie *Carrie* by noting, "Certainly I will never again take for granted that audience males identify solely or even mainly with screen males and audience females with screen females. If Carrie, whose story begins and ends with menstrual imagery and seems in general so painfully girlish, is construed by her author as a latter-day variant on Samson, the biblical strong man who overcame all manner of handicap to kill at least six thousand Philistines in one way or another, and if her target audience is any high school boy who has been pantsed and had his glasses messed with, then we are truly in a universe in which the sex of a character is no object. No accident, insofar as it is historically and, above all, politically overdetermined, but also no object—no impediment whatever to the audience's experience of his or her function. That too is one of the bottom-line propositions of horror, a proposition that is easily missed when you watch mainstream cinema but laid bare in exploitation cinema and, once registered, never lets you see any movie 'straight' again" (20).

24. Jameson's list of the most significant postmodern artists—"Cage, Ashbery, Sollers, Robert Wilson, Ishmael Reed, Michael Snow, Warhol, or even Beckett himself"—does not question its own politics of representation, a difficult move to justify as so many postmodern works have been written or created by socially or culturally marginalized subjects (26).

25. While one of my desires in this chapter is to examine what these works might add to more politically astute forms of analysis, I should also acknowledge that what little attention such works have received from those who do work on avant-garde writing has tended to present them as the advanced guard of dominant culture and not as works written in opposition, not as works of resistance, not even as works deeply embedded in discussions of everyday and political decisions. So a work like *DICTEE* has tended to be read as if it had nothing to do with colonialism and everything to do with poststructuralism. Elaine Kim complains: "I am far less tolerant of readers who, in their eagerness to explore the affinities between *Dictée* and other 'postmodern' texts, have found it possible to discuss Cha's work without alluding in a significant way to her Korean heritage, for it is they, and not the Korean journalist who compares Cha with South Korean writer Yi Sang, who will rush their views into print in widely read literary journals" ("Poised on the In-Between," 22). Kim does not footnote who she is talking about, but Allen deSouza, Stephen-Paul Martin, Robert Siegle, Michael Stephens, Rob Wilson, and Susan Wolf (although none of these articles are published in widely read literary journals; but to my knowledge there have been no articles on Cha in anything I would call widely read) all seem to be reading *DICTEE* more generally as experimental and less specifically as postcolonial or Korean nationalist. I assume the Korean journalist she refers to is Walter Lew, former editor of Kaya, literary critic, and the translator of Yi Sang.

26. Yung-Hee Kim recently informed me that Yu is often referred to as Korea's Joan of Arc in Korea.

27. Yung-Hee Kim translated this for me.

28. There are, for instance, three different narratives about this photograph in *Writing Self Writing Nation*. See Elaine Kim ("Poised on the In-Between" 25 n. 9), Kang (99 n. 7), and Wong (107).

29. Shih interestingly points to a connection between this passage and the ritual of "blood writing" (*hyulso*) that revolutionaries like Ahn Joong Kim used to symbolize their commitment to Korean self-determination. While one could argue that blood writing might reaffirm a clear relation between blood and nation, it seems crucial also to consider the bilingual emphasis on permeability in this passage. For more on blood in *DICTEE* see Lisa Lowe's "Decolonization, Displacement, Disidentification: Asian American 'Novels' and the Question of History." For more on Ahn Joong Kim and blood writing see Walter Lew's *Excerpts from* Δikth /딕테/딕티/ DIKTE for DICTEE (1982).

Works Cited

Abel, Elizabeth. "Black Writing, White Reading: Race and the Politics of Feminist Interpretation." *Critical Inquiry* 19 (1993): 470–498.

Adams, Henry. *The Education of Henry Adams.* Boston: Houghton Mifflin, 1961.

"Advertisement." *Transition* 7 (1927): 171–172.

Allen, Donald. *The New American Poetry.* New York: Grove, 1960.

Altieri, Charles. "Some Problems about Agency in the Theories of Radical Poetries." *Contemporary Literature* 37.2 (1996): 207–236.

———. "Without Consequences Is No Politics: A Response to Jerome McGann." *Politics and Poetic Value.* Ed. Robert von Hallberg. Chicago: U of Chicago P, 1987. 301–308.

Anderson, Amanda. "Cosmopolitanism, Universalism, and the Divided Legacies of Modernism." *Cosmopolitics: Thinking and Feeling beyond the Nation.* Ed. Pheng Cheah and Bruce Robbins. Minneapolis: U of Minnesota P, 1998. 265–289.

Andrews, Bruce. *Give Em Enough Rope.* Los Angeles: Sun & Moon P, 1987.

———. *I Don't Have Any Paper So Shut Up (Or, Social Romanticism).* Los Angeles: Sun & Moon P, 1992.

———. *Paradise & Method: Poetics & Praxis.* Evanston: Northwestern UP, 1996.

———. *Public Constraint and American Policy in Vietnam.* Beverly Hills: Sage, 1976.

Andrews, Bruce, and Charles Bernstein, eds. *The L=A=N=G=U=A=G=E Book.* Carbondale: Southern Illinois UP, 1984.

Andrews, Bruce, Charles Bernstein, Ray DiPalma, Steve McCaffery, and Ron Silliman. *Legend.* New York: L=A=N=G=U=A=G=E/Segue, 1980.

Andrews, Julie. "My Favorite Things." By Richard Rogers and Oscar Hammerstein II. *The Sound of Music.* New York: BMG/RCA, 1995.

Angelou, Maya. "On the Pulse of Morning." *The Complete Collected Poems of Maya Angelou.* New York: Random House, 1994. 269–273.

Anzaldúa, Gloria. *Borderlands: La Frontera: The New Mestiza.* San Francisco: Spinsters/ Aunt Lute, 1987.

Arteaga, Alfred. *Cantos.* Chusma House Publications, 1991.

———. "An Other Tongue." *An Other Tongue: Nation and Ethnicity in the Linguistic Borderlands.* Ed. Alfred Arteaga. Durham: Duke UP, 1994. 9–33.

Asad, Talal. "The Concept of Cultural Translation in British Social Anthropology." *Writing Culture: The Poetics and Politics of Ethnography.* Ed. James Clifford and George E. Marcus. Berkeley: U of California P, 1986. 141–164.

Ashton, Jennifer. "Gertrude Stein for Anyone." *ELH* 64 (1997): 289–331.

Awkward, Michael. *Negotiating Difference: Race, Gender, and the Politics of Positionality.* Chicago: U of Chicago P, 1995.

Balaz, Joe. *Ola.* Honolulu: Tinfish Network. December 5, 1997. http://wings.buffalo.edu/epc/ezines/tinfish/balaz/ (17 May 1999).

Banggo, Kathy Dee Kaleokealoha Kaloloahilani. *4-Evas, Anna.* Honolulu: Tinfish Network, 1997.

Baraka, Amiri, "Introduction: Pfister Needs to Be Heard." *Beer Cans, Bullets, Things, and Pieces,* by Arthur Pfister. Detroit: Broadside P, 1972. 4–6.

———. "Notes on Lou Donaldson and Andrew Hill." *Cricket* (1969): 46.

Barthes, Roland. *The Pleasure of the Text.* Tr. Richard Miller. New York: Noonday P, 1975.

Bataille, Georges. *Manet.* Tr. Austryn Wainhouse and James Emmons. Cleveland: World Publishing Company, 1955.

Beach, Christopher. *Poetic Culture: Contemporary American Poetry Between Community and Institution.* Evanston: Northwestern UP, 1999.

Beatles, The. "Matchbox." *Pastmasters.* Vol. 1. New York: EMI Records, 1988.

Berger, John. *Ways of Seeing.* London: British Broadcasting Corporation and Penguin Books, 1972.

Bernstein, Charles. *Artifice of Absorption.* Philadelphia: Paper Air, 1987.

———. "A Blow Is Like an Instrument." *Daedalus* 126.4 (1997): 177–200.

———. *Content's Dream: Essays 1975–1984.* Los Angeles: Sun & Moon, 1986.

———. *A Poetics.* Cambridge: Harvard UP, 1992.

———. "Poetics of the Americas." *Modernism/Modernity* 3.3 (1996): 1–23.

———. "What's Art Got to Do with It? The Status of the Subject of the Humanities in an Age of Cultural Studies." *Beauty and the Critic: Aesthetics in an Age of Cultural Studies.* Ed. James Soderholm. Tuscaloosa: U of Alabama P, 1997. 21–45.

Bhabha, Homi K. "The World and the Home." *Dangerous Liaisons: Gender, Nation, and Postcolonial Perspectives.* Ed. Anne McClintock, Aarnir Mufti, and Ella Shohat. Minneapolis: U of Minnesota P, 1997. 445–455.

Biarujia, Javant. "Purges." *Chain* 6 (1998): 9–12.

Blackmur, Corinne E. "African Masks and the Arts of Passing in Gertrude Stein's 'Melanctha' and Nella Larsen's *Passing.*" *Journal of the History of Sexuality* 4.2 (1993): 230–263.

Bloom, Lynn Z. "Auto/Bio/History: Modern Midwifery." *Autobiography and Questions of Gender.* Ed. Shirley Neuman. London: Frank Cass, 1991. 12–24.

Brathwaite, Kamau. *Trench Town Rock.* Providence: Lost Roads, 1994.

Brennan, Tim. *At Home in the World: Cosmopolitanism Now.* Cambridge: Harvard UP, 1997.

———. "Off the Gangsta Tip: A Rap Appreciation, or Forgetting about Los Angeles." *Critical Inquiry* 20 (1994): 663–693.

Bridgman, Richard. *Gertrude Stein in Pieces.* New York: Oxford UP, 1970.

Bürger, Peter. *Theory of the Avant-Garde.* Tr. Michael Shaw. Minneapolis: U of Minnesota P, 1984.

Byers, Thomas B. "The Closing of the American Line: Expansive Poetry and Ideology." *Contemporary Literature* 33.2 (1992): 396–415.

Cabacungan, Darryl Keola. "He Song of Parting Ma M-akaha" *Hybolics* 1 (1999): 42–43.

Cage, John. *Themes and Variations.* Barrytown: Station Hill P, 1982.

Campbell, David A. *Greek Lyric.* Vol. 1. Cambridge: Harvard UP, 1982.

Cariaga, Catalina. *Cultural Evidence.* Honolulu: Subpress, 1999.

Césaire, Aimé. *Return to My Native Land.* Paris: Présence Africaine, 1968.

Cha, Theresa Hak Kyung, ed. *Apparatus: Cinematographic Apparatus: Selected Writings.* New York: Tanam P, 1980.

———. *DICTEE.* Berkeley: Third Woman, 1995.

Cheah, Pheng, and Bruce Robbins, eds. *Cosmopolitics: Thinking and Feeling beyond the Nation.* Minneapolis: U of Minnesota P, 1998.

Chessman, Harriet Scott. *The Public Is Invited to Dance: Representation, the Body, and Dialogue in Gertrude Stein.* Stanford: Stanford UP, 1989.

Christian, Barbara. "The Race for Theory." *Feminist Studies* 14.1 (1988): 67–79.

Clark, Hilary. "The Mnemonics of Autobiography: Lyn Hejinian's *My Life*." *Biography* 14 (1991): 315–335.

Clash, The. *Give 'Em Enough Rope.* New York: Sony Music, 1987.

Clifford, James. *The Predicament of Culture: Twentieth-Century Ethnography, Literature, and Art.* Cambridge: Harvard UP, 1988.

Clover, Carol J. *Men, Women, and Chainsaws: Gender in the Modern Horror Film.* Princeton: Princeton UP, 1992.

Clovers, The. "Lovey Dovey." By Memphis Curtis. *The Very Best of the Clovers.* New York: Wea/Atlantic/Rhino, 1998.

Cohn-Bendit, Daniel, and Gabriel Cohn-Bendit. *Obsolete Communism: The Left Wing Alternative.* Tr. Arnold Pomerans. New York: McGraw-Hill, 1968.

Coltrane, John. *My Favorite Things.* New York: Rhine, 1987.

Conolly-Smith, Peter. "'Ersatz-Drama' and Ethnic (Self-)Parody: Adolf Philipp and the Decline of New York's German-Language Stage, 1893–1918." *Multilingual America: Transnationalism, Ethnicity, and the Languages of American Literature.* Ed. Werner Sollers and Marc Shell. New York: New York UP, 1998. 215–239.

Conrad, Bryce. "Gertrude Stein in the American Marketplace." *Journal of Modern Literature* 19.2 (1995): 215–233.

Corn, Alfred. *Autobiographies.* New York: Viking, 1992.

Cortissoz, Royal. *American Artists.* New York: AMS P, 1970.

Crawford, James. *Hold Your Tongue: Bilingualism and the Politics of "English Only."* New York: Addison-Wesley, 1992.

Crystal, David. *English as a Global Language.* New York: Cambridge UP, 1997.

Daly, Lew, Alan Gilbert, Kristin Prevallet, and Pam Rehm. "Editorial." *Apex of the M* 2 (1994): 5–8.

Damon, Maria. "Avant-Garde or Borderguard: (Latino) Identity in Poetry." *American Literary History* 10.3 (1998): 478–496.

——. *The Dark End of the Street: Margins in American Vanguard Poetry.* Minneapolis: U of Minnesota P, 1993.

——. "Poetic Canons: Generative Oxymoron or Stalled-Out Dialectic?" *Contemporary Literature* 39.3 (1998): 146–151.

——. "When the NuYoricans Came to Town: (Ex)Changing Poetics." *XCP* 1 (1997): 16–40.

Davidson, Michael, Lyn Hejinian, Ron Silliman, and Barrett Watten. *Leningrad.* San Francisco: Mercury House, 1991.

Davis, Angela. *Blues Legacy and Black Feminism: Gertrude "Ma" Rainey, Bessie Smith, and Billie Holiday.* New York: Pantheon Books, 1998.

de Certeau, Michel. *The Practice of Everyday Life.* Tr. Steven Rendell. Berkeley: U of California P, 1984.

DeKoven, Marianne. *A Different Language: Gertrude Stein's Experimental Writing.* Madison: U of Wisconsin P, 1983.

Delany, Samuel R. *Times Square Red Times Square Blue.* New York: New York UP, 1999.

Deleuze, Gilles, and Félix Guattari. *Kafka: Towards a Minor Literature.* Tr. Dana Polan. Minneapolis: U of Minnesota P, 1986.

deSouza, Allan. "The Spoken Word: Theresa Hak Kyung Cha's *Dictée*." *Third Text* 24 (1993): 73–79.

Dickens, Charles. *David Copperfield.* 1850. *Project Gutenberg.* Ed. Jo Churcher. December 1996. October 2, 1999. <http://promo.net/pg/__authors/dickens__ charles__.html>.

Dobyns, Stephen. *Body Traffic: Poems.* New York: Penguin, 1990.

——. *Velocities: New and Selected Poems.* New York: Penguin, 1994.

Douglas, Ann. *Terrible Honesty: Mongrel Manhattan in the 1920s.* New York: Farrar, Straus, Giroux, 1995.

Douglass, Frederick. *Narrative of the Life of Frederick Douglass, an American Slave, Written by Himself.* New York: Signet, 1968.

Drucker, Johanna. *History of the/My World.* New York: Granary Books, 1995.

Du Bois, Page. *Sappho Is Burning.* Chicago: U of Chicago P, 1995.

Du Bois, W. E. B. *The Souls of Black Folk.* New York: Bantam Classics, 1989.

Dydo, Ulla. "Landscape Is Not Grammar: Gertrude Stein in 1928." *Raritan* 7 (1987): 97–113.

——. "*Stanzas in Meditation:* The Other Autobiography." *Chicago Review* 35.2 (1985): 4–20.

——, ed. *A Stein Reader.* Evanston: Northwestern UP, 1993.

Eichhoff, Jürgen. "The German Language in America." *America and the Germans: An Assessment of a Three-Hundred-Year History.* Vol. 1. Philadelphia: U of Pennsylvania P, 1985. 223–240.

Eliot, T. S. "Charleston, Hey! Hey!" *Nation and Athenaeum* 29 January 1927: 595.

——. "The Waste Land." *The Complete Poems and Plays: 1909–1950.* New York: Harcourt, Brace and World, 1962. 37–55.

Evans, Steve. "1978: Reading Stein." *Aerial* 8 (1999): 247–283.

Figiel, Sia. *Where We Once Belonged.* Aukland: Pacifika P, 1996.

Finkelstein, Norman. *The Utopian Moment in Contemporary American Poetry.* 2nd ed. Lewisburg: Bucknell UP, 1993.

Fish, Stanley. *Is There a Text in This Class? The Authority of Interpretive Communities.* Cambridge: Harvard UP, 1980.

Fishkin, Shelley Fisher. "Interrogating 'Whiteness,' Complicating 'Blackness': Remapping American Culture." *American Quarterly* 47.3 (1995): 428–466.

——. *Was Huck Black? Mark Twain and African-American Voices.* New York: Oxford UP, 1993.

Fiske, John. *Understanding Popular Culture.* Boston: Unwin Hyman, 1989.

Franklin, Cynthia. "Recollecting *This Bridge* in an Anti-Affirmative Action Era: Literary Anthologies, Academic Memoir, and Institutional Autobiography." Unpublished manuscript in the forthcoming *This Bridge Called My Back: Twenty Years Later.*

——. "Review of *Women/Autobiography/Theory.*" *Biography* 22.3 (1999): 399–406.

——. "Turning Japanese/Returning to America: Race and Nation in Memoirs by Cathy Davidson and David Mura." Unpublished manuscript.

Free [Abbie Hoffman]. *Revolution for the Hell of It.* New York: Dial, 1968.

Freedman, Diane P. "Writing in the Borderlands: The Poetic Prose of Gloria Anzaldúa and Susan Griffin." *Constructing and Reconstructing Gender: The Links among*

Communication, Language, and Gender. Ed. Linda A. M. Perry, Lynn M. Turner, and Helen M. Sterk. Albany: State U of New York P, 1992. 211–217.

Freud, Sigmund. *Dora: An Analysis of a Case of Hysteria.* New York: Collier Books, 1997.

Friere, Paulo, and Donald Macedo. *Literacy: Reading the Word and the World.* South Hadley: Bergin and Garvey, 1987.

Frost, Elizabeth. "Signifyin(g) on Stein: The Revisionist Poetics of Harryette Mullen and Leslie Scalapino." *Postmodern Culture* 5.3 (1995): 40 pars. http:// jefferson. village.virginia.edu/pmc/text-only/issue.595/frost.595 (13 Oct. 1997).

Gass, William H. "Gertrude Stein and the Geography of the Sentence." *The World within the Word.* Boston: David R. Godine, 1979. 63–123.

Gates, Henry Louis, Jr. *The Signifying Monkey: A Theory of Afro-American Literary Criticism.* New York: Oxford UP, 1988.

Gilbert, Sandra M., and Susan Gubar. *No Man's Land: The Place of the Woman Writer in the Twentieth Century.* Vol. 2: *Sexchanges.* New Haven: Yale UP, 1989.

Gilroy, Paul. *The Black Atlantic: Modernity and Double Consciousness.* Cambridge: Harvard UP, 1993.

Ginsberg, Allen. "Wichita Vortex Sutra." *Collected Poems, 1947–1980.* New York: Harper and Row, 1984. 394–411.

Gioia, Dana. *Can Poetry Matter? Essays on Poetry and Culture.* St. Paul: Graywolf, 1992.

Gitlin, Todd. *Campfires of Resistance: Poetry from the Movement.* New York: Bobbs-Merrill, 1971.

———. *The Sixties: Years of Hope, Days of Rage.* New York: Bantam, 1987.

Gladman, Renee. *Arlem.* San Francisco: Idiom, 1998. 22 Feb. 1999, http:// www. idiomart.com/issue__1/renee__contents.html (11 Nov. 1999).

———. *Not Right Now.* San Francisco: Second Story Books, 1998.

———. "RE: Hejinian's Influence." E-mail to author. 15 Sept. 1999.

Glancy, Diane. "A Fieldbook of Textual Migrations." *Chain* 5 (1998): 79–84.

———. "The Woman Who Was a Red Deer Dressed for the Deer Dance." *XCP* 2 (1998): 89–104.

Glissant, Édouard. *Caribbean Discourse: Selected Essays.* Charlottesville: UP of Virginia, 1989.

———. *Poetics of Relation.* Tr. Betsy Wing. Ann Arbor: U of Michigan P, 1997.

Golding, Alan. *From Outlaw to Classic: Canons in American Poetry.* Madison: U of Wisconsin P, 1995.

Goldman, Anne. "'I Yam What I Yam': Cooking, Culture, and Colonialism." *De/ Colonizing the Subject: The Politics of Gender in Women's Autobiography.* Ed. Sidonie Smith and Julia Watson. Minneapolis: U of Minnesota, 1992. 169–195.

Goldman, Emma. "The Individual, Society, and the State." *Red Emma Speaks: An*

Emma Goldman Reader. Ed. Alix Kates. Atlantic Highlands, NJ: Humanities P, 1996. 109–123.

Greer, Michael. "Ideology and Theory in Recent Experimental Writing, or the Naming of 'Language Poetry.'" *Boundary 2* 16.2–3 (1989): 335–355.

Grenier, Robert. "On Speech." *This* 1 (1971): 86–87.

Griffin, Farah, Michael Magee, and Kristen Gallagher. *Combo* 1 (1997). http://wings. buffalo.edu/epc/authors/mullen/interview-new.html (14 Sept. 1999)

Hampsten, Elizabeth. "Considering More Than a Single Reader." *Interpreting Women's Lives: Feminist Theory and Personal Narratives*. Ed. Personal Narrative Group. Bloomington: Indiana UP, 1989. 129–138.

Harryman, Carla. *In the Mode Of.* La Laguna: Zasterle P, 1991.

Hartley, George. *Textual Politics and the Language Poets*. Bloomington: Indiana UP, 1989.

Hebdige, Dick. *Cut N Mix: Culture, Identity, and Caribbean Music*. New York: Routledge, 1990.

Hejinian, Lyn. *My Life*. Los Angeles: Sun & Moon P, 1980.

——. "My Life in the Early Nineties." *Lingo* 1 (1993): 97–99.

——. "The Rejection of Closure." *Poetics Journal* 4 (1984): 134–143.

——. *Two Stein Talks*. Santa Fe: Wenselsleeves P, 1995.

Henning, Barbara. "An Interview with Harryette Mullen." 21 June 1999. http://www.poetryproject.com/mullen.html (23 Sept. 1999).

Holub, Robert C. *Reception Theory: A Critical Introduction*. New York: Methuen, 1984.

Homans, Margaret. "'Women of Color' Writers and Feminist Theory." *New Literary History* 25 (1994): 73–94.

hooks, bell. *Black Looks: Race and Representation*. Boston: South End P, 1992.

Hoʻomanawanui, Kuʻualoha Meyer. "Electric Lava" and "Lei Waiʻaleʻale." *ʻOiwi* 1 (1999): 123–127.

——. "Wailuanuiahoʻāno ('The-Great-Twin-Waters-of-[the-Chief] Hoʻāno')." *ʻOiwi* 1 (1999): 177–182.

Howe, Susan. "Bride's Day." *The Europe of Trusts*. Los Angeles: Sun & Moon P, 1999. 139–146.

——. "Melville's Marginalia." *The Nonconformist's Memorial*. New York: New Directions, 1993. 86–150.

——. *My Emily Dickinson*. Berkeley: North Atlantic Books, 1985.

——. *Pierce-arrow*. New York: New Directions, 1999.

——. "Some Notes on Visual Intentionality in Emily Dickinson." *How(ever)* 3.4 (1986): 13–17.

——. "These Flames and Generosities of the Heart: Emily Dickinson and the Illogic of Sumptuary Values." *Sulfur* 28 (1991): 134–153.

———. "Women and Their Effect in the Distance." *Ironwood* 28 (1986): 58–91.

Hubbard, Stacy. "Trimmings." *St. Mark's Poetry Project Newsletter* February/March 1992: 3–4.

Hughes, Langston. *The Weary Blues.* New York: Knopf, 1926.

Hunt, Eric. "Notes for an Oppositional Poetics." *The Politics of Poetic Form: Poetry and Public Policy.* Ed. Charles Bernstein. New York: Roof Books, 1990. 197–211.

Ignatiev, Noel, and John Garvey. "Abolish the White Race by Any Means Necessary." *Race Traitor.* Ed. Noel Ignatiev and John Garvey. New York: Routledge, 1996. 9–14.

Jameson, Fredric. "Periodizing the Sixties." *The Sixties, without Apology.* Ed. Sohnya Sayers, Anders Stephenson, Stanley Aronowitz, and Fredric Jameson. Minneapolis: U of Minnesota P, 1984. 178–209.

———. *Postmodernism: Or, The Cultural Logic of Late Capitalism.* Durham: Duke UP, 1991.

Jameson, Fredric, Anders Stephenson, and Cornell West. "A Partial Chronology." *The Sixties, without Apology.* Ed. Sohnya Sayers, Anders Stephenson, Stanley Aronowitz, and Fredric Jameson. Minneapolis: U of Minnesota P, 1984. 210–215.

Jett, Joan. "Bad Reputation." By Joan Jett, Laguna, Cordell, Kupersmith. *Bad Reputation.* New York: Blackheart Records, 1981.

Johnson, Linton Kwesi. *Inglan Is a Bitch.* London: Race Today Publications, 1980.

Jolas, Eugene. "Vertigral Workshop." *Transition* 24 (1936): 109–112.

Jones, Le Roi. *Blues People: Negro Music in White America.* New York: Morrow Quill Paperbacks, 1963.

Joyce, James. *Finnegans Wake.* New York: Viking, 1958.

Joyce, Joyce. "The Black Canon: Reconstructing Black American Literary Criticism." *New Literary History* 18.2 (1987): 335–344.

Kachru, Braj B. *The Alchemy of English: The Spread, Functions, and Models of Non-Native Englishes.* New York: Pergamon Institute of English, 1986.

———. "The Bilingual's Creativity: Discoursal and Stylistic Strategies in Contact Literatures." *Discourse across Cultures: Strategies in World Englishes.* Ed. Larry E. Smith. New York: Prentice Hall, 1987. 125–140.

———. "Models for Non-Native Englishes." *The Other Tongue: English across Cultures.* Ed. Braj Kachru. Urbana: U of Illinois P, 1992. 48–74.

———. "World Englishes 2000: Resources for Research and Teaching." *World Englishes 2000.* Ed. Larry E. Smith and Michael Lawrence Foreman. Honolulu: U of Hawai'i/East-West Center, 1997. 209–237.

Kaipa, Summi. *The Epics.* San Francisco: Leroy P, 2000.

Kane, Cheikh Hamidou. *Ambiguous Adventure.* Portsmouth, NH: Heinemann, 1972.

Kang, Li Hyun Yi. "The 'Liberatory Voice' of Theresa Hak Kyung Cha's *Dictée*." *Writing Self Writing Nation: Essays on Theresa Hak Kyung Cha's "DICTEE."* Ed. Norma Alarcón and Elaine H. Kim. Berkeley: Third Woman P, 1994. 73–99.

Keating, AnnLouise. "Interrogating 'Whiteness,' (De)Constructing 'Race.'" *College English* 57.8 (1995): 901–918.

——. "Interview with Anzaldúa." *Frontiers* 14.1 (1993): 105–130.

Kim, Elaine H. "Poised on the In-Between: A Korean American's Reflections on Theresa Hak Kyung Cha's *Dictée*." *Writing Self Writing Nation: Essays on Theresa Hak Kyung Cha's "DICTEE."* Ed. Norma Alarcón and Elaine H. Kim. Berkeley: Third Woman P, 1994. 3–30.

——. "Preface." *Writing Self Writing Nation: Essays on Theresa Hak Kyung Cha's "DICTEE."* Ed. Norma Alarcón and Elaine H. Kim. Berkeley: Third Woman P, 1994. ix–xi.

Kim, Myung Mi. *The Bounty*. Minneapolis: Chax P, 1996.

——. *Under Flag*. Berkeley: Kelsey Street P, 1991.

Kingston, Maxine Hong. *The Woman Warrior: Memoirs of a Girlhood among Ghosts*. New York: Vintage, 1989.

Lavie, Smadar. *The Poetics of Military Occupation*. Berkeley: U of California P, 1990.

Lazer, Hank. "The Lyric Valuables: Soundings, Questions, and Examples." *Modern Language Studies* 27.2 (1997): 25–50.

——. *Opposing Poetries*. Vol. 2, *Readings*. Chicago: Northwestern UP, 1996.

Leithauser, Brad. "The Confinement of Free Verse." *New Criterion* May 1987: 4–14.

Lejeune, Philippe. *On Autobiography*. Minneapolis: U of Minnesota P, 1989.

Lew, Walter. *Excerpts from Δikth / 딕테 / 딕티 / DIKTE for DICTEE (1982)*. Seoul: Yeul Eum Publishing Company, 1992.

Lewis, Wyndham. *Time and Western Man*. Los Angeles: Black Sparrow P, 1993.

Llona, Victor. "Foreigners Writing in French." *Transition* 2 (1922): 169–174.

Logan, William. *Vain Empires*. New York: Penguin, 1998.

Lowe, Lisa. "Decolonization, Displacement, Disidentification: Asian American 'Novels' and the Question of History." *Cultural Institutions of the Novel*. Ed. Deidre Lynch and William B. Warner. Durham: Duke UP, 1996. 96–128.

——. "Heterogeneity, Hybridity, Multiplicity: Marking Asian American Differences." *Diaspora: A Journal of Transnation Studies* 1.1 (Spring 1991): 24–44.

Lu, Pamela. *Pamela: A Novel*. Berkeley: Atelos, 1999.

Lubiano, Wahneema. "Shuckin' Off the African-American Native Other: What's 'Po-Mo' Got to Do with It?" *Dangerous Liaisons: Gender, Nation, and Postcolonial Perspectives*. Ed. Anne McClintock, Aarnir Mufti, and Ella Shohat. Minneapolis: U of Minnesota P, 1997. 204–229.

Luoma, Bill. "Scanner Dan" Online posting. 12 Aug. 1999. Subpoetics-l. 12 Aug. 1999. <js@lava.net>

Mackey, Nathaniel. *Discrepant Engagement: Dissonance, Cross-Culturality, and Experimental Writing*. New York: Cambridge UP, 1993.

Mac Low, Jackson. *The Virginia Woolf Poems*. Providence: Burning Deck 1985.

Marcus, Greil. *Lipstick Traces: A Secret History of the Twentieth Century*. Cambridge: Harvard UP, 1989.

Martin, Stephen-Paul. *Open Form and the Feminine Imagination: The Politics of Reading in Twentieth-Century Innovative Writing*. Washington, D.C.: Maisonneuve, 1998.

McCaffery, Larry, and Brian McHale. "A Local Strangeness: An Interview with Lyn Hejinian." *Some Other Frequency: Interviews with Innovative American Authors*. Ed. Larry McCaffery. Philadelphia: U of Pennsylvania, 1996. 121–145.

McCaffery, Steve, and bpNichol. *Rational Geomancy: The Kids of the Book Machine. The Collected Research Reports of the Toronto Research Group, 1973–1982*. Vancouver: Talonbooks, 1992.

McCaffery, Steve, and Jed Rasula. *Imagining Language: An Anthology*. Cambridge: MIT P, 1998.

McGann, Jerome J. "Contemporary Poetry, Alternate Routes." *Politics and Poetic Value*. Ed. Robert von Hallberg. Chicago: U of Chicago, 1987. 253–276.

———. "Response to Charles Altieri." *Politics and Poetic Value*. Ed. Robert von Hallberg. Chicago: U of Chicago, 1987. 309–314.

McKenzie, F. A. *The Tragedy of Korea*. London: Holder and Stoughton, 1908.

Meese, Elizabeth A. *Crossing the Double-Cross: The Practice of Feminist Criticism*. Chapel Hill: U of North Carolina P, 1986.

Melnick, David. *Men in Aida, Book One*. San Francisco: Tuumba P, 1983.

Menchú, Rigoberta. *I, Rigoberta Menchú: An Indian Woman in Guatemala*. Tr. Ann Wright. New York: Verso Books, 1987.

Messerli, Douglas. *From the Other Side of the Century: A New American Poetry, 1960–1990*. Los Angeles: Sun & Moon, 1994.

———. *"Language" Poetries: An Anthology*. New York: New Directions, 1987.

———. "Stats on Hejinian's *My Life*." E-mail to author. 7 Sept. 1999.

Miller, Nancy. "Facts, Pacts, and Acts." *Profession* (1992): 10–14.

———. *Subject to Change: Reading Feminist Writing*. New York: Columbia UP, 1988.

Morris, Meaghan. "Banality in Cultural Studies." *Discourse* 10.2 (1988): 3–29.

Morris, Tracie. *Intermission*. New York: Soft Skull P, 1999.

Morrison, Toni. *Beloved*. New York: Knopf, 1987.

———. *Playing in the Dark: Whiteness and the Literary Imagination*. New York: Vintage, 1992.

Mullen, Harryette. "Imagining the Unimagined Reader: Writing to the Unborn and

Including the Excluded." *Boundary 2: 99 Poets/1999: An International Symposium* 26.1 (1999): 198–203.

——. *Muse & Drudge*. Philadelphia: Singing Horse P, 1995.

——. "Poetry and Identity." *West Coast Line* 30.1 (1996): 85–89.

——. "Runaway Tongue: Resistant Orality in *Uncle Tom's Cabin, Our Nig, Incidents in the Life of a Slave Girl,* and *Beloved.*" *The Culture of Sentiment: Race, Gender and Sentimentality in Nineteenth-Century America*. Ed. Shirley Samuels. New York: Oxford UP, 1992. 244–264.

——. "Solo Mysterioso Blues." *Callaloo* 19.3 (1996): 651–669.

——. *S*PeRM**K*T*. Philadelphia: Singing Horse P, 1992.

——. *Tree Tall Woman*. Galveston: Earth Energy Communications, Inc., 1981.

——. *Trimmings*. New York: Tender Buttons, 1991.

Naylor, Paul. *Poetic Investigations: Singing the Holes in History*. Evanston: Northwestern UP, 1999.

Nealon, Jeffrey T. *Alterity Politics: Ethics and Performative Subjectivity*. Durham: Duke UP, 1998.

——. *Double Reading: Postmodernism after Deconstruction*. Ithaca: Cornell UP, 1993.

Ngai, Sianne. "Raw Matter: A Poetics of Disgust." *Open Letter: A Canadian Journal of Writing and Theory* 10.1 (1998): 98–122.

Ngũgĩ wa Thiong'o. *Decolonising the Mind: The Politics of Language in African Literature*. Portsmouth: Heinemann, 1986.

Nielsen, Aldon Lynn. *Black Chant: Languages of African-American Postmodernism*. New York: Cambridge UP, 1997.

——. "Black Margins: African-American Prose Poems." *Reading Race in American Poetry: "An Area of Act."* Ed. Aldon Lynn Nielsen. Champaign: U of Illinois P, 2000. 148–62.

——. *Reading Race: White American Poets and the Racial Discourse in the Twentieth Century*. Athens: U of Georgia P, 1988.

——. *Writing between the Lines: Race and Intertextuality*. Athens: U of Georgia P, 1994.

Nielson, Melanie. *Civil Noir*. New York: Roof Books, 1991.

Niranjana, Tejaswini. *Siting Translation: History, Post-structuralism, and the Colonial Context*. Berkeley: U of California P, 1992.

Noland, Carrie. "Poetry at Stake: Blaise Cendrars, Cultural Studies, and the Future of Poetry in the Literature Classroom." *PMLA* 112.1 (1997): 40–55.

North, Michael. *The Dialect of Modernism: Race, Language, and Twentieth-Century Literature*. New York: Oxford UP, 1994.

Nussbaum, Martha C. *Love's Knowledge: Essays on Philosophy and Literature*. New York: Oxford UP, 1990.

Omi, Michael, and Howard Winant. "On the Theoretical Status of the Concept of Race." *Race, Identity, and Representation in Education.* Ed. Cameron McCarthy and Warren Crichlow. New York: Routledge, 1993. 3–10.

Paikeday, Thomas M. *The Native Speaker Is Dead!* New York: Paikeday, 1985.

Parsons, Marnie. *Touch Monkeys: Nonsense Strategies for Reading.* Toronto: U of Toronto P, 1994.

Pearcy, Kate. "A Poetics of Opposition? Race and the Avant-Garde." *Poetry and the Public Sphere: The Conference on Contemporary Poetry.* (27 Apr. 1997). http://english.rutgers.edu/pierce.htm. (13 Oct. 1997).

Perelman, Bob. *The Marginalization of Poetry: Language Writing and Literary History.* Princeton: Princeton UP, 1996.

———. "Parataxis and Narrative: The New Sentence in Theory and Practice." *American Literature* 65.2 (1993): 313–324.

———. *The Trouble with Genius: Reading Pound, Joyce, Stein, and Zukofsky.* Berkeley: U of California P, 1994.

Perloff, Marjorie. "Can(n)on to the Right of Us, Can(n)on to the Left of Us." *New Literary History* 18.3 (1987): 633–56.

———. "Conversation with Bob Perelman at Kelly Writer's House." 20 Oct. 1999. http://www.english.upenn.edu/~wh/webcasts/

———. *The Dance of the Intellect: Studies in the Poetry of the Pound Tradition.* New York: Cambridge UP, 1985.

———. "'Logocinēma of the Frontiersman': Eugene Jolas's Multilingual Poetics and Its Legacies." October 1998. http://wings.buffalo.edu/epc/authors/perloff/jolas.html (21 Oct. 1997).

———. *The Poetics of Indeterminacy: Rimbaud to Cage.* Princeton, Princeton UP, 1981.

———. "Whose New American Poetry? Anthologizing in the Nineties." September 1996. http://wings.buffalo.edu/authors/perloff/anth.html (21 Oct. 1997).

Personal Narrative Group. *Interpreting Women's Lives: Feminist Theory and Personal Narratives.* Bloomington: Indiana UP, 1989.

Peterson, Carla. "The Remaking of Americans: Gertrude Stein's 'Melanctha' and African-American Musical Traditions." *Criticism and the Color Line: Desegregating American Literary Studies.* Ed. Henry B. Wonham. New Brunswick: Rutgers UP, 1996. 140–157.

Philip, Marlene Nourbese. *She Tries Her Tongue: Her Silence Softly Breaks.* Charlottetown: Ragweed P, 1989.

Pollock, Griselda. *Vision and Difference: Femininity, Feminism, and Histories of Art.* New York: Routledge, 1988.

Pratt, Mary Louis. *Imperial Eyes: Travel Writing and Transculturation.* New York: Routledge, 1992.

Quartermain, Peter. *Disjunctive Poetics: From Gertrude Stein and Louis Zukofsky to Susan Howe.* New York: Cambridge UP, 1992.

———. "Getting Ready to Have Been Frightened: How I Read Bruce Andrews." *Aerial* 9 (1999): 161–182.

Radway, Janice. *Reading the Romance: Women, Patriarchy, and Popular Literature.* Chapel Hill: U of North Carolina P, 1984.

Rafael, Vicente L. *Contracting Colonialism: Translation and Christian Conversion in Tagalog Society under Early Spanish Rule.* Durham: Duke UP, 1992.

Rasula, Jed. *The American Poetry Wax Museum: Reality Effects, 1940–1990.* Urbana: National Council of Teachers, 1996.

———. "The Politics of, the Politics in." *Politics and Poetic Value.* Ed. Robert von Hallberg. Chicago: U of Chicago, 1987. 315–322.

Reid, B. L. *Art by Subtraction.* Norman: U of Oklahoma P, 1958.

Retallack, Joan. *How to Do Things with Words.* Los Angeles: Sun and Moon, 1998.

———. *Mongrelisme.* Providence: Paradigm P, 1999.

———. "The Poethical Wager." *Onward: Contemporary Poetry and Poetics.* New York: Peter Lang, 1996. 293–306.

Riding, Laura. *Contemporaries and Snobs.* New York: Doubleday, Doran, 1928.

Robbins, Bruce. "Comparative Cosmopolitanisms." *Cosmopolitics: Thinking and Feeling beyond the Nation.* Ed. Pheng Cheah and Bruce Robbins. Minneapolis: U of Minnesota P, 1998. 246–264.

———. *Secular Vocations: Intellectuals, Professionalism, Culture.* New York: Verson, 1993.

Rodriquez, Richard. *Hunger of Memory: The Education of Richard Rodriquez.* New York: Bantam, 1983.

Roffé, Mercedes. "Love Poem in Twelve Tongues." *Chain* 5 (1998): 196–198.

Rorty, Richard. *Contingency, Irony, and Solidarity.* New York: Cambridge UP, 1989.

Rothenberg, Jerome. *Technicians of the Sacred: A Range of Poetries from Africa, America, Asia, Europe, and Oceania.* Berkeley: U of California P, 1985.

Rose, Tricia. *Black Noise: Rap Music and Black Culture in Contemporary America.* Hanover: Wesleyan UP, 1994.

Ross, Andrew. "The New Sentence and the Commodity Form: Recent American Writing." Ed. Cary Nelson and Lawrence Grossberg. *Marxism and the Interpretation of Culture.* Urbana: U of Illinois P, 1988. 361–380.

Royle, Nicholas. *Telepathy and Literature: Essays on the Reading Mind.* Cambridge: Blackwell, 1991.

Ruddick, Lisa Cole. *Reading Gertrude Stein: Body, Text, Gnosis.* Ithaca: Cornell UP, 1990.

Rushdie, Salman. "'Commonwealth Literature' Does Not Exist." *Imaginary Homelands: Essays and Criticism, 1981–1991.* New York: Viking Penguin, 1991. 61–70.

Sabina, María. *The Midnight Velada*. Tr. Alvaro Estrada, Eliona Estrada de Gonzalez, and Henry Munn. *Poems for the Millennium*. Vol. 2. Ed. Jerome Rothenberg and Pierre Joris. Berkeley: U of California P, 1998. 487–490.

Sagarin, Edward, and Robert J. Kelly. "Polylingualism in the United States of America: A Multitude of Tongues amid a Monolingual Majority." *Language Policy and National Unity*. Ed. William R. Beer and James E. Jacob. Totowa: Rowman and Allanheld, 1985. 20–44.

Said, Edward. "The Politics of Knowledge." *Race, Identity, and Representation in Education*. Ed. Cameron McCarthy and Warren Crichlow. New York: Routledge, 1993. 306–314.

Saldívar, José. *Border Matters: Remapping American Cultural Studies*. Berkeley: U of California P, 1997.

Samuels, Lisa. "Eight Justifications for Canonizing *My Life*." *Modern Language Studies* 27.2 (1997): 103–119.

Samuels, Lisa, and Jerome McGann. "Deformance and Interpretation." *New Literary History* 30 (1999): 25–56.

Sappho. *Sappho: A New Translation*. Tr. Mary Barnard. Berkeley: U of California P, 1958.

Sarris, Greg. *Keeping Slug Woman Alive: A Holistic Approach to Native American Texts*. Berkeley: U of California P, 1993.

——. "'What I'm Talking about when I'm Talking about My Baskets': Conversation with Mabel McKay." *De/Colonizing the Subject: The Politics of Gender in Women's Autobiography*. Ed. Sidonie Smith and Julia Watson. Minneapolis: U of Minnesota, 1992. 20–33.

Sayers, Sohnya, Anders Stephenson, Stanley Aronowitz, and Fredric Jameson, eds. *The Sixties, without Apology*. Minneapolis: U of Minnesota P, 1984.

Scalapino, Leslie, and Ron Silliman. "What/Person: From an Exchange." *Poetics Journal* 9 (1991): 51–68.

Schmitz, Neil. *Of Huck and Alice: Humorous Writing in American Literature*. Minneapolis: U of Minnesota P, 1983.

Schueller, Malini. "Questioning Race and Gender Definitions: Dialogic Subversions in *The Woman Warrior*." *Criticism* 31.4 (1989): 421–437.

——. "Theorizing Ethnicity and Subjectivity: Maxine Hong Kingston's *Tripmaster Monkey* and Amy Tan's *The Joy Luck Club*." *Genders* 15 (1992): 72–85.

Schultz, Susan. "'Called Null or Called Vocative': A Fate of the Contemporary Lyric." *Talisman* 14 (1995): 70–80.

——. "Gertrude Stein's Self-Advertisement." *Raritan* 12 (1992): 71–87.

Sex Pistols. "Anarchy in the U.K." *Never Mind the Bollocks, Here's the Sex Pistols*. New York: Warner Brothers, 1988.

Shell, Marc. "Babel in America: Or, The Politics of Language Diversity in the United States." *Critical Inquiry* 20 (1993): 103–127.

———. "Hyphens: Between Deitsch and American." *Multilingual America: Transnationalism, Ethnicity, and the Languages of American Literature.* Ed. Werner Sollers and Marc Shell. New York: New York UP, 1998. 258–271.

Shelley, Mary. *Frankenstein.* London: Henry Colburn and Richard Bentley, 1831. http://etext.lib.virginia.edu/modeng0.browse.html, 1994 (29 June 1999).

Shih, Shu-Mei. "Nationalism and Korean American Women's Writing: Theresa Hak Kyung Cha's *Dictée.*" *Speaking the Other Self: American Woman Writers.* Ed. Jeanne Campbell Reesman. Athens: U of Georgia P, 1997. 144–162.

Siegle, Robert. *Suburban Ambush: Downtown Writing and the Fiction of Insurgency.* Baltimore: Johns Hopkins UP, 1989.

Silliman, Ron. "Disappearance of the Word, Appearance of the World." *The New Sentence.* New York: Roof Books, 1987. 7–18.

———. *In the American Tree.* Orono: National Poetry Foundation, 1986.

———. *The New Sentence.* New York: Roof Books, 1987.

———. "Poetry and the Politics of the Subject." *Socialist Review* 18.3 (1988): 61–68.

———. "Post-Reading Discussion: January 22, 1998. Writer's House, Philadelphia." *Philly Talks* 6 (1998): 9–17.

———. "Re: Reading the Essay." E-mail to author. 9 Feb. 1998.

Silliman, Ron, Carla Harryman, Lyn Hejinian, Steve Benson, Bob Perelman, and Barrett Watten. "Aesthetic Tendency and the Politics of Poetry: A Manifesto." *Social Text* 7.1–2 (1988): 261–275.

Smedman, Lorna J. "'Cousin to Cooning': Relation, Difference, and Racialized Language in Stein's Nonrepresentational Texts." *Modern Fiction Studies* 42.3 (1996): 569–588.

Smith, Larry E., ed. *Discourse across Cultures: Strategies in World Englishes.* New York: Prentice Hall, 1987.

Smith, Larry E., and Michael L. Forman. *World Englishes 2000.* Honolulu: U of Hawai'i/East-West Center, 1997.

Smith, Michael. *It A Come.* San Francisco: City Lights, 1986.

Smith, Rod. "Introduction." *Aerial* 9 (1999): v.

Smith, Sidonie. "The Autobiographical Manifesto: Identities, Temporalities, Politics." *Autobiography and Questions of Gender.* Ed. Shirley Newman. London: Frank Cass, 1991. 186–212.

Smith, Sidonie, and Julia Watson, eds. *De/Colonizing the Subject: The Politics of Gender in Women's Autobiography.* Minneapolis: U of Minnesota, 1992.

———, eds. *Getting a Life: Everyday Uses of Autobiography.* Minneapolis: U of Minnesota, 1996.

——, eds. *Women/Theory/Autobiography: A Reader.* Madison: U of Wisconsin, 1999.

Smith, Valerie. "Gender and Afro-Americanist Literary Theory and Criticism." *Within the Circle: An Anthology of African American Literary Criticism from the Harlem Renaissance to the Present.* Ed. Angelyn Mitchell. Durham: Duke UP, 1994. 482–498.

——. *Self-Discovery and Authority in Afro-American Narrative.* Cambridge: Harvard UP, 1987.

Solomons, Leon M., and Gertrude Stein. *Motor Automatism.* New York: Phoenix Book Shop, 1969.

Sommer, Doris. "Textual Conquests: On Readerly Competence and 'Minority' Literature." *Modern Language Quarterly* 54.1 (1993): 141–153.

——. "Who Can Tell? Filling in Blanks for Villaverde." *American Literary History* 6.2 (1994): 213–233.

Spillers, Hortense J. "Mama's Baby, Papa's Maybe: An American Grammar Book." *Diacritics* 17.2 (1987): 65–81.

Spivak, Gayatri Chakravorty. *In Other Worlds: Essays in Cultural Politics.* New York: Routledge, 1988.

Stefans, Brian Kim. "Korean American Poetry." *Korean Culture* 18.4 (1997): 4–16.

Stein, Gertrude. *As Fine as Melanctha.* New Haven: Yale UP, 1954.

——. *The Autobiography of Alice B. Toklas.* New York: Harcourt Brace and Company, 1933.

——. *Bee Time Vine and Other Pieces [1917–1927].* New Haven: Yale UP, 1953.

——. *Composition as Explanation.* London: Hogarth P, 1926.

——. *Everybody's Autobiography.* New York: Cooper Square Publishers, 1971.

——. *Fernhurst, Q.E.D., and Other Early Writings.* New York: Liveright, 1971.

——. *First Reader and Three Plays.* Dublin: Maurice Fridberg, 1946.

——. *The Geographical History of America; or, The Relation of Human Nature to the Human Mind.* Baltimore: Johns Hopkins UP, 1995.

——. *Geography and Plays.* Boston: Four Seas, 1922. 178–188.

——. *Gertrude Stein's America.* Ed. Gilbert A. Harrison. New York: Liveright, 1974.

——. *GMP: Matisse Picasso and Gertrude Stein with Two Shorter Stories.* Barton: Something Else P, 1972. 13–116.

——. *How to Write.* New York: Dover, 1975.

——. *How Writing Is Written.* Los Angeles: Black Sparrow P, 1974.

——. *Lectures in America.* Boston: Beacon, 1985.

——. *The Letters of Gertrude Stein and Carl Van Vechten: 1913–1946.* Ed. Edward Burns. New York: Columbia UP, 1986.

——. *Lifting Belly.* Ed. Rebecca Mark. Tallahassee: Naiad P, 1989.

——. *The Making of Americans: Being a History of a Family's Progress.* Normal: Dalkey Archive P, 1995.

———. *Narration*. Chicago: U of Chicago P, 1969.

———. *A Novel of Thank You*. New Haven: Yale UP, 1958.

———. *Painted Lace and Other Pieces*. New Haven: Yale UP, 1955.

———. "Patriarchal Poetry." *The Yale Gertrude Stein*. New Haven: Yale UP, 1980. 106–146.

———. *A Primer for the Gradual Understanding of Gertrude Stein*. Los Angeles: Black Sparrow P, 1971.

———. *Reflections on the Atomic Bomb*. Los Angeles: Black Sparrow P, 1973.

———. "Stanzas in Meditation (Selections)." *A Stein Reader*. Ed. Ulla Dydo. Evanston: Northwestern UP, 1993. 568–587.

———. *Tender Buttons*. Los Angeles: Sun & Moon Classics, 1990.

———. *Three Lives*. New York: Signet Classics, 1985.

———. *Useful Knowledge*. Barrytown: Station Hill P, 1988.

Stein, Herbert. "The Cubist Republican: What Gertrude Stein and I Share—Beyond a Last Name." *Salon*. http://www.slate.com/itseemstome/97-02-06/ itseemstome. asp. (6 Feb. 1997).

Stein, Leo. *Journey into the Self*. New York: Crown, 1950.

Stephens, Julie. *Anti-Disciplinary Protest: Sixties Radicalism and Postmodernism*. New York: Cambridge UP, 1998.

Stephens, Michael. *The Dramaturgy of Style: Voice in Short Fiction*. Carbondale: Southern Illinois UP, 1986.

Stepto, Robert B. *From behind the Veil: A Study of Afro-American Narrative*. Urbana: U of Illinois P, 1979.

Steve Miller Band, The. "Gangster of Love." By Johnny "Guitar" Watson. *Sailor*. New York: Capitol Records, 1990.

Stevens, Wallace. "The House Was Quiet and the World Was Calm." *The Collected Poems of Wallace Stevens*. New York: Knopf, 1957. 358–359.

Stewart, Susan. "The State of Cultural Theory and the Future of Literary Form." *Profession* 93 (1993): 12–15.

Stimpson, Catharine R. "Gertrude Stein and the Lesbian Lie." *American Women's Autobiography: Fea(s)ts of Memory*. Ed. Margo Culley. Madison: U of Wisconsin P, 1992. 152–166.

———. "The Mind, the Body, and Gertrude Stein." *Gertrude Stein: Modern Critical Views*. Ed. Harold Bloom. New York: Chelsea House, 1986. 131–144.

Stoll, David. *Rigoberta Menchú and the Story of All Poor Guatemalans*. Boulder: Westview P, 1999.

Stowe, Harriet Beecher. *Uncle Tom's Cabin*. New York: Bantam Classics, 1983.

Tardos, Anne. *Uxudo*. Berkeley and Oakland: Tuumba P and O Books, 1999.

Taussig, Michael. *Mimesis and Alterity: A Particular History of the Senses*. New York: Routledge, 1993.

Taylor, Reuben T. "Black Rhythms." *Transition* 21 (1932): 312–317.

Todorov, Tzvetan. "Dialogism and Schizophrenia." *An Other Tongue: Nation and Ethnicity in the Linguistic Borderlands.* Ed. Alfred Arteaga. Durham: Duke UP, 1994. 203–214.

Tompkins, Jane. *Reader Response Criticism: From Formalism to Post Structuralism.* Baltimore: Johns Hopkins UP, 1981.

Torgovnick, Marianna. "The Politics of the 'We.'" *South Atlantic Quarterly* 91 (1992): 43–63.

Torres, Edwin. "Portorico N Prague." *Chain* 5 (1998): 248–251.

——. "Seeds Sown Long Ago: Are You the Layer?" *XCP* 1 (1997): 89–91.

——. "Taxi-Toxic-Tiction." *XCP* 1 (1997): 92.

Torres, Lourdes. "The Construction of the Self in U.S. Latina Autobiographies." *Third World Women and the Politics of Feminism.* Ed. Chandra Talpade Mohanty, Ann Ruso, and Lourdes Torres. Bloomington: Indiana UP, 1991. 271–287

Tosches, Nick. *Country: The Twisted Roots of Rock 'n' Roll.* New York: Da Capo P, 1996.

Trask, Haunani-Kay. *Light in the Crevice Never Seen.* Corvallis: Calyx Books, 1994.

Trinh T. Minh-ha. *Woman, Native, Other: Writing Postcoloniality and Feminism.* Bloomington: Indiana UP, 1989.

Tsurumi, Patricia E. "Colonial Education in Korea and Taiwan." *The Japanese Colonial Empire, 1895–1945.* Ed. Ramon H. Myers and Mark R. Peattie. Princeton: Princeton UP, 1984. 275–311.

Turner, Frederick. *Natural Classicism: Essays on Literature and Science.* New York: Paragon House P, 1985.

Twain, Mark. *Life on the Mississippi.* New York: Bantam Classics, 1997.

Valcarel, Luis E. "There Are Several Americas." *Transition* 24 (1936): 131–138.

Vetsch, Florian. "Desultory Correspondence: An Interview with Paul Bowles." *Modern Fiction Studies* 42.3 (1996): 627–645.

Vicuña, Cecilia. *Quipoem: The Precarious: The Art and Poetry of Cecilia Vicuña.* Hanover: UP of New England, 1997.

Villaverde, Cirilio. *Cecilia Valdes: O, la loma del Angel; Novela de costumbres Cubanas.* New York: Las Americas Pub., 1964.

Von Hallberg, Robert. *American Poetry and Culture, 1945–1980.* Cambridge: Harvard UP, 1985.

Wald, Priscilla. *Constituting Americans: Cultural Anxiety and Narrative Form.* Durham: Duke UP, 1995.

Wallace, Mark. "On the Lyric as Experimental Possibility," July 1996. http:// wings. buffalo.edu/epc/authors/wallace/lyric.html (19 Sept. 1999).

Washington, Booker T. *Up from Slavery.* New York: Viking, 1986.

Watten, Barrett. "The Bride of the Assembly Line: From Material Text to Cultural Poetics." *The Impercipient Lecture Series* 1.8 (1997).

Weiner, Hannah. *Clairvoyant Journal*. Lenox: Angel Hair Books, 1978.

Weir, David. *Anarchy and Culture: The Aesthetic Politics of Modernism*. Amherst: U of Massachusetts P, 1997.

Weiss, M. Lynn. *Gertrude Stein and Richard Wright: The Poetics and Politics of Modernism*. UP of Mississippi, 1998.

West, Cornel. "The New Cultural Politics of Difference." *Out There: Marginalization and Contemporary Culture*. Ed. Russell Ferguson and Martha Gever. New York: MIT P, 1991. 19–36.

Whitman, Walt. *An American Primer*. San Francisco: City Lights, 1970.

———. *The Complete Poems*. New York: Penguin Books, 1975.

Williams, Raymond. *The Politics of Modernism: Against the New Conformists*. New York: Verso, 1989.

Willinsky, John. *Learning to Divide the World: Education at Empire's End*. Minneapolis: U of Minnesota P, 1998.

Wilson, Edmund. *The Shores of Light: A Literary Chronicle of the Twenties and Thirties*. New York: Farrar, Straus, and Young, 1952.

Wilson, Rob. "Falling into the Korean Uncanny." *Korean Culture* 12 (1991): 33–37.

———. "RE: broodings on 'Autonomy.'" E-mail to author. 11 May 2000.

Wilson, Rob, and Wimal Dissanayake. *Global/Local: Cultural Production and the Transnational Imaginary*. Durham: Duke UP, 1996.

Wolf, Susan. "Recalling Telling Retelling." *Fire Over Water*. New York: Tanam P, 1986.

Wong, Shelley Sunn. "Unnaming the Same: Theresa Hak Kyung Cha's *Dictée*." *Writing Self Writing Nation: Essays on Theresa Hak Kyung Cha's "DICTEE."* Ed. Norma Alarcón and Elaine H. Kim. Berkeley: Third Woman P, 1994. 103–140.

Wright, Richard. "Gertrude Stein's Stay Is Drenched in Hitler's Horrors." *PM's Sunday Magazine Section* March 11, 1945: M15.

Xu Bing. "Introduction to New English Calligraphy and A Book from the Sky." *Chain* 5 (1998): 275–282.

Yamanaka, Lois Ann. *Blu's Hanging*. New York: Farrar, Straus, and Giroux, 1997.

———. *Saturday Night at the Pahala Theatre*. Honolulu: Bamboo Ridge P, 1993.

Young Bear, Ray A. *The Invisible Musician*. Duluth: Holy Cow! P, 1990.

Zinn, Howard. *A People's History of the United States*. New York: Harper Perennial, 1980.

Index

Abel, Elizabeth, 189 (n. 32)

Adams, Henry, 68, 76, 176 (n. 29)

Alcheringa, 162 (n. 5)

Alexander, Will, 97

Ali, Muhammad, 34

Allen, Donald, 73

Allen, Lewis, 188 (n. 30)

Althusser, Louis, 154

Altieri, Charles, 58–59, 72, 171–172 (n. 10)

anarchy, 13–14, 66, 71, 154–155

Anderson, Amanda, 192 (n. 20)

Andrews, Bruce, 4, 6, 8, 9, 13, 50, 51, 52, 54, 57, 61, 69, 124, 162 (n. 4), 173 (n. 16), 175 (n. 25), 177 (n. 31), 183 (n. 57); "Confidence Trick," 10, 53, 60, 63–66, 71, 81–85; "Constitution/Writing, Politics, Language, the Body," 55; and critique of whiteness, 81–86; *I Don't Have Any Paper So Shut Up,* 183 (n. 56); "Poetry as Explanation, Poetry as Praxis," 55; *Public Constraint,* 75; and punk, 65–66; "Revolution Only Fact Confected," 55; "Text & Context," 54–55; and Vietnam, 74–75, 179 (n. 42)

Angelou, Maya, 82

Anzaldúa, Gloria, 5, 76, 156, 180 (n. 45)

Apex of the M, 57, 171 (n. 6), 175–176 (n. 25)

Aronowitz, Stanley, 179 (n. 38)

Arteaga, Alfred, 156, 191 (n. 15)

Asad, Talal, 191 (n. 12)

Ashton, Jennifer, 39, 167 (n. 15)

Augustine, St., 113

autobiography, 9, 75–76, 80–81, 91, 179 (n. 43); and Gertrude Stein, 34–40; *DICTEE* as, 129; *My Life* as, 66–71, 75–81

avant-garde, 53, 66, 86–87, 155

Awkward, Michael, 186 (n. 14), 189 (n. 32)

Baker, Houston, 96

Baker, Josephine, 95, 186 (n. 12)

Bakhtin, Mikhail, 141

Balaz, Joe, 158

Baldwin, James, 96

Banggo, Kathy Dee Kaleokealoha Kaloloahilani, 156

Baraka, Amiri, 97, 171 (n. 8), 186 (n. 15), 187 (n. 20). *See also,* Jones, Le Roi

Barroso, Gustavo, 20

Barthes, Roland, 14, 141, 162 (n. 7)

Bataille, Georges, 188 (n. 24)

Beach, Christopher, 162 (n. 5), 176 (n. 27)

Beatles, The, 113
Beatty, Paul, 97
Benjamin, Walter, 135
Benson, Steve, 59, 61, 62
Berger, John, 188 (n. 24)
Bernstein, Charles, 56, 61, 169 (n. 1),
    173-176 (nn. 16, 18, 25); *Artifice
    of Absorption,* 56; "A Blow is Like
    an Instrument," 62; "A Defence of
    Poetry," 170 (n. 4); "Poetics of the
    Americas," 156–157, 182 (n. 51);
    "Professing Stein/Stein Professing,"
    165 (n. 9), 166 (n. 14); "What's
    Art Got to Do With It," 162 (n.
    5), 192 (nn. 18, 19)
Bhabha, Homi K., 147
Biarujia, Javant, 156
Black Arts movement, 92, 97
Black Fire, 93
Blackmur, Corinne E., 163–165 (n. 6)
Black Panther Party, 73
Bloom, Lynn Z., 179–180 (n. 43)
Bowles, Paul, 165 (n. 8)
bpNichol, 56
Brathwaite, Kamau, 62, 156, 158, 182
    (n. 51)
Brennan, Tim, 142, 188 (n. 22), 192
    (n. 20)
Bridgman, Richard, 188 (n. 27)
Brooks, Gwendolyn, 93, 97
Bryant, Tisa, 97
Bürger, Peter, 175–176 (n. 26)
Buzzcocks, the, 65
Byers, Thomas B., 191 (n. 17)

Cabacungan, Darryl Keola, 156
Cage, John, 4, 72, 156
Campbell, David A., 188 (n. 28), 189
    (n. 31)

Cariaga, Catalina, 152
Carrie, 193 (n. 23)
Cerf, Bennett, 167 (n. 19)
Césaire, Aimé, 140
Cha, Theresa Hak Kyung, 5, 13, 50,
    87, 162 (n. 4); *Apparatus: Cinema-
    tographic Apparatus: Selected Writ-
    ings,* 123, 140, 162 (n. 4), 189 (n.
    3); and colonialism, 124–127, 131,
    133, 140, 145–150, 152; *DICTEE,*
    10, 11, 119–152, 189 (n. 2); and
    nationalism, 124, 129, 147, 150;
    nonstandard English in *DICTEE,*
    130–133, 143, 148, 151, 152
Cheah, Pheng, 192 (n. 20)
Chessman, Harriet Scott, 165 (n. 9)
Choy, Sam, 124
Christian, Barbara, 77, 82
Clark, Hillary, 176 (n. 30)
Clash, The, 65, 73
Clifford, James, 128, 130
Clover, Carol, 192–193 (n. 23)
Clovers, The, 113
Cohn-Bendit, Daniel and Gabriel, 71
collage, 128–130
colonialism, 124–127, 131, 133, 140,
    145–150, 152
Coltrane, John, 94
Conolly-Smith, Peter, 165 (n. 8)
Conrad, Bryce, 168 (n. 25)
Coolidge, Clark, 173 (n. 16)
Corn, Alfred, 174 (n. 19)
Cortissoz, Royal, 17, 19
cosmopolitan, 19, 20, 25, 31, 127,
    141–143, 147, 154, 157, 158, 192
    (n. 20)
Crane, Hart, 20
Crawford, James, 191 (n. 13)
Crystal, David, 190 (n. 9)

Culler, Jonathan, 12
cultural studies, 7, 42, 54, 87, 91

Daly, Lew, 171 (n. 6)
Damon, Maria, 8, 22, 162 (n. 5), 166
    (n. 10), 169 (n. 27), 174–175 (n.
    20), 192 (n. 21)
Davidson, Michael, 61
Davies, Kevin, 183 (n. 57)
Davis, Angela, 188 (n. 30)
de Certeau, Michel, 11, 162 (n. 9)
deconstruction, 11–13, 54, 74, 102
DeKoven, Marianne, 41, 188 (n. 26)
Delany, Samuel, 161 (n. 2)
Deleuze, Gilles, 48, 169 (n. 27)
Derksen, Jeff, 183 (n. 57)
Derrida, Jacques, 102
deSouza, Allen, 193 (n. 25)
Dickinson, Emily, 72
DiPalma, Ray, 61
Dissanayake, Wimal, 192 (n. 20)
Dobyns, Stephen, 176 (n. 27)
Domino, Fats, 114
Douglas, Ann, 182 (n. 54)
Douglass, Frederick, 2–4, 161 (n. 1)
Drucker, Johanna, 181 (n. 49)
Dryer, Carl, 148
Du Bois, Page, 188 (n. 31)
Du Bois, W. E. B., 95, 102, 185–186
    (n. 8)
Dydo, Ulla, 76, 165 (n. 9), 180 (n. 44)

Eco, Umberto, 12
Eichhoff, Jürgen, 163 (n. 2)
Eliot, T. S., 18, 20, 31, 138, 158, 191
    (n. 16); "The Waste Land," 20, 163
    (n. 3)
Ellis, Thomas Sayers, 97
English language, 19, 23, 24, 31, 41,
137, 157; and dialect, 19, 21, 31,
155; "English First," 137, 138; as
a second language for Stein, 20,
26, 27, 31; nonstandard English
in *DICTEE*, 130–133, 143, 148,
151, 152
ethnopoetics, 53
Evans, Steve, 169 (n. 1), 178 (n. 36)

Falconetti, Maria, 148
Faulkner, William, 113
Ferlinghetti, Lawrence, 73
Fields, Julia, 97
Figiel, Sia, 190 (n. 10)
Finkelstein, Norman, 62, 169 (n. 3)
Fish, Stanley, 11–13, 162 (n. 7)
Fishkin, Shelley Fisher, 182 (nn. 53, 54)
Fiske, John, 162 (n. 7)
Foreman, Michael L., 190 (n. 8)
Foucault, Michel, 52
Franklin, Cynthia, 180 (n. 43), 181
    (n. 48), 183 (n. 55)
Free, 53. *See also* Hoffman, Abbie
Freedman, Diane P., 180 (n. 45)
French language, 23, 26, 151, 157
Freud, Sigmund, 95, 147, 186 (n. 11)
Friere, Paulo, 51
Frost, Elizabeth, 184 (n. 1), 188
    (n. 23)

Gallagher, Kristin, 98, 184 (n. 3), 185
    (n. 4), 187 (n. 21)
Garvey, John, 83
Gass, William, 188 (n. 26)
Gates, Jr., Henry Louis, 92, 95–98,
    100, 161 (n. 1), 186 (n. 15). *See
    also* signifyin(g)
German language, 19, 21–23, 26, 157,
    165 (n. 8)

Gilbert, Alan, 171 (n. 6)
Gilbert, Sandra M., 41, 168 (n. 22)
Gillespie, A. Lincoln, 20
Gilroy, Paul, 91, 97
Ginsberg, Allen, 57–58, 73, 74, 171
    (n. 8); "Wichita Vortex Sutra," 57–
    58, 179 (n. 39)
Gioia, Dana, 8
Giscombe, C. S., 97
Gitlin, Todd, 171 (n. 8), 179 (n. 38)
Gladman, Renee, 81, 97, 181 (n. 50)
Glancy, Diane, 62, 137, 156
Glissant, Édouard, 114–115, 138, 140–
    141, 145–146, 162 (n. 5)
globalism, 127, 141–143, 148, 159,
    192 (n. 20)
Godard, Jean-Luc, 123
Golding, Alan, 57, 170 (n. 5), 174
    (n. 20)
Goldman, Anne, 180 (n. 43)
Goldman, Emma, 14
Goldman, Judith, 183 (n. 57)
Greer, Michael, 172 (n. 14), 173
    (n. 16)
Grenier, Rob, 173 (n. 16), 178 (n. 35)
Griffin, Farah, 98, 184 (n. 3), 185 (n.
    4), 187 (n. 20)
Guattari, Félix, 48, 169 (n. 27)
Gubar, Susan, 41, 168 (n. 22)

Hagen, Nina, 65
Hampsten, Elizabeth, 179–180 (n. 43)
Harcourt, Alfred, 35
Harley, George, 57
Harryman, Carla, 59, 61, 62, 152,
    175–176 (n. 25)
Hartley, George, 171 (n. 7), 179
    (n. 41)
Hebdige, Dick, 188 (n. 22)

Hejinian, Lyn, 9, 50, 56, 59, 60, 61,
    62, 72, 86, 124, 169 (n. 1), 175–
    176 (n. 25), 178 (n. 33), 181 (n.
    50); My Life, 9, 52, 53, 54, 60, 66–
    71, 75–81, 169 (n. 1), 174 (n. 19),
    176–177 (nn. 27, 31), 181 (nn.
    47, 49); "Rejection of Closure,"
    56, 69; Two Stein Talks, 169 (n. 1).
    See also autobiography
Hell, Richard. See Richard Hell and
    the Voidoids
Henning, Barbara, 184 (n. 3)
Hensley, Larry, 113
Hermogene, 112
Hills, 173 (n. 17)
Ho'omanawanui, Ku'ualoha Meyer, 156
Hoffman, Abbie, 53, 66
Holiday, Billy, 113
Holub, Robert C., 163 (n. 9)
Homans, Margaret, 189 (n. 32)
hooks, bell, 82
Howe, Susan, 62, 72, 175 (nn. 21, 23,
    25), 177 (n. 31), 179 (n. 37)
Howlin' Wolf, 114
Hubbard, Stacy, 105, 176 (n. 29), 188
    (n. 23)
Hughes, Langston, 131
Hungarian language, 157
Hunt, Erica, 97, 115, 169 (n. 4)
Hunt, Sidney, 20
Hyung Soon Huo, 129, 132, 148

identity, 2, 6, 7, 36–40, 50, 71, 74,
    90–93, 104, 108, 115, 151, 192
    (n. 23); African-American, 89–101,
    108–111, 184 (n. 3), 186 (n. 16);
    and language writing, 71–72, 75–
    87, 92, 94, 115, 171–173 (nn. 10,
    16), 175 (n. 22); "multiple subjec-

tivity," 76–77; "white studies," 77, 81–85, 87, 182 (nn. 52, 53, 54), 183 (n. 55). *See also* autobiography

Ignatiev, Noel, 83

immigration, 17, 19–21, 23, 26, 31, 41, 43, 45–46, 48, 122, 125–127, 130, 131, 133, 139, 145, 146, 150, 152

Iser, Wolfgang, 12

James, Henry, 31

Jameson, Fredric, 57–58, 72–73, 179 (nn. 38, 40), 193 (n. 24); *Postmodernism: Or the Cultural Logic of Late Capitalism,* 57, 143–146, 162 (n. 7), 171 (n. 7)

Jefferson, Blind Lemon, 113

Joan of Arc, 148, 194 (n. 26)

Jogglars, 173 (n. 16)

Johnson, Robert, 114

Jolas, Eugene, 20, 21, 163 (n. 4). See also *Transition*

Jonas, Stephen, 97

Jones, Le Roi, 103, 171 (n. 8). *See also* Baraka, Amiri

Joy Division, 65

Joy to the World, 94, 185 (n. 5)

Joyce, James, 20, 41, 96–98, 155

Kachru, Braj B., 131, 167 (nn. 16, 18), 190 (nn. 7, 8)

Kaipa, Summi, 81

Kane, Cheikh Hamidou, 190 (n. 10)

Kang, Li Hyun Yi, 125, 129, 190 (n. 5), 194 (n. 28)

Keating, AnnLouise, 180 (n. 45), 183 (n. 55)

Kelly, Robert J., 165 (n. 8)

Kennedy, John F., 73

Kim, Ahn Joong, 194 (n. 29)

Kim, Elaine, 124, 129, 189 (n. 1), 193 (n. 25), 194 (n. 28)

Kim, Myung Mi, 115, 146, 152

Kim, Yung-Hee, 194 (nn. 26, 27)

Kingston, Maxine Hong, 76

Korea, 120, 122, 123, 125, 126, 149–150

Korean language, 149

Kropotkin, Peter, 13

L=A=N=G=U=A=G=E, 61, 73, 165 (n. 9), 169 (n. 1), 173 (n. 16, 17)

language writing, 52–63, 73–74, 92; and Stein, 52, 169 (n. 1); the term "language writing," 60–61

Lavie, Smadar, 14

Lazer, Hank, 57, 66, 175–176 (n. 25), 178 (n. 36)

Leithauser, Brad, 191 (n. 17)

Lejeune, Philippe, 75, 80

Lew, Walter, 124, 152, 193 (n. 25), 194 (n. 29)

Lewis, Jerry Lee, 113

Lewis, Wyndham, 18

literacy, 2

Llona, Victor, 20

localism, 19, 31, 143, 148, 155, 158

Loftin, Elouise, 97

Lowe, Lisa, 180 (n. 45), 194 (n. 29)

Lu, Pamela, 81

Lubeski, Lori, 183 (n. 57)

Lubiano, Wahneema, 96, 100, 186–187 (n. 18)

Luoma, Bill, 174 (n. 19)

Mac Low, Jackson, 72, 156, 175 (n. 23)

Macedo, Donaldo, 51

Mackey, Nathaniel, 97, 187 (n. 20)

Magee, Michael, 98, 184 (n. 3), 185 (n. 4), 187 (n. 20)

Manet, Édouard, 104–107, 188 (n. 24), 188 (n. 25)

Marcus, Greil, 65

Martin, Stephen-Paul, 193 (n. 25)

May 1968, 73

McCaffery, Larry, 56, 61, 177 (nn. 31, 32), 178 (n. 36)

McGann, Jerome, 58, 171–172 (n. 10), 175 (n. 23)

McHale, Brian, 177 (nn. 31, 32)

McKenzie, F. A., 120, 121

McLaren, Malcolm, 65

Meese, Elizabeth, 13

Melnick, David, 156

Menchú, Rigoberto, 76, 189 (n. 33)

Messerli, Douglas, 173 (n. 17), 174 (n. 19), 176 (n. 27)

Miller, Nancy, 80, 179 (n. 43)

Miller, Steve. *See* Steve Miller Band

Milton, John, 4

modernism, 20, 41, 50, 52, 74, 103, 105, 155; and race, 20–21, 92, 104–105

Molisa, Grace, 8

Morris, Meaghan, 42, 189 (n. 33)

Morris, Tracee, 97

Morrison, Toni, 82–83, 146, 182 (n. 52), 190 (n. 10)

Mtume, James, 113

Mullen, Harryette, 6, 8, 10, 50, 87, 89–118, 124, 143, 162 (n. 4); and Gertrude Stein, 92, 99, 100, 102, 104–108, 109, 110; "Imaging the Unimagined Reader: Writing to the Unborn and Including the Excluded," 90; *Muse & Drudge,* 89, 93, 94, 95, 98, 99, 101, 102, 103, 110, 111–114; "Poetry and Identity," 186 (n. 18); "*Runaway Tongue: Resistant Orality in* Uncle Tom's Cabin, Our Nig, Incidents in the Life of a Slave Girl, *and* Beloved," 101, 115, 187 (n. 19); "Solo Mysterioso Blues," 103, 110; *S*PeR M**K*T,* 93, 94, 95, 99, 102, 108–111, 112; *Tree Tall Woman,* 92–93, 98, 99, 108, 185 (n. 4), 186 (n. 16); *Trimmings,* 93, 94, 95, 98, 99, 101, 102, 104–111

multilingual. *See* polylingual

"My Favorite Things," 94, 185 (n. 6)

nationalism, 124, 129, 147, 150, 155, 158, 193 (n. 25)

Naylor, Paul, 178 (n. 33), 182 (n. 51)

Nealon, Jeffrey T., 169 (n. 2), 179 (n. 41), 181 (n. 46)

New American Poetry, 57, 73, 81, 84, 179 (n. 39)

New Criticism, 11–13, 122

New Formalism, 191 (n. 17)

New York School, 92

Newman, Roy, and His Boys, 113

Ngũgĩ wa Thiong'o, 126, 127

Ngai, Sianne, 84, 183–184 (n. 57)

Nichol, bp. *See* bpNichol

Nielsen, A. L., 90, 97, 109, 110, 163–165 (n. 6), 186 (n. 17), 187 (n. 20)

Nielson, Melanie, 175 (n. 23)

Niranjana, Tejaswini, 133

Noland, Carrie, 7

No More Masks, 93

North, Michael, 19, 21, 163–165 (n. 6), 182 (n. 54)

NOW, 73
Nowak, Mark, 163 (n. 9), 182 (n. 51).
    See also *XCP: Cross Cultural Poetics*
Nussbaum, Martha, 162 (n. 3)

Oden, Gloria, 97
Oliver, Akilah, 97
Omi, Michael, 90
Ong, Walter, 103
orality, 101, 103

Paikeday, Thomas M., 130, 131
Palmer, Michael, 173 (n. 16)
Parsons, Marnie, 68
Patton, Julie, 97
Pearcy, Kate, 184 (n. 1), 188 (n. 23)
pedagogy, 9, 43–44, 62–63, 129, 159,
    175 (nn. 23, 24)
Perelman, Bob, 32–34, 57, 59, 60–61,
    62, 82, 84, 85, 168 (n. 22), 170
    (n. 4), 171 (n. 7), 172 (nn. 13, 15),
    175 (n. 21), 178 (n. 35), 182 (n. 51)
Perkins, Carl, 113
Perloff, Marjorie, 22, 52, 57, 68, 163
    (n. 4), 166 (n. 11), 171 (n. 8)
Perse, St.-John, 20
Personal Narratives Group, 179 (n. 43)
Peterson, Carla, 163–165 (n. 6)
Philip, M. Nourbese, 62, 156
Phipps, Wanda, 98
Picasso, Pablo, 37, 40
Pitcher, Oliver, 97
pluralism, 38–40, 71, 74, 82, 84,
    151, 154
Poetics Journal, 173 (n. 17)
poetry, 7–9
Pollock, Griselda, 106, 188 (n. 25)
polylingual, 19, 23, 26, 31, 32, 47–48,

136–140, 155–156; *DICTEE* as,
    126, 127, 139–140, 143–146, 148,
    152; Jameson on, 143–146; and
    reading, 139–140, 143–146
Pop Group, 65
Port Huron Statement, 73
Postell, Tom, 97
postmodernism, 77, 78, 97, 143, 144,
    145, 146, 192 (n. 21)
poststructuralism, 12, 97, 127
Pound, Ezra, 20, 31, 138, 159, 186
    (n. 15), 191 (n. 16); *Cantos,* 20
Pratt, Mary Louise, 129
Prevallet, Kristin, 171 (n. 6)
punk, 65–66

Qu, 173 (n. 17)
Quartermain, Peter, 23, 64, 165 (n. 9),
    166 (n. 12)

Radway, Janice, 162 (n. 7)
Rafael, Vicente L., 136
Rankine, Claudia, 98
Rasula, Jed, 56, 57, 61, 170 (n. 5),
    171–172 (nn. 8, 10), 174 (n. 19),
    178 (n. 36)
Ray, Man, 35
Rayor, Diane J., 114
reader response, 11–13, 122
reading, 51, 54–56, 71–72, 91, 115–
    118, 134, 148, 154–155, 159; and
    anarchy, 6, 13–14, 154–155; and
    autonomy, 9, 11, 12, 50, 53, 72,
    77, 85, 91–92, 98–101, 154–155;
    and collage, 128–130; as communal
    3, 5, 6; and cosmopolitanism, 143;
    decolonizing, 122, 125–126, 144–
    145; as exchange, 5; and language

writing, 54–57, 60–63, 69, 71–72;
and multilingual works, 139–140,
144–145; and race, 98–101, 115–118
Reed, Ishmael, 102
Rehm, Pam, 171 (n. 6)
Reid, B. L., 33, 167 (n. 20)
Retallack, Joan, 137, 138, 156, 175
(n. 23)
Reznikoff, Charles, 155
Rich, Adrienne, 5, 93
Richard Hell and the Voidoids, 65
Riding (Jackson), Laura, 20, 165 (n. 8)
Riffaterre, Michael, 12
Robbins, Bruce, 141–142, 143, 192
(n. 20)
Robinson, Kit, 61
Rodriquez, Richard, 189 (n. 33)
Roffé, Mercedes, 156
Roof, 173 (n. 17)
Roosevelt, Theodore, 22, 165 (n. 8)
Rorty, Richard, 101
Rose, Tricia, 188 (n. 22)
Ross, Andrew, 57, 171 (n. 9)
Rothenberg, Jerome, 73, 162 (n. 5),
171 (n. 8)
Rousseau, Jean Jacques, 76
Royle, Nicholas, 50
Ruddick, Lisa, 41, 188 (n. 26)
Rushdie, Salman, 126, 127
Rushin, Kate, 98

Sabina, María, 156
Said, Edward, 90
Saldívar, José, 162 (n. 6)
Samuels, Lisa, 68–69, 175 (n. 23),
176–177 (nn. 27, 31), 181 (n. 47)
Sanchez, Sonia, 93, 97
Sanders, Ed, 171 (n. 8)

Sappho, 100, 103, 111, 112–114, 124,
188 (n. 31)
Sarris, Greg, 14, 162 (n. 5), 180 (n. 43)
Sayers, Sohnya, 179 (n. 38)
Scalapino, Leslie, 85–87, 182 (n. 50)
Schmitz, Neil, 35, 165 (n. 9)
Schueller, Malini, 180 (n. 45)
Schultz, Susan, 168 (n. 22)
Schwitters, Kurt, 20
Sex Pistols, 14, 65, 66
Shaffer, Roy, 113
Shell, Marc, 19, 137, 165 (n. 8), 191
(n. 14)
Shelley, Mary, 1–4; *Frankenstein* 1, 2
Shelton Brothers, the, 113
Shelton, Joe, 113
Shih, Shu-Mei, 125, 190 (n. 4), 194
(n. 29)
Siegle, Robert, 193 (n. 25)
signifyin(g), 95–98, 100, 184 (n. 1)
Silliman, Ron, 54, 57, 59, 61, 62, 69,
74, 86, 87, 170 (n. 4), 173 (nn.
16, 17), 177 (n. 31), 178 (nn. 34,
35); "Disappearance of the Word,
Appearance of the World," 56; *The
New Sentence,* 56; "Poetry and the
Politics of the Subject," 86
Simon, Claude, 144
singleton, giovanni, 98
Smedman, Lorna J., 163–165 (n. 6)
Smith, Bessie, 100, 103, 111, 112, 114
Smith, Larry, 131, 190 (n. 8)
Smith, Patricia, 98
Smith, Rod, 66
Smith, Sidonie, 180 (nn. 43, 45)
Smith, Valerie, 161 (n. 1)
Snyder, Gary, 73, 171 (n. 8)
Solomons, Leon M., 44

Sommer, Doris, 116–118, 126, 189 (n. 33)
Spellman, A. B., 97
Spillers, Hortense, 90, 91, 102, 114
Spivak, Gayatri Chakravorty, 107
Stefans, Brian Kim, 189 (nn. 2, 4)
Stein, Gertrude, 9, 13, 15, 18–50, 64, 72, 80, 92, 99, 100, 102, 109, 124, 133, 155, 159; "And Now," 168 (n. 24); and authority, 43–44, 47; and autobiography, 34; *The Autobiography of Alice B. Toklas*, 23, 35, 37, 40, 42, 46, 75, 165 (n. 7), 168 (n. 26); "Business in Baltimore," 22, 29; childhood, 19–20; *Composition as Explanation*, 18; and disruption, 27–31, 41–48; and English language, 20, 23, 24, 43–44; *Everybody's Autobiography*, 10–11, 33, 34, 35, 36–39, 78, 167 (n. 19), 168 (n. 25); *First Reader and Three Plays*, 30, 162 (n. 8); and feminism, 34, 46, 48, 168 (n. 26); and French language, 23, 25; and German language, 20, 21, 22, 23; *Geographical History of America*, 34, 46, 48; *Geography and Plays*, 18, 24, 25; *GMP*, 44; and grammar, 40, 46–48, 50; *Gertrude Stein's America*, 166 (n. 13); *How to Write*, 22, 29, 30, 40, 45; "In," 42; "An Instant Answer or a Hundred Prominent Men," 38; and language writing, 52, 169 (n. 1); and languages, 19–20, 23; *Lectures in America*, 32, 38, 39, 40, 44, 45, 107, 162 (n. 4), 167 (n. 15); and lesbianism, 22, 45, 168 (n. 26); *Lifting Belly*, 45; *The Mak-*

ing of Americans, 22, 27, 32, 39, 166 (n. 15); *Narration*, 162 (n. 4); "Natural Phenomena," 30; "No," 28; and nonsense, 13, 33; *A Novel of Thank You*, 44; "Patriarchal Poetry," 29; and patriotism, 23; *A Primer for the Gradual Understanding of Gertrude Stein*, 22, 30, 32; "Stanzas in Meditation," 76; and subversion, 41–42; and travel, 37–38; *Tender Buttons*, 15, 21, 22, 41, 42, 43, 50, 104–108, 110, 188 (nn. 26, 27); *Three Lives*, 21, 26, 45, 163–165 (nn. 6, 7); "We Came. A History," 27–28. *See also* Mullen, Harryette
Stein, Herbert, 166 (n. 13)
Stein, Leo, 33, 167 (n. 20)
Stephens, Julie, 179 (n. 38)
Stephens, Michael, 193 (n. 25)
Stephenson, Anders, 179 (nn. 38, 40)
Stepto, Robert B., 161 (n. 1)
Steve Miller Band, 113
Stevens, Wallace, 154
Stewart, Susan, 162 (n. 6)
Stimpson, Catharine, 22–23, 163–165 (n. 6), 168 (n. 22, 23)
Stoll, David, 76
Stowe, Harriet Beacher, 95, 186 (n. 9)
Students for a Democratic Society, 73
Sumner, Bernard, 65
"Swing Low, Sweet Chariot," 94, 185 (n. 7)
Syrianus, 112

Tardos, Anne, 156, 157–158
Taussig, Michael, 14
Taylor, Reuben T., 163 (n. 5)

Teenage Jesus and the Jerks, 65
The Sound of Music, 94
Thérèse de Lisieux, St., 148
This, 73, 173 (nn. 16, 17), 178 (n. 35)
This Bridge Called My Back, 93
Thomas, Lorenzo, 92, 97, 184 (n. 2)
Titian, 106
Todorov, Tzvetan, 191 (n. 16), 192
  (n. 22)
Toklas, Alice B., 23, 35, 37, 39, 46
Tompkins, Jane, 163 (n. 9)
Torgovnick, Marianna, 172 (n. 11)
Torres, Edwin, 115, 156
Torres, Lourdes, 180 (n. 45)
Tosches, Nick, 188 (n. 29)
Tottel's, 173 (nn. 16, 17)
Transition, 20, 168 (n. 24)
Trask, Huanani-Kay, 131, 158
Trinh T. Minh-ha, 120, 121, 122, 152
Trujillo-Lusk, Dorothy, 183 (n. 57)
Tsurumi, Patricia F., 190 (n. 6)
Tubes, the, 65
Turner, Frederick, 191 (n. 17)

universalism, 147–152, 154

Van Vechten, Carl, 33, 37, 167 (n. 19)
Velvet Underground, 65
Vetsch, Florian, 165 (n. 8)
Vicuña, Cecilia, 136, 156
Vietnam, 73, 74–75
Villaverde, Cirilio, 189 (n. 33)
Von Hallberg, Robert, 171 (n. 8)

Wald, Priscilla, 44, 166 (n. 15)
Waldman, Anne, 73

Wallace, Mark, 175–176 (n. 25)
Washington, Booker T., 95, 185 (n. 8)
Watson, Julia, 180 (n. 43)
Watten, Barrett, 34, 59, 61, 62, 170
  (n. 4), 173 (n. 16), 175–176 (n.
  25), 178 (n. 35), 182 (n. 51)
Weiner, Hannah, 181 (n. 49)
Weir, David, 13
Weiss, Lynn M., 163–165 (n. 6)
West, Cornel, 90, 101, 179 (n. 40)
Whitman, Walt, 26, 34, 73
Williams, Raymond, 20
Williams, William Carlos, 20, 23
Willinsky, John, 130, 131
Wilson, Edmund, 17, 19
Wilson, Rob, 154, 192 (n. 20), 193
  (n. 25)
Winant, Howard, 90
Wolf, Susan, 193 (n. 25)
Wong, Shelley Sunn, 189–190 (nn. 4,
  11), 194 (n. 28)
Wright, Richard, 102, 163–165 (n. 6)

XCP: Cross Cultural Poetics, 162 (n. 5),
  163 (n. 10), 182 (n. 51). *See also*
  Nowak, Mark
Xu Bing, 156

Yamanaka, Lois-Ann, 175 (n. 23), 190
  (n. 10)
Yiddish language, 22, 26, 166 (n. 10)
Yu Guan Soon, 120, 121, 194 (n. 26)

Zinn, Howard, 19, 163 (n. 1), 179
  (n. 41)
Zukofsky, Louis, 23, 155

About the Author

JULIANA SPAHR is a critic and a poet. She teaches in the Department of English at the University of Hawai'i, Mānoa, and has written extensively on poetry and poetics. She has had articles published in numerous places, including *American Literature* and *College Literature*. She co-edits the journal *Chain* with Jena Osman. Her other books include *Response* (Sun & Moon Press), *Spiderwasp or Literary Criticism* (Explosive Books), and the tentatively titled *Fuck You-Aloha-I Love You* (forthcoming, Wesleyan University Press).